Alfonso Gálvez

Sermons for
a World in Decline

New Jersey
U.S.A. - 2017

Sermons for a World in Decline by Alfonso Gálvez. Copyright © 2017 by Shoreless Lake Press. American edition published with permission. All rights reserved. No part of this book may be reproduced, stored in retrieval system, or transmitted, in any form or by any means, electronic, mechanical, photocopying, recording or otherwise, without written permission of the Society of Jesus Christ the Priest, P.O. Box 157, Stewartsville, New Jersey 08886.

CATALOGING DATA

Author: Gálvez, Alfonso, 1932–
Title: Sermons for a World in Decline

Library of Congress Control Number: 2017957592

ISBN–13: 978-0-9972194-6-3

Published by
Shoreless Lake Press
P.O. Box 157
Stewartsville, New Jersey 08886

INTRODUCTION

This compilation of essays begins with June 2015, the occasion of the fifty–ninth anniversary of my priestly ordination, the date of the first of the homilies —Sermons— transcribed here.

What prompted me to gather these essays into a book was my desire to put into writing some of the homilies I had preached, starting with the one just mentioned, but without following any particular order of dates, depending on the length of time God would grant me.

Written language, while losing the freshness and spontaneity proper to the spoken language, is better when it comes to explaining topics in a more detailed and organized way. Disadvantages and advantages which, after all, perhaps compensate each other for those who want to take advantage of the fruits of a work that is the result of a great effort.

As I have said, these *Sermons* have been culled from homilies I have preached on various occasions. Their written form has maintained essentially the same line of thought as the original homilies; nevertheless, it seemed convenient to add footnotes and commentaries which augmented the content and took on a different format. Obviously, when the homilies were preached the limitations imposed by the attention span of the listeners compelled me to dispense with those additions; hence the present title.

The biblical quotations are an accurate transcript of the official text of the Church, the Latin Neovulgate. I have also secured the best available versions in vernacular languages and occasionally consulted the original Greek for rather difficult or controversial texts.

Finally, I must acknowledge that this work does not intend to be a theological treatise, but only a transcription into written language of what were once oral homilies and which are now presented here in a somewhat more extensive and developed form.

At any rate, I offer the result of my efforts to the greater glory of God and the salvation of souls.

At Mazarrón, Murcia, June 2015

THE PRIESTHOOD[1]

Introduction

My dear spiritual children,

Today is the fifty–ninth anniversary of my ordination to the priesthood; this is a good opportunity, therefore, to speak about the mystery of the ministerial priesthood.

Let us start by acknowledging that our Lord Jesus Christ placed an extraordinarily difficult task upon the shoulders of those men chosen by Him when He entrusted them with the mission of carrying out the priestly ministry. Continuing the mission of Jesus Christ and evangelizing the world —*As the Father hath sent me, I also send you*[2]— is such a demanding and arduous undertaking that it can overcome the strength of any man, unless he is willing to obey out of love the mandate he has received and open his soul to the sufficient graces that will provide him with the fortitude necessary to fulfill it.

One cannot expect that the ordinary faithful will understand the magnitude of this issue which becomes a veritable *tragedy* in the life of any priest; actually, the faithful is not compelled to understand it. Not even young priests come to realize the terrible burden that awaits them, which is something good; God is so kind as to wrap

---

[1] Preached on June 10, 2015.
[2] Jn 20:21.

in the soft haze of the enthusiasm typical of the early years of the priesthood the severe pain and suffering involved in their sharing with Jesus Christ the weight of the Cross. It happens here something similar to what take place in marriage, with the joy of the early days of marriage when one is not mindful of the burdens and hard times which marriage will bring later on.[3]

At any rate, the priestly office is a *total immolation* accepted out of love for Jesus Christ, and consequently out of love for all men, and an absolute self-forgetfulness on the part of the priest.

He who is willing to undertake this incredible Adventure should not attempt it unless he is urged to do so by love, for there can be no other reason or motivation; moreover, this one is more than enough. If it is indeed true that man was created to love, it is even more true that only he who longs to fall in love with Jesus Christ Our Lord can have access to the priesthood; always trusting in the help from grace, without which it would be utter folly to undertake and impossible to carry out the Adventure we are talking about.

One of the times when a man feels firsthand just how diminished his limitations are is when he tries to describe sublime realities. Precisely because they are sublime they are difficult to express; much more so when these realities reach beyond the supernatural, that is, when one faces the impossible. If one tries to describe these realities, he can still resort to Poetry which comes to the aid of Prose; nevertheless, this alternative only manages to sew patches on the cloth of a narrative that fails to conceal the arrangements. For this reason, a long time ago and moved by the ardor and recklessness proper to young people, I dared to write a stanza concerning the

---

[3]Hence a lack of enthusiasm in the first years of priesthood may be an indication that the desire to share the Cross of Our Lord will not exist in the near future. This would be an early sign of the total failure of a priestly life.

The Priesthood 9

Priesthood. It is known that what Prose cannot accomplish, Poetry will attempt; nevertheless both run into the unspeakable, and hence the latter soon discovers that it has managed to reach only a little further than the spot where the former had to stop:

> *To speak of it and not live it is sadness,*
> *To live it and not speak of it is sublime,*
> *Guardian of my dreams,*
> *Come and tell me in time*
> *How to attain this beautiful existence.*

It is sad, indeed, and futile trying to talk about a Priestly Ministry without living it according to the spirit of Christ. Any discourse about this topic will merely be a collection of platitudes and empty and meaningless words.

But living that Priesthood, without talking about it, that is, without fanfare, quietly and in the humility of a hidden and self-giving life, is truly sublime. And it happens that sublime things are quite difficult to explain. And more so when the sublime borders what seems unattainable; it is then that speaking about it becomes an almost impossible task. And if, in spite of that impossibility, one does talk about it, or at least tries, it is because he has placed his confidence in the grace of God and, as in the present case, is acting out of obedience to the imperative of preaching, which is one of the heaviest loads that Jesus Christ has put on the shoulders of priests.

When I look back and think of the years before my ordination to the priesthood, sweet memories of youth come inevitably to my mind. They would undoubtedly be the happiest of my life, were they not far outweighed by what I am experiencing now in my old age. Six long years at the Seminary; I thought they would never end.

They passed slowly, one after another, while I was consumed with impatience and enthusiasm for reaching a goal that seemed ever more distant. Years, months, and weeks passed one after another in an increasingly slow succession which I counted longingly until finally the last twenty–four hours before my dreamed–of ordination arrived.

Time went by and things began to appear under another perspective, no different, but certainly more complete. It is proper to human nature to mature, thus the individual grows and develops, acquiring greater capacity for judgment and discernment. The same also happened to Jesus Christ the Man, Who, the gospels say, *advanced in wisdom, and age, and grace before God and men.*[4] This is surely why a young priest has an idea about the Priesthood that is as correct, adequate, and fair... as it is incomplete; very different, indeed, from the idea acquired when one reaches my advanced age which has seen many years of priestly ministry: fifty–nine years of pastoral work may very well be said to be enough and more than sufficient years to have a deeper knowledge of the Priesthood.

A brand new young priest who has just begun his ministerial work rightly thinks with enthusiasm about his priesthood. He considers his future life as a series of activities carried out enthusiastically for the salvation of souls, working as a faithful instrument of the Church, and rescuing countless souls from sin. These and other enthusiastic dreams, as correct as they are incomplete, are proper to young priests.

But years pass and there comes a time when one begins to understand that the priesthood is a much heavier and more difficult burden than anyone could have imagined. However, it is a job entrusted by God to the priest as he continues the mission of Jesus

---

[4] Lk 2:52.

Christ. To carry it out, he counts on the fact that he is accomplishing it for Him, with Him, and in Him. With the passage of time, the many activities of the ministry —worship, preaching, hearing confessions, visiting the sick, catechesis, and the various pastoral and parish activities— are still considered and valued as irreplaceable works to be done. But, at the same time, the priest also learns that the most important thing of all, in fact the only essential thing, is to love God. And while it is true that this attitude implies a higher level of maturity in the life of any Christian, it is even more so true for the priest; after all, he is a man *taken* from among men (Heb 5:1) to be *another Christ*.

Indeed, the love of God is the only and most important thing. When, according to the Gospel account, Martha complained to Jesus Christ that her sister Mary had left her alone with the housework, the Master replies, *Martha, thou art careful, and art troubled about many things, but one thing is necessary.* And Jesus Christ added, *Mary hath chosen the best part.*[5]

This passage has been discussed for centuries in connection with the distinction between contemplative and active life, and which should be given pride of place. And as expected, Doctrine, taking into account the clear message of the words of Jesus Christ, has always chosen to give priority to contemplative life over active life, while recognizing, at the same time, the importance and necessity of apostolic action.[6] However, this discussion is somewhat trivial, since there must be no incompatibility within Christian existence between the life of action and the life of contemplation.

---

[5] Lk 10: 41–42.

[6] An exception to be noted here are the aberrations of the prevailing modernist theology in the Church today that advocates contempt of prayer, especially contemplative prayer.

Be that as it may, one thing is very clear in the words of the Lord, which is that *only one thing is needed*; our love for Jesus Christ must be love to the point of madness. After all, as Saint John says in his gospel, Jesus Christ, *having loved his own who were in the world, he loved them unto the end.*[7] Finally, when this ideal has taken root deeply in his heart so as to determine his life, the priest comes to realize —after many labors, hardships, and sufferings endured for love of God and souls— that *everything else follows on its own*. The priest finally discovers that through the life of prayer, of intimacy, affection, friendship, and being *face to face* with Jesus, it is the only essential thing.

Jesus Christ said, referring to the concerns about the needs of each day or of tomorrow (food, clothing, etc.) *Seek ye therefore first the kingdom of God, and his justice, and all these things shall be added unto you.*[8] Note here that the adverb *first* must be understood primarily as what occupies prime space in the order of succession; but more properly as what is primary or essential. Secondarily, and according to the actual words of the Lord, the adverb means that everything else *will be given in addition*. Our Lord does not say that one can get everything else, or anything like that, but simply that *all these things shall be added unto you.*

This confirms, without assuming any abandonment of necessary activities, the obvious reality that a priest in love with his Lord, entirely true to His teachings, will soon gather the fruits of his efforts; simply and without further ado. Conversely, the activities carried out without love for the Lord or with insufficient love are absolutely fruitless.

---

[7] Jn 13:1.
[8] Mt 6:33.

Hence the question that an old priest often asks himself: *What should I have done in my life but love Jesus Christ more and more ardently every day...?* And, as if by paradox, as he advances in old age, he understands —or so he thinks— that his yearnings for loving his Master fail to turn off the feeling that he loves Him less and less. And even as the road that reaches the End becomes shorter, it seems to him that this goal is less accessible, more torturous, a mere glimpse from far away. And yet, he continues in his heart the tireless struggle for loving Jesus, as the commandment says, *with all your heart, with all your soul and with all your mind.*[9] More love, and more desire to love; more fire in the heart, and more longings for feeling the heart totally burnt; sometimes closer to the Lord, although at the price of feeling Him many times much farther away; seeing himself as more and more loved, but suffering the pain of not knowing how to reciprocate such love; always with the clear notion that everything that has not been love has been a waste of time:

> *Wholly bathed in tears from woe*
> *My heart cries in distress, wounded, by love burned,*
> *Feeling grief and great sorrow*
> *For time, which passed undiscerned,*
> *Spent thus, without loving, is never returned.*

Loving not in any way but as Jesus Christ did, Who *having loved his own who were in the world, he loved them unto the end;*[10] to the point of making his own the life of the Master, making real in himself Saint Paul's own words: *And I live, now not I; but Christ liveth in me.* Having achieved this, everything else would have been worthwhile.

---

[9] Mt 22:37.
[10] Jn 13:1.

The great misfortune of Protestantism, which at the present time is also shared by a broad sector of the Church and even by a vast majority of Catholic priests, has been to ignore the fact that the priest is *different* from his fellow men —*taken from among men*.[11] This becomes indeed a veritable *tragedy* in the life of a priest (Bernanos captured it well in his *Diary of a Country Priest*); at the same time, it is also both the glory that elevates him and the misfortune that immolates him, sinking him into the deep pain of a crucified existence which also is the promise of abundant fruit. The priest who, deceived by the fallacies of the world, is determined to appear as *equal* to other men (thinking, perhaps, of a more profitable apostolate or maybe compelled by the relaxation brought about by the abandonment of his spiritual life) will ultimately be *swallowed up* by the environment and turned into the ridiculous histrionic character he was determined to become.

The Holy Mass

The Mass, besides being the vital principle that conforms the entire priestly existence, is the main event and the core of Christian worship. The priest communicates life to other men, his brothers, by making the Mass real in his own life as a result of making it an integral part of his existence.[12]

---

[11] Heb 5:1.

[12] The devil, fully aware that he cannot completely eliminate the Mass from the life of the Church, has worked hard to strip it of its character and its sacrificial meaning; which is tantamount to reducing it to almost nothing. He has used his well–known art of deception, providing false arguments: the comfort of the brevity of the Mass; that one must adapt to the new times and the mentality of the modern age; the greater accessibility of the Mass and better participation on the part of the faithful because of the use of vernacular languages; the freedom and spontaneity of the celebrant made possible due to the elimination of rubrics; etc. The disastrous consequences that followed proved the *timeliness* of the improvements.

With the passage of time, a change in perspectives takes place as far as the priest is concerned. But since we are still talking about priests according to Christ, it should be noted as an introduction to this subject, that the dawn of the priestly life usually begins with careful attention to ceremonies. Those of us who long ago received the inestimable grace of living this reality know that the Traditional Mass, unlike the *Novus Ordo* Mass, requires some knowledge of Liturgy and practicing the celebration of the Holy Mass as something necessary for the proper use of the liturgical ceremonies. Hence the care and delicacy that in ancient times used to be displayed in the liturgical rites, which were always considered as the introductory threshold to the world of the sacred.

Nobody within the Church, until recent times, could have thought that the Liturgy of the Church would ever admit elements incompatible with the devotion and splendor of worship such as hurried ceremonies, shortening or even removing prayers for the sake of brevity, vulgarity, improvisation, and coarseness.

As a seminarian I was *Master of Ceremonies*. I had to personally train my fellow seminarians near the time of their ordination to the priesthood in the ceremonies of the celebration of the Mass; therefore I had to devote much of the little time available to me to the study of the Liturgy. Anyway, we (as I suppose is true of today's young men) started our ministerial vocation with great care in celebrating the Mass, faithfully following the liturgical rules, as this is something which usually attracts the attention of a newly ordained and enthusiastic priest.

This is why in my early years as a priest I celebrated Mass so carefully and *correctly*, trying to follow faithfully the complex and detailed rules that had regulated the Traditional Mass for centuries. I wanted to celebrate it with as much respect and delicacy as I could and, if you will, even with devotion. However, once again and as always, over the years and with the maturity acquired with time, I began to understand that this way of celebrating the Sacrifice, though correct and not lacking in love for Jesus Christ, *did not yet correspond to the true exigencies of the Mass.* I was convinced that, although I was celebrating Mass with painstaking fidelity, my spirit was still far from having delved into the wealth of its content.

The Mass requires celebrating it fully identified with Jesus Christ, and *especially with His Death*, for the Mass is truly a *Holy Sacrifice*. Undoubtedly it is *Holy*, but a *Sacrifice* after all; not merely a symbolic Sacrifice, but an *absolutely real* one which equally affects both the main Victim, Who is Jesus Christ, and the priest himself. And if in ordinary catechesis it is justly said that the faithful attending Mass participate in their own way in the Sacrifice, since they have received a certain sharing in the Priesthood of Christ through baptism —a sharing *essentially different* from the one proper to the priest—, one can affirm with even more certainty that it is in the Mass where the celebrant *truly dies* with Jesus Christ; not a physical death, but one that can be called mystical, supernatural, spiritual, or otherwise, since there is no adequate terminology to express realities that go far beyond the natural world and the power of human understanding. It is possible that the content of this mystery is similar to what Jesus Christ meant when He spoke about *denying oneself* or *losing one's own life out of love for Him*, or to what the well–known expression affirmed by Saint Paul: *And I live, now not I; but Christ liveth in me*. Be that as it may, the truth is that the mere fact of celebrating Mass has as a consequence that the life of the Priest no longer belongs to him and, therefore, *is not his*. And yet the mystery will still be a mystery and all the tentative explanations will be insufficient. For it is not enough to say that the priest has given up his own life because he participates at Mass in the Death of Christ, for a true participation in the death of Jesus Christ implies —if words are not mere symbols— *a true participation in the Death of his Master* and all that the expression *take part* in the death of somebody means. As we can see, we are back to square one, and the mystery remains a mystery. One thing is clear though: the participation in the Death of Jesus Christ, which may be called mystical or given some other equivalent term, must always be somehow *painful and tremendous* for the Priest; which is the least —or perhaps the most— we can say with respect to a real death. And as the Death of Jesus Christ became Life for all Christians, when the Priest dies with his Lord through the Mass he also becomes the source of life for his parishioners.

This wonderful mystery and firm reality turns the existence of the ministerial priesthood into a *tragic* event which the priest understands only with the maturity that the passing of years provides. At which point the minister of Jesus Christ really begins to understand that the drama of the Priesthood involves the need to die with his Master as a condition for bearing fruit. For, as the *Letter to the Hebrews* says, *without the shedding of blood there is no remission.*[13] All other paths —*New Evangelizations?*— are secondary, incidental, contingent, circumstantial, temporary, casual, occasional, and the like, but actually useless if the primary and essential requirement, that is dying along with Jesus Christ, is absent.

Death in Christ and with Christ —which should never be interpreted in a symbolic or, as some would say, a *spiritual* sense— causes such a strong impact on the priestly life as to bring about an *immolation* that must also be taken in its truest and deepest sense. This is how the life of the priest, now turned into a real *death in*

---

[13] Heb 9:22.

Christ in all of his daily activities, reaches its most intense degree of reality at the time of the Sacrifice of the Mass, where the mystical death of the minister who offers it reaches its climax, which can actually affect the priest, when he lives following the spirit of Jesus Christ in all its depth, in the most painful way (even if such a thing should pass unnoticed, which is what usually happens). Nevertheless, behold, this is the moment of glory in any priestly life: to die out of love for the Beloved and along with Him: *Unless the grain of wheat falling into the ground die, itself remaineth alone. But if it die, it bringeth forth much fruit.*[14]

We are dealing with a number of sublime mysteries about which, as always happens with the most awe-inspiring things, the world usually knows nothing. There is here another overwhelming reality of Christian life which particularly affects the priest: the love and appreciation God has for His own is usually as intense as the contempt and hatred the world feels for them.

But the problem here is that Christians tend to give the words of Jesus a merely spiritual, symbolic, poetic significance if you will, without paying attention to their deepest meaning. This is why no consideration is given to the drastic content of His words or to their deriving consequences for real life: *Unless the grain of wheat falling into the ground die, itself remaineth alone. But if it die, it bringeth forth much fruit.*[15]

There is no other way for the life of a priest to produce an abundant and lasting fruit than to sacrifice his own life, as the words of Jesus Christ make abundantly clear, *I have chosen you; and have appointed you, that you should go, and should bring forth fruit; and*

---

[14] Jn 12:24.
[15] Jn 12:24.

your fruit should remain,[16] thus corroborating the prominence He gave to the roads leading to the Cross. And there really is no other means of apostolate that can be used as an effective instrument for the salvation of souls.

Now we can understand the futility of the efforts of the *New Evangelizations* which abundantly indicate that the modern Pastoral activity of the Church has lost its compass. The methods of Evangelization are clearly and adequately explained in the Gospel, and we have no need of resorting to new ones. Problems began when liberal Protestantism and Bultmann's methods of interpretation, on the one hand, and modernist historicism on the other first began to question the historicity of the scriptural testimonies and later to deny their veracity. Catholicism was soon seduced by the alleged *progress* of such research methods, resulting in the gradual loss of confidence in the conclusions of the Pontifical Biblical Commission, which finally ended up disappearing: further evidence that the so-called *modern novelties* have always been a temptation for the self-conscious and those weak in Faith.

Consequently, the fate that awaits the priest faithful to his vocation is to suffer death on the Cross with his Master, like the grain of wheat, as our Lord's commandment clearly affirmed. And since we are dealing with realities and not symbolisms or abstractions, it must be said that death, whether the physical death of the body or the mystical death of the soul, always refers to a real death; therefore, the latter must be no less painful and harrowing than the former.

The mystery of death to one's self out of love for Jesus Christ, valid for any Christian but in a special way for the priest, reaches its maximum level of reality in the latter through the celebration

---

[16] Jn 15:16.

of the Holy Sacrifice, which raises the priest to a different, supernatural world, so alien to what is ordinarily known that the limited human language is unable to describe it. It is a world which could be expressed as dreamlike, entirely withdrawn from time and space, and located on a plain different from all the things of this world.

The minister of Jesus Christ who, aided by grace, has made his own the words of the Apostle, *but God forbid that I should glory, save in the cross of our Lord Jesus Christ; by whom the world is crucified to me, and I to the world*[17] is overtaken by feelings of indescribable joy (which sometimes can be feelings of suffering, or both at the same time, and which defy any possible description) when he celebrates the Eucharistic Mystery. And what may seem a strange paradox is nothing other than those simultaneous feelings merging, alternately or at the same time, the anguish of death and the supreme joy of suffering for and with the beloved Person.

The fruit of the Holy Sacrifice depends largely on the *awareness* of the soul of the priest that these veritable mysteries must be part and parcel of his own life; which depends, in turn, on both the personal graces received by him to carry out his ministry and his willing *cooperation* with such graces. Something happens here which is similar to what happens with preaching, as we will explain later: a priest who does not feel himself painfully *wounded*, mystically but really, by the consequences and the effects the Mass has on him, can rest assured that the celebration of the Eucharistic Mystery has been reduced in his particular case to the effect caused by a liturgical ceremony of any kind.

The sublime reality that takes place during the Celebration of the Mass —the anguish of death and the joy of dying for and with Someone Whom one loves, sharing His life— is usually as much

---

[17] Gal 6:14.

overlooked by the common faithful as is the difference that exists between the common priesthood of all Christians and the ministerial priesthood of ordained Priests. We have here one of the most precious and unique graces of the ministerial priesthood which the fervent priest knows how to keep zealously hidden in his heart, according to the Old Testament which says that *it is good to keep the secrets of a king.*[18] Indeed, great and lofty graces in the life of a priest are reserved for God alone, as the Apostle advises us: *You are dead, and your life is hidden with Christ in God.*[19] Feeling oneself dead and unknown to the world befits a life *hidden* with Christ; it is, in the last analysis, *an essential condition in the life of a priest.*

Hence, the priest cannot expect recognition or reward from the world. Nor should he be surprised when the opposite happens and he is persecuted; he should feel overjoyed: *If you had been of the world, the world would love its own: but because you are not of the world, but I have chosen you out of the world, therefore the world hateth you.*[20] *Behold what love the Father hath bestowed upon us, that we should be called, and should be the sons of God. Therefore the world knoweth not us, because it knew not him.*[21]

Truly speaking, the priest will have to feel himself *alienated* and *exiled* by and for the world, and the diagram of his life must be outlined according to those parameters; which is but a copy of his Master's life, Who ended His life dying on the Cross, thus giving life to the world. For this reason, and above any other considerations the world may hold about him, favorable or unfavorable, the priest, although aware that he has been ordained for men *in the things that*

---

[18] Tob 12:7.
[19] Col 3:3.
[20] Jn 15:19.
[21] 1 Jn 3:1.

appertain to God, also knows that he has been placed in this world by God *in favor of men, that he may offer up gifts and sacrifices for sins*.[22]

Although the Holy Sacrifice of the Mass was instituted by Jesus Christ *for all the faithful*, some of its loftiest content is, as it were, reserved for the celebrant by way of a unique and delicate secret which is so sublime that not even the priest himself would be able to express it beyond his own inner world. For if it is appropriate to keep the king's secrets, according to the *Book of Tobias*, so much more must this secret be kept hidden because it holds within itself the inexpressible mystery of the sweetness and intimacy of the *face-to-face* spousal relationship of divine–human love:

> *We shall go at once*
> *To the deep caverns of the rock*
> *Which are all secret,*
> *There we shall enter in*
> *And taste of the new wine of the pomegranate.*[23]

Confession

I remember the first time I sat in the confessional. Although they say there is a first time for everything, nervousness is more than justified when one begins to delve as a priest into the sublime and unfathomable sacrament of Penance. As a twenty-four-year-old totally rookie priest, with confidence in God and ready to do my job well, I thought I would easily start my office in the world of this Comforting Sacrament by hearing the confession of some

---

[22] Heb 5:1.
[23] Saint John of the Cross, *Spiritual Canticle*.

boring pious old lady, whose sins would be nothing more than mere childishness or nun's scruples. Who would have thought at that time of the great number of challenging and difficult penitents whom I would have to help, sometimes with great anguish for me, in my pastoral wanderings through various countries and so many singular places!

This sacrament of mercy and forgiveness, which throughout the history of Christianity has brought peace of heart to countless Christians by reconciling them with God; this sacrament, the most sublime and Joy–bearing of all the sacraments after the Eucharist, has been virtually eliminated in the New Church re-founded at the occasion of the Second Vatican Council. And we must admit that this is one of the greatest scores achieved by Satan against the true Church, with consequences for the salvation —and damnation— of souls which are known to God alone. Woe to those responsible for such larceny! It is seemingly impossible to think that there will be any repentance of guilt, even at the time of death, by those who made such a great effort to open the gates of Hell for so many unfortunates whose number, were it known, would completely terrify the living.

But let us go back to the early days of the ministry of a young priest, when the unseasoned minister of the Lord would take great care in helping the penitents with all the love of his heart. He welcomes them with kindness, listens to them carefully, and procures from them their integral confession, looking after the good of their souls —which is sometime quite laborious—, and finally dismisses them with the best possible brief exhortation drawn from his best repertoire. This aspect of the priesthood is not always easy, but the faithful usually do not realize the problems involved in carrying it out. Quite often penitents approach the confessional with some fear and even shame, which is understandable given the condition of human nature. The minister of the Sacrament who, in addition to being judge carries out at the same time his duties as father and doctor, will have to draw on all his love and all variety of understanding and patience with souls so that they will prepare themselves for true repentance and confess all their sins.

The exercise of this ministerial task will be very far from easy or simple; so much so that the particular attention given to the penitents, each considered as a special and unique case, usually causes great inner tension and tiredness, which becomes more intense and serious when the priest is hearing confessions for hours on end. But this is no longer the case in modern times, now that the Pastoral activity of the New Church, infected with modernism, has brought about both the massive defection of priests from the ministry of confession and the abandonment on the part of the faithful, often encouraged by priests themselves, of this sacrament or the rejection of the necessary integral confession.

But this was not the case in past, more joyful times; nor is it happening now in a few isolated hubs scattered around the world which are still true to Catholicism. As far as I am concerned, I have spent many hundreds of hours sitting in the confessional during my long ministerial life. Sometimes for even more than twenty hours with hardly any interruption, sustained by a few cups of coffee that good souls would bring to my confessional. After those hours I would lie down on my bed or on a couch for a couple of hours without taking off my cassock; but the stimulation of the coffee did not allow me to rest. During my stay in the Andes, my Indian parishioners remained lined up for two or three days to be able to get to confession. And it was not unusual that sometimes I fell asleep in the confessional —perhaps unconscious, I could not tell— for hours while the penitents continued coming for confession without interruption and without being aware of my condition. For my part, I never harbored any doubts about the validity of those confessions.

During the early years of my ministry, before any of this happened, I had what I initially thought was a good idea by which the fatigue caused by long hours spent in the confessional might be overcome, at least in part. At the end of the day I was a human being after all, and it is well known that human nature is always imagining the possibility of practicing the law of least effort, in the mistaken belief that the most beautiful and lofty things can be achieved at a low cost. And so I wrote a short standard speech as an admonition to be allocated to each penitent, which would save me the complicated issue of concocting special considerations for each one.

An *intelligent* resource that ended in absolute failure since I could never apply it, not even once. I realized in each case that I had before me a *particular person* who was also a faithful Christian and a child of God with his particular problems and anxieties, in need of consolation and peace and with the hope and assurance that he would find them in the confessional. How could I then just apply a standard recipe and dismiss those faithful souls...? Little heart and even less love for Jesus Christ and those souls should I have if I were to do so. So I had to conclude that the ingenious process that I had initially considered had to be cancelled.

And we continue with the theme of maturity and the passing of years. There comes a time when the priest finally understands the true depth and meaning of the sacrament of Penance. It is a real and unfathomable abyss that must mean for him, once again, yet another way of participating intensely in the mystery of sharing the sufferings of the Lord on the Cross. It is now that the priest finally realizes that this sacrament is not simply to absolve and forgive sins;

he himself, like his Lord, *must also carry them*. For if Jesus Christ took upon Himself the sins and miseries of all men, making them His own and making Himself sin for man's sake, appearing before His Father —He being the Innocent among the innocent— as if He were guilty and bearing all human rottenness, thus bringing about the salvation of the world...;[24] and if the priest's mission is *identical to that of his Master* (Jn 20:21), then the life that souls receive through the sacrament of Penance requires only one condition: that he also bears the sins of others *and the consequent suffering that such a thing implies*. It is in this way that what the *Letter to the Hebrews* said is fulfilled: *without the shedding of blood there is no remission.*[25] Consequently, the sins of his fellow men are meant to cause more sorrow in his own heart than in the heart of those who committed them. The result is not difficult to infer: it is quite clear that the work of any priest produces little fruit through this sacrament as long as he does not understand *and live* the reality of these mysteries.

Preaching

This is another heavy load that the Lord has entrusted to His ministers. And again I feel the need of highlighting that the preaching of a new priest will be ineffective, or will produce very little fruit, until he is truly convinced that preaching is a veritable *heavy burden*. For many years I have persistently taught young priests a principle that may not convince everyone but which I consider safe: *the fruit of the preaching of a priest is inversely proportional to the personal satisfaction he experiences about his own oratory. Conversely, this fruit is directly proportional to the feeling of his own ineptitude and*

---

[24] Cf., for example, Ps 22:2; 7–9; 7: 17,b; Is 53: 5–6.
[25] Heb 9:22.

his own personal failure, by virtue of which he is forced to trust in the Lord and in Him alone.

Nevertheless, if we take into account the way in which human nature behaves, it is understandable and even natural that the novice priest begins his oratorical tasks with enthusiasm.

In times past, when one could still talk of sacred oratory in the Church and of true homilies, it was not unusual that a priest wanted to look good in front of the faithful and sought the success of his sermons; and he was naturally filled with satisfaction when he thought he had been successful. It could even happen that some priests became famous and were then asked to preach in this or that place; which in no way could be considered a bad event *provided that the priest would not feel satisfied with his triumphs, attributing them to the good qualities with which he was gifted.* After all, those were normal times.

Older people will think, rightly, that it was appropriate to attribute these peculiarities, sometimes fortunate and other times less fortunate, to *past times,* because there is no point in dealing with these issues with what is happening in the New Church, where it is impossible to talk about preaching since there is nothing in the New Church which may even remotely resemble sacred oratory. Indeed, not even the term *poor preaching* can be applied to the manifold *chattering* with which the few faithful who still attend Sunday Mass are being punished; they are insubstantial at best or full of nonsense most of the time, where they speak about everything except the Word of God: *They are of the world: therefore of the world they speak, and the world heareth them,* said Saint John in his *First Letter.*[26]

---

[26] 1 Jn 4:5.

But let us go back to normality and imagine that we still live in the happy times about which a new Don Quixote would have said, recalling the famous Speech of the Arms and Letters, *Blessed age and those times...!* where there was still a Christian people who enjoyed the gift of Faith and attended sacred worship with devotion. But be that as it may, it is absolutely normal that the young priest begins his work of preaching with enthusiasm and the desire to do good to souls... and even in the mood for looking good.

But years pass and again the priest begins to understand better what Preaching the Word of God is and what it means. The transmission of the words and teachings of Jesus Christ to the sheep entrusted to him is anything but an easy task. The priest realizes that his words are heard sometimes, while many other times they are not. It is true that Jesus told His disciples that just as some people had heard His own doctrine, they would also listen to theirs (Jn 15:20). But it is true that He also complained that His Word had not been heard, with the obvious rejection of the truth: *If I tell the truth, why do you not believe me...?*[27] *If I had not come, and spoken to them, they would not have sin; but now they have no excuse for their sin.*[28] And also the Baptist is said to be the *voice of one crying in the wilderness.*[29]

The conclusion to be drawn from this is that although preaching is indeed important —*Woe is unto me if I preach not the gospel* said Saint Paul[30]— the priest need not worry too much about the results.

---

[27] Jn 8:46.
[28] Jn 15:22.
[29] Mt 3:3.
[30] 1 Cor 9:16.

The priest must be ready to preach the Word drawing on the deepest feelings of his heart, after having taken the Word to prayer, and through a life devoted to working for the good of the faithful. This is not an easy task for it demands from him the *sweating of blood*, being beset by responsibility and zeal for souls, elaborating his work again and again in the dialogue of prayer and through the efforts of study... and always with the feeling, impossible to dispel, that, after all, *what he has said* was not what he would have liked to communicate to the faithful. Therefore, aware of his inability to carry out an undertaking which transcends him completely, the priest is forced to put his trust in the Lord; *and only then is when his preaching begins to bear fruit.*

Bernanos said, in his *Diary of a Country Priest*, that it was necessary that the Word of God should *wound deeply* the hearts of listeners in order to bear fruit, and that, consequently, the priest who preaches it must be the first to be affected by it. For if the Word does not pierce his heart, it is quite likely that his preaching does not have a real impact on his listeners. Preaching is not *uttering a speech*, as any man of this world might do, but an act of submission and obedience to God in order to spread His Word which will always entail the personal immolation of the priest.

With regard to what in times past was called *sacred oratory* it is necessary to recognize that quite often more emphasis was laid on *oratory* than on *sacred*. Unlike what happens in the new post-conciliar Church, where *oratory* has no meaning at all, let alone *sacred*.

Nevertheless, when his preaching is authentic the priest tries to deliver and transmit to the faithful his own life through an act in regard to which, with a view to obtaining a greater effect and a more intense participation in the Cross of Christ and his sheep, God

Himself allows the priest to consider it sometimes as useless (though in reality it never is).

When the priest culminates his life and reaches old age, if by chance he looks back, he will better understand many things of the past with reason enough to start mourning. *But why...?* some may ask. Probably because then his existence appears as a failure, given the many things left to be done and the time that he could have used to love God more intensely. But in reality, on second thought, not everything in the past was bad; there were even many good things, in greater abundance, than bad things. And as to mourning... as Gandalf said in Tolkien's epic, *not all tears are an evil*, as they are often the fruit of joy and the result of the truer consideration that God is good. But also, if the priestly life were not to end in failure, it would not have had any worth, since failure and nothing else was the life of Jesus Christ, culminating in His Death on a Cross which was what gave life to the world.

The existence and the culmination of the life of the priest cannot be different from that of his Master. And if, once he has reached the end of the road, he humbly thinks that he has done too little, he can be sure that he would hear at that moment these most sweet and loving words from the mouth of the Lord: *Well done, good and faithful servant, because thou hast been faithful over a few things, I will place thee over many things: enter thou into the joy of thy lord.*[31]

---

[31] Mt 25:21.

Conclusion

The priestly life as tragedy

It was certainly Bernanos, in his *Diary of a Country Priest*, who best described the life of a priest as *tragic*.

Perhaps it would be convenient, before anything else, to note that the noun *tragedy* or its adjective *tragic* is not taken here in its usual meaning, but rather in its derivative, although true, sense. The same applies to the word *failure* when applied, as has been done throughout this work, to the balance of a priestly life exacted at its culmination.

If we stick to the current and usual meaning of these words, true tragedy and complete failure must be properly applied to the existence of a bad priest. God alone knows the possibility, explanation, and causes of this unfortunate event as well as its final destiny.

Nevertheless, Bernanos' work inevitably brings about some pessimism in the reader, or some sorrow at least, not easy to dispel. But this feeling, referring as it does to a supernatural vocation and destiny, has no reasonable explanation, *for it is impossible to find the slightest shadow of pessimism in any supernatural reality*. Hence it must be said that the character of the Curé of Ambricourt, despite the well–deserved grandeur it holds in Universal Literature, inevitably fails at some point.

It would be easy to start looking for possible causes of the said pessimism in the serious illness of the character, the terrible loneliness in which he lived, and his pastoral failure regarding the faithful entrusted to him. But these explanations can easily be refuted, for none of them can justify the feelings of dejection and sadness that seem to surround the character. One might even say that loneliness, illness, or pastoral failures are the usual conditions that must accompany a holy priestly life.

Probably the real reason for the pessimism that seems to emerge from the work is more complex and even impossible to explain by anyone who cannot look at this issue and judge it from the right perspective.

First, it is not often noted that the Curé of Ambricourt was a priest; consequently, it would be quite difficult for anyone who is not a priest to determine the situation of his alleged *tragedy*. And Bernanos was not a priest, though no one would question his status as a true Christian. However, the fact is that the heart of a priest, because of the sacramental character he receives at his ordination, *can only be known by another priest*. Therefore, a layman, even if he has more sanctity than any particular priest, never ceases to be a layman to whom the mysterious sanctuary of a priestly soul remains inaccessible.

Second, and the most important point which Bernanos failed to consider when he created his character, the tragedy of a priest is not like any other tragedy, differing only to the greater or lesser degree of severity each could reach, which, at this point, would be inconsequential; it is an entirely *sui generis* tragedy which is in no way comparable to any other tragedy, for the simple reason that the tragedy of a priest is *a copy of the tragedy that took place at Golgotha* and which, although being a real tragedy, belongs to an order higher and more sublime than all other orders, in that, in addition to other circumstances and peculiarities, it was precisely this tragedy that *gave life to the World*.

It is for this reason that the existence of a priest can never give rise to a pessimistic attitude; on the contrary, his life will be the less pessimistic and *his priestly existence* indeed *the more triumphant and glorious* the more the world regards it as a failed and sad existence.

Both points, as one might expect, escaped the genius of Bernanos; hence the unmistakably pessimistic atmosphere that surrounds his character. Thus, when one considers the novel as a whole, while recognizing its undisputable literary value, it is hard to deny that the semblance of the character depicted by Bernanos, despite its unquestionable greatness, misses important features that render that semblance incomplete, making it —at least from a certain perspective, from which Bernanos should have looked at his character— unreal and merely fictional; for one cannot think that Bernanos wanted make the Curé of Ambricourt appear as a failure in his vocation and his priestly existence, which certainly was alien to the mind of Bernanos.

It is true, however, that the apparent pessimism of the novel is partly redeemed at the end of its Epilogue, when his friend and former priest, in the attic of whose house in Paris the dying Curé of Ambricourt had taken refuge, informed him that the requested priest from the neighboring parish would not arrive in time to give him the last rites. The Country Priest, already in the throes of his agony, responds with words which Charles Moeller rightly terms as the most beautiful phrase of the entire twentieth–century Literature: *Does it matter? Grace is everywhere...*

In effect, priestly life as a *tragedy* goes unnoticed to the world if we understand this term in the sense explained here and which is unknown to anyone other than a priest.

The enmity of Jesus Christ with the world is repeatedly narrated in the Scriptures: *He came unto his own, and his own received him not.*[32] *He was in the world, and the world was made by him, and the*

---

[32] Jn 1:11.

world knew him not.[33] *If the world hateth you, know ye, that it hath hated me before you.*[34] *In the world you shall have distress: but have confidence, I have overcome the world.*[35] So it is not surprising that being unknown and even despised by the world is a destiny which takes shape in a special way in the life of a priest as he continues His mission, as Saint Paul wrote in a rather descriptive way: *But in all things let us exhibit ourselves as the ministers of God, in much patience, in tribulation, in necessities, in distresses, in stripes, in prisons, in seditions, in labours, in watchings, in fastings, in chastity, in knowledge, in long suffering, in sweetness, in the Holy Ghost, in charity unfeigned, in the word of truth, in the power of God; by the armour of justice on the right hand and on the left; by honour and dishonour, by evil report and good report; as deceivers, and yet true; as unknown, and yet known; as dying, and behold we live; as chastised, and not killed; as sorrowful, yet always rejoicing; as needy, yet enriching many; as having nothing, and possessing all things.*[36]

The priest lives in the world and gives his life for his brethren. But he does not expect —he cannot expect— any recognition or appreciation from them or from the world. His life is hidden in Christ —the only thing his heart longs for and which can satisfy him— and he is dead to the world. Therefore, what Saint Paul said to the Colossians can be especially applied to him: *You are dead, and your life is hidden with Christ in God.*[37] And speaking of himself the Apostle added something which is meant for any Christian but which affects in a unique way and to a greater degree those who exercise the office of priesthood: *But God forbid that I should glory,*

---

[33] Jn 1:10.
[34] Jn 15:18.
[35] Jn 16:33.
[36] 2 Cor 6: 4–10.
[37] Col 3:3.

save in the cross of our Lord Jesus Christ; by whom the world is crucified to me, and I to the world.[38]

The great secret of the life of a priest, quite contrary to what the spirit of the world or even he himself might think, is not merely the fact that he sees his life as a *tragedy*, as in fact it certainly is, but that *he finds in this fact his glory and joy, wanting nothing else*. The Apostle said of himself, as we have seen, that he *gloried* in being crucified with Christ to the world. Consequently, the priest *will never bear fruit in his ministry or find the secret of Joy even in this life* as long as he does not consider it his glory to be forgotten, despised, and even persecuted. We can also affirm here that the fruit of the priestly ministry is in inverse ratio to his attempt to live his own life. The number of sacred ministers who, because of their desire for prominence, have ruined their existence, *perhaps for eternity*, is another mystery of the History of the Church known to God alone and providentially ignored by those still active and exercising their ministry within the Church.

The central point concerning this issue, as can easily be deduced from what has been said, is *the love of Jesus Christ*. The priest is not only convinced that his mission is to continue the mission of his Lord, which, being a great weight in itself, would be little for him; precisely because he is another Christ —*Alter Christus*, as the right Doctrine has always called him—, he ardently wants nothing other than to *identify himself with his Master*, urged by his love for Him; for love passionately longs to unite the destiny of the lover to the fate of the Loved One. And if *tragedy* was the life of his Master and Lord, *tragedy* and nothing else is what the priest wants as the culmination of his own life.

---

[38] Gal 6:14.

The *tragic* destiny of the priest entails that he needs to live on hope. As we have repeated throughout this essay, although the basic virtues of Christian life are the heritage of all Christians, they belong in a special and peculiar way to the priestly existence, so much so that some features of those virtues will affect the life of the priest exclusively; which is what happens, in a way, with the virtue of hope.

Hope is necessary for the practice of any virtue; therefore, *a heroic virtue must be accompanied by a heroic hope*, like Abraham *who against all hope believed in hope*.[39] Furthermore, hope is a theological virtue and therefore closely related to love. All this is confirmed by the words of Saint Paul in a text referring especially to the priestly life: *And not only so; but we glory also in tribulations, knowing that tribulation worketh patience; and patience trial; and trial hope; and hope confoundeth not.*[40]

But hope longs securely for *what it does not have and what is yet unseen*. For, as the Apostle says, *a hope that is seen is not hope. For what a man seeth, why doth he hope for?*[41] We have reached the central point that turns the existence of the priest into a *tragedy*. His heart, which is supposed to be in love with Jesus Christ, is yearning because he does not yet feel himself fully identified with Him, or because he does not love Christ as ardently as he should or as he would like to love Him. And most painful of all, as the feeling which most deeply overwhelms his soul: *because he does not yet see Him face to face or fully own Him.* And is there anything which would inflame more with burning fire a loving soul than to suffer the absence of the Loved One...?

---

[39] Rom 4:18.
[40] Rom 5: 3–5.
[41] Rom 8:24.

Someone may rightly think that we are stepping into the realm of mysticism to which, strictly speaking, the priest is not bound. Catholic Doctrine, however, has assiduously repeated that the priest is *Alter Christus* and *must be holy*. The problem is that these and similar expressions have degenerated into mere clichés to which nobody pays any attention, hence the tremendous consequence: the priest who from the very beginning has not set his sights on reaching an *intimate union and loving friendship with Jesus Christ has given up forever a life abundant in fruits and graces from Heaven for both himself and the faithful*. And any minister of the Lord, since he has been called to a vocation of intense apostolate —*That you should bring forth fruit; and your fruit should remain*[42]— who has not undertaken at the beginning of his consecrated life the necessity of being holy would find himself in a situation that would make him the most miserable of men.

Saint John of the Cross, a mystic truly in love with Jesus Christ, expressed with his wonderful verses these sentiments:

> *Upon a gloomy night,*
> *With all my cares to loving ardours flushed,*
> *(O venture of delight!)*
> *With nobody in sight*
> *I went abroad when all my house was hushed.*[43]
>
> *Where can your hiding be,*
> *Beloved, that you left me thus to moan*
> *While like the stag you flee*
> *Leaving the wound with me?*
> *I followed calling loud, but you had flown.*[44]

---

[42] Jn 15:16.
[43] Saint John of the Cross, *Dark Night of the Soul*.
[44] Saint John of the Cross, *Spiritual Canticle*.

In this way, the priestly existence, even though it is called to end in a tragic destiny —in the truest and deepest sense of the word— can never be regarded as tragic as the world understands this term. Truly speaking, it is a road on which somebody walks and which is verily marked by the Cross and suffocated by labors and sufferings; a road which, at the same time is studded —by a strange and inexplicable paradox— with sweet and wonderful feelings that love alone can cause in the soul of the traveler, now savored only in earnest, but intended to deflagrate, once it finally reaches its End, into the Fire of Infinite Love.

Between success and the possibility of an easy life, including the approval of the world and even a harvest of abundant fruits of apostolate and, conversely, the spectacular failure of an existence, useless in the eyes of the world, filled with work and suffering, and in the end culminating in a life and death that never went beyond being totally indifferent and unknown to the world, the priest in love with the Lord Jesus will certainly choose this latter destiny for no other reason than that it is the same as that of his Master.

It is for this reason that here, as happened with the actors in the Ancient World who were involved in Greek tragedy, some kind of *cothurnus* is needed to represent this tragedy; which is precisely the absolute necessity and indispensable willingness to open one's heart to true Love. And this is why the *aptitude to fall in love* would be the only criterion for evaluating the authenticity of a true vocation to the priesthood.

THE GREAT DINNER AND THE DISCOURTEOUS GUESTS[1]

Dear brethren in the Hearts of Our Lord and the Blessed Virgin Mary, Our Mother:

Today, the second Sunday after Pentecost, and as prescribed by the Extraordinary Form of the Roman Rite of the Mass, the Church invites us to consider the Gospel passage from Saint Luke which tells the story of the guests invited to a great banquet who, contrary to what would have been logical to expect, one after another began to make excuses under various pretexts.

According to one of them, he had bought a farm and had to go see it; so he offered his apologies. Another argued that he had just acquired five yoke of oxen and wanted to try them, and so he also begged to be excused. A third explained that he had married and consequently he considered himself justified for not attending.

The *householder*, the host who had invited them to the great wedding banquet, became so angry that he ordered his servant: *Go out quickly into the streets and lanes of the city, and bring in hither the poor, and the feeble, and the blind, and the lame.* The servant carried out his master's bid and then he said: *Lord, it is done as thou hast commanded, and yet there is room.* And the Lord said to the servant: *Go out into the highways and hedges, and compel them to come in, that my house may be filled.*

---

[1] Preached on June 7, 2015.

The parable or story is quite expressive and, as always happens with the teachings of the Lord, lends itself to many detailed considerations.

The first thing that calls one's attention is the fact that the guests were called to a great supper —*cenam magnam*—, whereby the evangelical teaching begins by underlining one transcendental fact: God offers man the Love of His own Heart. But man, in the vein of the invited to the great supper of the parable, usually responds by declining the offer and inventing the most diverse excuses to justify his behavior. This causes us to think about the need for every Christian to consider himself as one of the reluctant guests, because most people respond with a negative answer to the offer God makes of His Love and Friendship.

What is inexplicable is the fact that someone might believe that the projects he has imagined for himself can be more interesting than what God offers him. And in this respect, anyone can look at those around him, and especially at his own person, to verify that this is precisely what usually happens. For when God offers the Whole, man chooses the part; if God grants him the possibility of greatness, man prefers smallness; and when God opens the way of perfect Joy, man tends to pay no attention and considers it a better choice to grasp the tiny pleasures offered by his earthly existence: *For my people have done two evils. They have forsaken me, the fountain of living water, and have digged to themselves cisterns, broken cisterns, that can hold no water.*[2] Man does not want to realize that his thoughts, plans, and projects are always small and even laughable compared to the thoughts and projects that God has prepared for him, despite the fact that Christ warns us in one of His teachings, which always seem to fall on deaf ears since almost nobody pays any attention to

---

[2] Jer 2:13.

them, that *he that findeth his life, shall lose it: and he that shall lose his life for me, shall find it.*³

Here lies the great tragedy of mankind. On the one hand, there is the option for the supernatural, spiritual, and durable goods which are able to provide man with the true meaning of his life and the keys to Perfect Joy (as a pledge in this world and with the promise of Its fulfillment in the other). On the other hand, man is offered material and sensitive goods that surround him and continually require his attention, whose goodness and beauty are undeniable, as things created by God and thus reflections of His Goodness and Beauty, but also ephemeral and thus unable to satisfy man's heart.

It is here that the mystery of human freedom comes into play along with the unfathomable and unpredictable feelings of man's heart, making it possible that one of the most important instructions of the Apostle Saint Paul, which defines the entire human existence, may remain forgotten and not taken into account: *Seek the things that are above; where Christ is sitting at the right hand of God; mind the things that are above, not the things that are upon the earth.*⁴

In this passage, special attention must be paid to the reason given by the Apostle for seeking the things that are Above: *Christ is sitting there at the right hand of God.* For Jesus Christ is the Life of man (Col 3:4), the only thing that fills the longings of his heart, the sum of all his hopes, and the key to the Perfect Joy that he has always sought. Christians are convinced of this much, but then the reality of the necessary struggle to put what has been said into practice makes itself felt, and not everyone is willing to put up that fight.

---

[3] Mt 10:39.
[4] Col 3: 1–2.

The weakness and frailty of human nature lead man to be easily captivated by the things of this world, which are easier to acquire and within one's reach; and man does not mind much that they lack the sublime greatness of supernatural things. This can be seen, for example, in human love: no matter how pure and elevated this love may be, it can never be compared with the Divine love or with divine–human love, given the immeasurable difference that mediates between them. And herein lies the need to fight that urges the Christian, a pilgrim member of the Militant Church after all, walking through labors and sweat on the path that leads to Life (Mt 7:14) until he reaches the End, which is attained only by those who shall *persevere to the end* (Mt 24:13).

Thus the life of every man who comes into this world is faced with the inexorable dilemma: either the things *above* or the things *below*. This is why the *Book of Job* says that the life of every man during his stay on earth is a warfare (Job 7:1); and hence also the promise that the Spirit repeatedly makes, contained in the Seven Letters to the Churches, in the Book of the *Apocalypse*: the prize will only be awarded to him that *overcometh*.[5]

We have already seen that those invited to the banquet declined their attendance, alleging various excuses. These pretexts are but a small example of the infinite number of justifications, each one more varied than the next, frequently invoked by man to reject God's offer, which, in turn, are nothing more than one of the many means man uses to deceive himself; deceiving one's neighbor is the result of an evil state of mind, difficult to explain; but self–deception is the consequence of suffering from supreme stupidity, impossible to explain.

---

[5] Rev 2:7; 2:11; 2:17, etc.

This implies a *tragic* situation for man, for having been created for and destined to *eternal joy* he has traded this end for *temporal joy*, which he thinks *definitive* but which is doomed to end in *eternal failure without any possibility of mending*; all this because man's capacity for self–deception is nearly boundless.

Consequently, Jesus' words are forgotten according to which, *he that findeth his life, shall lose it: and he that shall lose his life for my sake, shall find it* (Mt 16:25). Unfortunately humans are not very drawn to paradoxes, let alone to those affecting their own existence. And the problem becomes more complicated when, as in this case, love is involved; for it is not enough to be willing to lose one's life, it must be lost *out of love*.

We should not forget that man has been created to love and be loved. But sin shielded the human soul with a refractory layer of love, pushing man to *enclose* himself in his egotism when actually he had been destined to *open* himself to the roads that lead to self–surrender. Roads whose viability necessarily requires the *other*, a key component without which the dialogue of love —the ultimate and defining element of human existence— cannot happen.

The words of Jesus Christ may seem harsh to human nature suffering from weakness caused by sin. Therefore, man is reluctant to believe them, despite the fact that Jesus Christ Himself said that they are *spirit and life*,[6] and without considering that their rejection has brought about, among other things, the so–called *culture of death* and aberrations such as abortion and euthanasia. Therefore, His words are hard to hear, too profound to be understood, and difficult to explain. This last consequence can be easily seen in the fact that His teachings are no longer preached; they have been abandoned by modern Pastoral activity that is muzzled for fear of hurting the

---

[6] Jn 6:63.

ears of the world: a categorical demonstration that this Pastoral has stopped believing in them.

Since the twentieth century until today preaching in Spain has gone through several phases that can be summarized in three. The first would extend well into the twentieth century and exemplifies a period of *sacred oratory* in which it was customary to put more emphasis on *oratory* than on *sacred*. The second would reach to the end of General Franco's era and the first years of the so-called transition; *anti-Franco political preaching*, essentially Marxist, was all the rage, followed by a period of years of *preaching platitudes*. The third stage comprises the entire post-conciliar period and is characterized by the absolute dominance of *modernist preaching*. It is true that in some places, here and there, there has been a *Catholic preaching* of the Gospel teaching, but it is the exception. No wonder the words of the Apostle Saint John are still relevant today: *They are of the world: therefore of the world they speak, and the world heareth them.*[7]

But the harsh reality of existence imposes itself upon every man. If one wants to find the meaning of life, to escape the emptiness that the world and its things cause in the soul, to free himself from the clutches of an environment in which lies and falsehoods prevail, to escape from the darkness that blinds the mind and hardens the heart, to eliminate the feelings of anxiety and gloom with which the spirit of modernity tries to drown one's personality..., one will have to turn to the words of Jesus Christ as the only recourse that will lead him to the true Life which He Himself came to bring us (Jn 10:10).

Preferring the life one has chosen for himself and ignoring the will of God leads to the *failure of one's own existence* without any

---

[7] 1 Jn 4:5.

possibility of return, since no man has been granted the option to live another life; and the absurdities and platitudes espoused by strange philosophies as the acceptance of *reincarnation*, in which almost no one believes, are not worth a thought. The truth is that each man decides his own life on a roadmap that his choices outline but in which there is no possibility of return once man has reached the end. Neither will the pretext of *having made a mistake* be accepted as a valid argument. Ultimately, what is at stake here is nothing more and nothing less than the problem of *eternal salvation or damnation.*

Facing the possibility of making the *mistake* of choosing the path that leads to eternal damnation, it is absolutely necessary for every man to think of the reality of Hell, which is included within the scope of the eternity *without time*, which in turns precludes any speculation about endless time in it. This place does not brook posing the possibility of an *end* since there is no *beginning* (both are factors that necessarily depend on the concept of *time*); it is merely a *being there*, with a total abstraction of realities now nonexistent, as *before* or *afterwards, beginning* or *end.* All possibility of hope gone, the damned has no other choice but to consider his past life as a wasted opportunity, now turned into an insufferable curse that will last *without taking any duration into consideration.*

Many try to deceive themselves and negate the existence of Hell.

But reality is equally indifferent to man's hopes and to his bad omens. He may choose freely: dreaming of a better future or fearing a rather miserable tomorrow; living on dreams or being anchored in reality; affirming what he pleases or denying what he wants; opting for truth or agreeing with the lie. But the world of reality does not depend on what he thinks or does not think about it, but *on what things really are and how they are.* The real disaster for Humanity began when man abandoned the Philosophy of being and decided that thought does not depend on reality, but that reality is determined and defined by thought. Of course, these Philosophies always bumped into something so obvious and evident as are the conclusions of *common sense*, which is the power given by God to man to walk through the world with open eyes, without falling into ravines or rushing into the abyss. When man decides that his power of perception *does not depend on the reality of things*, and that *the reality of things depends on his own perception*, man has properly become blind, with the consequences already known: *Can the blind lead the blind? Do they not both fall into the ditch?*[8] As can easily be seen in the events of daily life, putting aside common sense leads inevitably to madness of mind and absurd stupidity.

The parable goes on to say that the master of the house was so angry because his guests had rejected his call that he said to his servant:

—Go out quickly into the streets and lanes of the city, and bring in hither the poor, and the feeble, and the blind, and the lame.

The parable, which is quite expressive, shows quite clearly that it is usually not the rich who answer the call to attend the divine banquet. Rather they are the ones who despise the divine offer and choose the things of this world which they regard as the only *wealth* that can satiate the longings of their heart. The bought farm, the acquired five yoke of oxen, the recently celebrated wedding are merely rhetorical figures that the parable uses to express the preferences of those who opt for the world and despise Jesus Christ. Small wonder that Saint Paul painfully complains about the behavior of one of his disciples: *Demas hath left me, loving this world.*[9]

---

[8] Lk 6:39.
[9] 2 Tim 4:10.

The fact that the *poor* are the ones who are subsequently called and accept the invitation of the master of the house, thus replacing those who being *rich* did not want to come to the supper, is another of the mysterious paradoxes that intersperse Christian life. This leads us to the enigmatic announcement of the Gospel stating that the Kingdom of Heaven belongs to the poor: *Blessed are the poor, for yours is the kingdom of God*;[10] which poses a complex issue present throughout the Message of Jesus Christ: the confrontation between the *love of the world*, with its pomp and works and all its elements, on the one hand, and Christian *poverty*, on the other.

Poverty is the closest virtue to *charity* and is so intimately linked to it that one can say that poverty is somehow second to charity in importance. He who loves surrenders everything out of love and becomes a destitute person who possesses nothing because he has given his belongings to the beloved; this is the key element of poverty as a prerequisite to enter the Kingdom of Heaven: *Every one of you that does not renounce all that he possesseth, cannot be my disciple.*[11] And Saint Paul clearly affirms: *For see your vocation, brethren, that there are not many wise according to the flesh, not many mighty, not many noble; but the foolish things of the world hath God chosen, that he may confound the wise; and the weak things of the world hath God chosen, that he may confound the strong.*[12] An approach which is confirmed by the little appreciation Jesus Christ showed for the rich: *Amen, I say to you, that a rich man shall hardly enter into the kingdom of heaven. It is easier for a camel to pass through the eye*

---

[10] Lk 6:20.
[11] Lk 14:33.
[12] 1 Cor 1: 26–27.

of a needle.[13] And in another place He said: *You cannot serve God and mammon.*[14]

This issue cannot be resolved in a simplistic way, but Saint Thomas offers a well–thought answer to it in his treatise *De Perfectione Vitae Spiritualis*;[15] there the Saint reminds us that Saint Matthew, Saint Bartholomew, and Zacchaeus were rich and, nevertheless, entered into the Kingdom of Heaven.

However, and admitting that a clear concept of poverty based on the words and conduct of Jesus Christ has not always been given, the question arises: what exactly is the doctrine of the Founder of Christianity on the apparently opposing concepts of *wealth* and *poverty*?

If one attentively examines the text of Matthew 6:24: *You cannot serve God and mammon*, one can easily see that it is not a matter of *possessing or not possessing* wealth but of *being intent on serving* it, which would imply a preference of wealth over God, which, in turn, would preclude entering the Kingdom of Heaven. In fact, this is what happens with most of those who in addition to having riches dedicate their lives to serving them; hence their danger. On the other hand, the text of Matthew 5:3, where the *poor in spirit* are mentioned, clarifies Saint Luke's passage introducing the true concept of Christian poverty. Saint Thomas also makes reference to an observation made by Saint Augustine regarding the words of Jesus Christ stating that it is easier for a camel to pass through the eye of a needle than for a rich man to enter into the kingdom of heaven: according to Saint Augustine (*De quæst. Evang.*), the

---

[13] Mt 19: 23–24.

[14] Mt 6:24.

[15] This issue is amply studied in my book *The Importunate Friend*, Shoreless Lake Press, New Jersey, 1995, pp. 134 and ff.

disciples understood that they who covet riches are included in the number of the rich; otherwise, considering how small is the number of the wealthy in comparison to the vast multitude of the poor, they would not have asked: *Who then shall be saved?* Jesus Christ Himself mingled and ate with the poor as well as the rich.

The underlying problem here is the corruption of the idea of *poverty* that Evil has managed to introduce into the Christian mindset in order to create serious confusion. Poverty being the closest virtue to charity and entirely linked to it, and charity being the nuclear element of Christian life, the manipulation of the meaning of poverty has dealt a blow to the Faith of Christian people, who have come to be suspicious of anything that has to do with wealth.

The severity of this issue is better understood when one considers that of all the cardinal virtues poverty is the most important for Christian existence as a course of action that connects it to charity. Its importance gives rise to its sublime beauty and to the preference that the Gospel shows for the poor, the humble, and the little ones of this world: *I confess to thee, O Father, Lord of heaven and earth, because thou hast hidden these things from the wise and prudent, and hast revealed them to little ones. Yea, Father, for so it hath seemed good in thy sight.*[16] Poverty's dependence on charity surrounds it with a special aura of love and sweetness, as well as a particular charm that oozes out of its nature and clothes it with an extraordinary power of attraction. Far from demanding anything, poverty is rather willing to give everything; alien to any rebellious spirit, poverty rejoices with meekness, humility, love of neighbor, fixing its hopes on God alone Whom poverty loves.

Marxist poverty, on the contrary, lacks any vestige of charity and love of neighbor. The so–called *option for the poor* of Marxist

---

[16] Lk 10:21.

ideology, adopted, in turn, by those Catholic doctrines infected with Marxism, is nothing short of a corruption and manipulation of Christian poverty. This *option*, fed as it is by feelings of hatred and rebellion against others, is ready to reclaim what it asserts to have been deprived of, while it is convinced that it owes nothing to anyone. It grows on the assumption that it has been subjected to economic and social misery because of the injustices inflicted upon it by the bourgeoisie as the main oppressor class, *being absolutely indifferent as to whether such injustice is real or fictitious*; this indifference was foreseen by the Marxist doctrine as a fundamental and essential principle of the so–called *class struggle*, which demands that a *situation of injustice be created where it does not really exist*, as the most efficacious instrument in vanquishing the *bourgeoisie* and the Christian principles which support it. In short, it is a concept of poverty concocted by Marxist ideologies, based on hatred against any kind of Christian values and the desire to eliminate everything that is based on them, namely the most fundamental rights of human nature affecting the dignity of persons and the elimination of all vestiges in favor of freedom.

This is the *poverty* that has been introduced into Catholicism mainly through *Liberation Theology* and which has become a basic principle of the Doctrine and Pastoral action of the modern Church; it is being disseminated freely and unopposed by her most high–ranking Shepherds. Many years of continuous preaching along this line of thought has managed to bring about in the majority of the faithful a concept of poverty energized by malice and falsehood that withholds from them the sublime treasure of grandeur and eternal life that could effect in them the practice of true Christian poverty.

According to the parable, the invited guests offered various excuses not go to the feast to which they had been summoned. All three excuses, and many others that could have been put forward, agree on preferring the life that each guest has chosen for himself to the life intended for him by our loving God; despite the pettiness and vulgarity of a purely natural existence, devoid of lofty horizons, compared to the greatness of a supernatural destiny which can raise man to heights he has never imagined in his mind or in his heart.

Unfortunately Christians often disregard the otherwise essential words of Jesus Christ which shape not only their lives in this world but also their eternal destiny. Every man begins his existence by planning how to face the future of his ordinary life: getting the best preparation to perform in the world in which he lives, choosing a profession, raising a family, reaching a certain position in society, etc.

But man often forgets that his personal existence encompasses two different but tightly connected and interdependent stages. The first one, short and ephemeral, is very important, for it is the determinant of the second, which is eternal and decisive. The second is his final destination or end station, unlike the first which is only a stopover.

Man's tragedy is precisely that he believes that the stopover is his final destination; therefore, his existence is already truncated from the start. But man's destiny remains eternal; consequently his destiny does not end at the stopping place which now becomes merely a location for changing the tracks that will lead the train of his life to another destination: damnation. And this will happen because man made the tremendous blunder of planning his existence for only the first part (short, fleeting) that actually is merely a preparation and determinant of the second (final and eternal). In short, one faces the tremendous mistake of planning one's *entire existence* while ignoring Jesus Christ's statement that *he who seeks his own life, will lose it.* Some of the words Jesus Christ uttered, which apparently at least are the hardest and most paradoxical statements of the entire Gospel, emphatically declare that the only way to win one's own life is to *lose it out of love for Him*. Hence it is necessary to recognize that the willingness to lose one's own life is one of the unique mysteries of human existence, whose only explanation is love. If love means giving, giving up what man is most fond of —his own life— is the greatest love: *Greater love than this no man hath, that a man lay down his life for his friends.*[17]

The situation described continues to pose a major problem. For what might seem a *heroic* act becomes, instead, *normal*, something that belongs to the essence of Christian life. This means that Christian life is always *naturally heroic*, even if it transpires through the most ordinary circumstances that define the existence of any ordinary Christian. And surprisingly enough, trying to understand in any other way the Christian Faith is to turn away from the Sources of Revelation that contain the doctrine preached by Jesus Christ.

This doctrine and Modernism are poles apart. Modernism denies the sacrificial and propitiatory character of Redemption, the existence of sin, the need of repentance for salvation; it advocates instead a naturalistic ethics of comfort incompatible with any vestige of personal effort and struggle on the part of the Christian and any means conducive to sharing the Cross of Jesus Christ as an instrument of salvation. Jesus Christ Himself, Who said of His own Person that He was the Way and the only way to the Father (Jn 14:6), also taught that the way that leads to Life goes through a *narrow gate and few there are that find it.*[18]

---

[17] Jn 15:13.
[18] Mt 7:14.

This configuration of Christian existence is far from divine whim. We have said that the heroism inherent to Christian life is the result of love, which is by nature *totality* and absence of any kind of conditions: *You shall love the Lord with "all" your heart, with "all" your soul, with "all" your mind... Love one another "as I have loved you"... Jesus, having loved his own who were in the world, "he loved them to the end"... As the Father has loved me, "so I have loved you"... I no longer call you servants, "but friends"...* Christianity, contrary to what many believe, is not a doctrine to take or leave according to taste, but only to take: *He that is not with me is against me; and he that gathereth not with me, scattereth;*[19] which puts aside any middle–of–the–road positions and states of indecision or indifference while establishing a categorical statement, whether fully with Christ or fully against Christ, according to the express and explicit teaching of the Lord Himself. One of the most characteristic features of the current modernist Church is its amphibological, misleading, verbose, and bombastic language; in stark contrast to the concise and clear language of Jesus Christ: *Let your speech be yea, yea; no, no; and that which is over and above these, is of evil.*[20] As the Apostle James said: *Let your speech be, yea, yea; no, no; that you fall not under judgement.*[21] The false theology and misplaced Pastoral action of the modernist Church dare to question not only the words of Jesus Christ but also His historical existence, which is clear evidence that the general Apostasy announced for the apocalyptic times has put its seal even upon the Hierarchy itself.

And the parable continues, saying that the master of the house became angry at the failure of his potential guests to attend the

---

[19] Mt 12:30.
[20] Mt 5:37.
[21] Jas 5:12.

call that he had extended to them. Apparently, according to the story, they were selected people and, therefore, they were expected to attend the magnificent banquet prepared for them. The disappointment of the host is humanly understandable, since his intention, certainly motivated by a burning and deep affection, was to offer an extremely expensive and exquisitely prepared gift which, even so, was rejected by those to whom it was offered, with the aggravating circumstances put forward by the irrelevant and clearly spurious excuses.

It should be noted that the master of the house —God, according to the meaning of the parable— had paid an extremely high price for the great supper prepared for His guests: nothing less than *the blood of His own Son*. On the other hand, the mendacious excuses of the guests did not constitute in this case a mere attempt to justify themselves but also had the intention of deceiving their host, God Himself, Whom they also affronted by the contempt shown towards the gift offered by Him.

There were, therefore, more than enough justifiable reasons for the irritation of the master of the house and for the invitations addressed to guests *never to be repeated*. This detail of the parable usually goes unnoticed, but it clearly shows, once again, that there are no second chances, or at least that there is the possibility that a second chance may not be offered, which is sufficient reason to not endanger one's existence to total failure. This is what Saint Augustine meant when he said *Fear that Jesus is passing because He may not pass by again*. If it is dangerous to put all one's eggs into one basket, it is even more risky to jeopardize one's personal eternal destiny for what may be a unique opportunity where *there is no return from failure*; which is precisely what millions of Christians do every day thinking, apparently, that life —the only life that has been granted to them and on which their entire existence depends— is just a children's game, as inconsequential as it is irrelevant and frivolous.

Rage compelled the master of the house to immediately address his servant and urge him to act quickly:

—*Go out quickly into the streets and alleys of the town and bring in here the poor, the crippled, the blind and the lame.*

The expression *quickly* uttered by the master of the house indicates anger because of the offense received and the desire to *never remember again* the first invited guests; which underlines what has been said about how risky despising God may become.

This second call, which is the ultimately effective summons, highlights a striking and peculiar fact which we have mentioned before but which still provides important considerations. What is clearly shown in the text is that the ones who respond positively to God's offer are not the rich and powerful of this world but the poor, that is those who are *despised and forgotten by the world*. In this way, it is evident, for those who want to see reality, that the Mystical Body of Christ, which is the Church to which all Christians officially belong, is divided into two major different and even antagonistic camps.

On one side are those who respond to God's call —the poor and wretched of this world—, the members of the first group; on the other side are those who despise that call —the rich and powerful of the world—, those who make up the second group. The bizarre thing about this situation is that the vast majority of Christians *strive earnestly to join the second group*, as if it were the better one and the key to their destiny, while they despise and flee from anything that could lead them to the first group, forgetting that this, and not the second group, is the only path that would lead them to Life and the ultimate existence for which they were created.

What has been said leads us to interesting as well as important conclusions. The various doctrines and theories on social classes (that began in earnest with the works of Karl Marx and Max Weber), their evolution and the role each has played at different times in history, the influence of the Marxist theory of *class struggle* in the twentieth century, etc., have shaped the world of sociology and politics. And yet this vast and overwhelming issue is eventually solved with the eschatological approach to the destiny of mankind —not only as the end point of history but also as the final judgment on it. This eschatological standpoint complies with the divine judgment as set forth in the Gospel of Saint Matthew (Mt 25: 31–46) whereby only two kinds of human beings are to be considered within the unchanging fabric that forms the structure of humanity. These two types, which will include all human beings, are described by the scriptural language as sheep and goats, that is, saved and damned.

This terminology coincides, ultimately, with the two different groups of guests who, according to the parable, reacted in such dissimilar ways to the divine call.

From a careful reading of the parable it is clear that both the doctrine and its application to the existence of those who claim to be Christians belong especially to the poor; only for them the doctrine and its application are intended and only by them are both received: *Hearken, my dearest brethren: hath not God chosen the poor according to the world, rich in faith, and heirs of the kingdom which God hath promised to them that love him?*[22] And as can be seen very clearly by the words of the Apostle James, the concepts of poor and poverty are to be understood in a Christian sense: *the poor according to the world*, says the Apostle, which is the same as saying those whom the world considers poor and despises as such.

---

[22] Jas 2:5.

And these poor are chosen to be made *rich in faith*, and not just in money. It is clear, once again, that the concept of poverty as the world considers it and the concept of Christian poverty are opposites and entirely incompatible.

Although Christians do not want to understand or admit this, Revelation in both its forms (Scripture and Tradition) repeats insistently that Christianity is contrary to the criteria on which the world operates. The most recent Doctrine, and primarily since the times of Modernism, strives to support the opposite; but the truth is that there is no possible reconciliation between Christianity and the World: *Adulterers, know you not that the friendship of this world is the enemy of God? Whosoever therefore will be a friend of this world, becometh an enemy of God.*[23] And Saint Paul said earlier that he preached only Christ crucified, knowing that such a thing represented a *stumbling block to Jews and foolishness to gentiles.*[24] This same madness and scandal have occurred throughout history, and today they have acquired an extraordinary momentum with an eruption within the Church of the modernist heresy which has not hesitated to destroy the foundations of Revelation and the Magisterium in order to build a *New Christianity* and a *New Church*, both governed by worldly standards foreign to any vestige of the supernatural; nevertheless, almost the entire Catholic Hierarchy, and millions of Catholics along with it, has blithely joined this heresy.

So we are back to the parable of the *Great Dinner* and its insistence on presenting the contrast between God and the world by expounding the two proposals that obtained such different results: the one offered to the rich (which ended in failure), and the subsequent call made to the poor (with its successful outcome).

---

[23] Jas 4:4.
[24] 1 Cor 1:23.

The *poor* Christian sees himself as stripped of everything and looks at the things of this world as entirely secondary; understanding well that *secondary* does not mean *unimportant* but rather a subordination of some things to another thing that is considered as the principal one to whom all other things make reference. Truly speaking, nobody gives more importance to the things of this world than the Christian, for he regards them as having been created by God and meant for his own salvation.

The worldly man uses things for his own benefit —or at least he thinks so—, but his only achievement is to get to the end of his life in utter nakedness that accompanies him to the grave because he cannot take any of them with him. The Christian, however, uses things to offer them to God and for His praise; therefore he reaches the culmination of his life surrounded by the glory and splendor which that *savoir faire* about things has given him.

All this is confirmed when one looks at the current situation of the world and the Church. Who are the poor and, therefore, true Christians? The Cardinals, Bishops, religious, or most of the secular clergy? But most of them deserted at one time to join the *New Church*...! Are perchance *poor* the rulers, politicians, or those who appear as heads of modern society and direct it? Perhaps the Powerful and the hoarders of money? Those who have taken over the media and are bent on deceiving and brainwashing the masses in favor of their ideologies, interest of money, or more or less shady political dealings but always for their own benefit? Those who consider themselves the architects of the world of the *intelligentsia* or the world of *Arts*? (But these modern *intellectuals* and self–proclaimed artists should be at least thanked because they have highlighted their own *foolishness* for the laughter of sensible people, which is the same ridiculousness in which the world lives.) Perhaps those worshipers of Evil who practice all kinds of degrading aberrations as they proclaim themselves the sole legislators of social Morality? The ones who in the shadows and through Secret Societies manage and direct the destinies of the world?

And who are those who hold positions of responsibility in both the civil society and the Church? Are they by chance the best, the most honest, the most intelligent, the most faithful to the true values, the more detached and concerned for the good of others...? Or rather are they the unprincipled, the flatterers, and the *climbers* of social ladders, the liars and the calculators? Are not the Freemasons, the unbelievers and wicked, the enemies of the highest human values, the scammers and deceivers, the racists and oppressors of the weak, those who run the governments of the world in which Christians never take part?

It is a not–surprising old adage which said that to understand how much God esteems money one has only to see to whom He gives it. We must always be aware and never forget something that is behind this whole issue: that money or wealth often go together with, or are almost synonymous with, what is called Power as it is understood and practiced by the World.

Here again, in summary, are the characters of the actions described by the parable; first, banquet guests: the brightest but those who did not want to go and who, in spite of that, are the only ones that count in the eyes of the World. Then, those who were called afterwards and accepted the invitation; they are the weakest and most unfortunate, nevertheless the only ones that count in the eyes of God.

But we must insist on the concept of *poverty*. Because when it is understood in a Christian sense, which is really the only sense that deserves to be taken into account, poverty is one of the most important and beautiful virtues of Christian life; and also the most difficult to understand and even more so to be practiced.

Precisely because poverty is so important —due to its great testimonial value—, it runs the risk of being easily given to histrionics, as indeed is happening today often by means of the demagogical work of the modernist Church, specifically by the Hierarchy. The false ministers and teachers of the liberal Church are the ones using poverty as a disguise to their own advantage; with remarkable success, we must admit. But the true poor are the weak and those despised by the world; they are often persecuted, as happens today to Christians loyal to their Faith, and beset by the modernist Church.

It is hardly surprising that the world persecutes those who live true poverty. Poverty, being a virtue with such a testimonial value, has the quality of evidencing the madness of a world that crazily pursues what it understands as wealth —Money and Power— but which can only cause the emptiness of the human soul. Moreover, since poverty is the most visible manifestation of *true love*, the latter is the most patent proof of the lie of a world that does not know it. Love being the supreme and authentic reality —God is the Truth and also Love—, he who does not have it remains in the lie, and who bears to be put forth as a liar?

Since poverty is a virtue linked to charity, of which the former is a prerequisite (he who loves gives up everything for love and is in a state of dispossession), it becomes as difficult to practice as it is essential to being a disciple of Jesus Christ, according to Whom, *every one of you that doth not renounce all that he possesseth, cannot be my disciple.*[25] Therefore, in order to understand poverty it is useful to know the person and the life of Saint Francis of Assisi,

---

[25] Lk 14:33.

also called the *Poverello* as one of the characters in the history of the Church who has lived poverty in the highest and most singular degree.

If poverty is both derivation and foundation of charity, and since true love means *totality*, true poverty requires *absolute dispossession*. People generally barely understand that only true love is identified with total, unconditional love for the beloved. Only he loves who has true love; and it is in divine or divine–human love where the conditions for perfect love are best met. Thus it can happen in the life of any Christian that the virtue of poverty, as any other virtue, is lowered to a lesser or even a minimum degree of perfection, which would introduce the drama of a mediocre existence governed by tepidity and immersed in vulgarity.

The teachings of Jesus Christ on this regard are, once again, so clear and categorical that they may seem even scandalous: *He that loveth father or mother more than me, is not worthy of me; and he that loveth son or daughter more than me, is not worthy of me.*[26] *If any man come to me, and hate not his father, and mother, and wife, and children, and brethren, and sisters, yea and his own life also, he cannot be my disciple.*[27] Words which show the peculiar, categorical, and unequivocal character of Christian life which demands authenticity and opposes mediocrities, conditions, hesitations, and, in general, everything that lacks generosity and does not bear the hallmark of love. Once again the *new commandment* appears as the touchstone of Christian existence, and hence perfect love has to pass the test: to put God *above all things*, as required by the first commandment. That is why Jesus said that parents should love God more than they love their children, children must love God more

---

[26] Mt 10:37.
[27] Lk 14:26.

than they love their parents, husbands should love Him more than they love their wives, and wives love Him more than they love their husbands, etc. In other words, the Christian must put his love for God *above what he loves the most in his life*. There have been many who have seen their lives destroyed forever because their parents, fully convinced that their children belonged to them as their property and exclusive possession, believed they could dispose of their children at whim.

Therefore, Christian life is a tension resulting from the enmity between the Christian and the world. Thus Saint Paul said: *In all these things we exhibit ourselves... by honour and dishonour, by evil report and good report; as deceivers, and yet true; as unknown, and yet known; as dying, and behold we live; as chastised, and not killed; as sorrowful, yet always rejoicing; as needy, yet enriching many; as having nothing, and possessing all things.*[28]

So, as the Apostle says, we appear *as deceivers, and yet true*; because the witness and confessor of truth, the disciple of Him Who said of Himself *I am the Truth*, and *I came into the world to bear witness to the truth*, must bear to be accused of lying, being a diffuser of myths, tricking people, and of all kinds of allegations connected with falsehood. It is not for nothing that the Evil one, the Spirit of the Lie who lives eternally immersed in the anguish of his own contradictions, usually attributes all his iniquities to Him Whom he hates. In the same fashion, the ideologies inimical to Christianity tend to accumulate against it all the abjections they commit.

The Apostle goes on to say that we are as *unknown, and yet known*. In effect, the disciples of the Evil one make every effort to accuse Christians of appearing as aliens to the world, living without paying attention to the course of history, ignoring the reality of

---

[28] 2 Cor 6: 8–10.

things, despising the scientific view of the cosmos to enclose themselves within their own universe of fantasy and false dreams, etc.

Moreover, when Christians perform works worthy of mention, the World is quick to discredit them or, at best, to subject them to the law of silence.

Of course iniquity is discovered in the lie of the world's own statements. In effect, if Christians mean nothing and do not count for the world, why bother to consume time and energy to prove it? On the other hand, Modernist heresy, now prevailing in the Church, bases its ideological foundations on the philosophies of Immanentism and Idealism is opposed to the philosophy of being, which is the best demonstration that it is Modernism which is *outside of reality.*

Finally, the Apostle also says that they are going to point at us *as sorrowful, yet always rejoicing.* The followers of the Evil One proclaim that only they know reality; that to them alone belong the present which can determine what the future will be. They believe themselves to be those who have rescued the world from its overreaching darkness and have discovered true human nature, which is for them merely worldly, lacking any supernatural connotation. They affirm that Christians are established in a mythological past filled with imaginary supernatural things which impels them to live in a world which is not real and which, consequently, impedes them from influencing today's world and building up the future. They consider Christianity as an ideology filled with pessimism and confusion —its most emblematic historical epoch is called the *Dark Age*— which has instilled in man feelings of bitterness and sufficient leeway to urge him to flee from this world to seek another one rooted in utopia.

But this materialistic concept of existence essential to these atheistic ideologies does not succeed in going beyond the horizon of a world entirely devoid of hope, which has nothing to offer apart from the sad reality in which those who inhabit it live. At the same time, the shortcomings and defects of which they accuse Christians are but their own, as if they were trying desperately to reflect in others what they see in themselves.

As for what life is, in reality there is no other life worthy of being called such but that which comes from the Author of Life (Jn 1:4), Who said of Himself that He was Life Itself (Jn 14:6) and had come into the world to grant it to men (Jn 10:10). Christians, on the contrary, in the midst of the trials and sufferings they endure while on pilgrimage in the world, are actually the true lords of this earth, as Saint Paul wrote to the Corinthians: *For all things are yours, whether it be Paul, or Apollo, or Cephas, or the world, or life, or death, or things present, or things to some; for all are yours; and you are Christ's; and Christ is God's.*[29]

Hence Perfect Joy is the unique heritage of Christians, as one of the fruits from the Holy Spirit (Gal 5:22) and as Jesus Christ Himself promised them.[30]

The parable goes on to say that the servant told his master that the banquet hall was filled with the poor and indigent, and yet there was still room. And his lord answered:

—*Go out into the highways and hedges, and compel them to come in, that my house may be filled with guests.*

It is worth noting that the expression *compel them to come in* nowadays sounds scandalous to the ears of a modernist Church that disregards the teachings of the Gospel whose doctrines, consequently, are rejected by the modern ecclesiastical Progressivism whose modernist approach inspired the Declaration on *Religious*

---

[29] 1 Cor 3: 22–23.
[30] Jn 16: 22.24; 17:13.

Freedom issued by the Second Vatican Council. This Declaration became a serious obstacle to the Pastoral Care of Evangelization of the Church which had remained steadfast and flourishing throughout twenty centuries.

In fact the Church has never understood apostolic zeal as an instrument for coercing souls into conversion. *The zeal of thy house hath eaten me up,*[31] in Psalm 69, refers to the very person who loves God (as easily follows from the same expression), and who is impelled by this love to work for the conversion of others. The evangelizing apostle only fulfills the command of Jesus Christ: *Going therefore, teach ye all nations; baptizing them in the name of the Father, and of the Son, and of the Holy Ghost. Teaching them to observe all things whatsoever I have commanded you.*[32] Nevertheless, the apostolic and evangelical spirit of the Church, however ardent and even justified it may be when the salvation of souls is at stake, has always taken into account the antecedent need for *freedom* of spirit of the evangelized. Actually the idea of an alleged coercion was surreptitiously introduced in the post–conciliar Catholic theology without foundation, using the customary recourse to methodological falsehoods and historical lies so much loved by Modernism.

The first obstacles to this centuries–old teaching of the Church were the ideas, rather discordant with Traditional Doctrine, contained in the Declaration *Dignitatis Humanæ* of Vatican II.

This Vatican Council declares that the human person has a right to religious freedom. This freedom means that all men are to be immune from coercion on the part of individuals or of social groups and of any human power, in such wise that no one is to be forced to act in a manner contrary to his own beliefs, whether privately or publicly, whether alone or

---

[31] Ps 69:10.
[32] Mt 28: 19–20.

in association with others, within due limits. The council further declares that the right to religious freedom has its foundation in the very dignity of the human person as this dignity is known through the revealed word of God and by reason itself. This right of the human person to religious freedom is to be recognized in the constitutional law whereby society is governed and thus it is to become a civil right.

Therefore the right to religious freedom has its foundation not in the subjective disposition of the person, but in his very nature. In consequence, the right to this immunity continues to exist even in those who do not live up to their obligation of seeking the truth and adhering to it and the exercise of this right is not to be impeded, provided that just public order be observed.[33]

As over fifty years of post–conciliar history shows, the consequences of this doctrine did not delay: confusion in the Church regarding her doctrine, liturgy, worship, self–identity, and confusion among the faithful with massive defections to Protestant sects. Much has been said and still can be said about this topic; perhaps it is best to offer an example of one of the most recent events at the time of this writing:

As the journalist Chris Jackson reports,[34] in Detroit, Michigan, a one–ton bronze monument dedicated to Satan, called Baphomet, has been uncovered in order to be exposed to a limited number of faithful worshipers. The writer tells us about the fiery protest of a number of well–known neo–Catholics and some Protestant groups, noting the discrepancy between this attitude of the neo–Catholics and their support of the doctrine taught by Vatican II and later confirmed by the post–conciliar Popes.

The chronicler affirms that if we were to literally stick to the Council's teaching then the satanists would have every right *to be*

---

[33] *Dignitatis Humanæ*, I. 2.

[34] Chris Jackson, web page of *The Remnant* newspaper, July 15, 2015.

immune from coercion on the part of individuals or of social groups and of any human power, in such wise that no one is to be forced or to be impeded to act in religious matters in a manner contrary to his own beliefs, whether privately or publicly, whether alone or in association with others, within due limits.

This right to immunity —the journalist adds quoting the Council— *continues to exist even in those who do not live up to their obligation of seeking the truth and adhering to it and the exercise of this right is not to be impeded, provided that just public order be observed.*

Someone might object that this argument is meaningless because it is clear that the intention of the Council, although not expressly stated, is referring exclusively to Divine worship, excluding elements that are not religious, properly speaking, as are those rendered to Satan. However, within the scope of the Laws, recourse to an alleged *implied* legislative intent is not valid when the text of the law is sufficiently clear and explicit. Perhaps one could resort to the complicated theories about legal interpretation of famous experts in Law, as Legaz Lacambra, Giorgio del Vecchio, and Hans Kelsen; but it would be to no avail, for the *Declaration* clearly states that nobody can be impeded in the exercise of his right to religious liberty when he acts *in accordance to his own conscience*, without even mentioning God, and according to the general obvious sense of the Document. There is no limitation of any kind to this right except the reference made to *due limits*; an expression that is clarified by what is added: *provided that just public order be observed.*

The statement that satanic cults are outside the strictly religious sphere does not correspond to reality, because Satan is a real being mentioned in Revelation. And the same happens with Hell; it is part of Revelation as a counterpoint of Heaven.

Moreover, it is difficult to deny that the Council takes account of all kinds of religions, including those that make no reference to the Divinity or are contrary to It, as its texts clearly confirm:

But the plan of salvation also includes those who acknowledge the Creator. In the first place amongst these there are the Mohammedans, who, professing to hold the faith of Abraham, along with us adore the one and merciful God, who on the last day will judge mankind.[35]

And in another place:

Thus in Hinduism, men contemplate the divine mystery and express it through an inexhaustible abundance of myths and through searching philosophical inquiry. They seek freedom from the anguish of our human condition either through ascetical practices or profound meditation or a flight to God with love and trust. Again, Buddhism, in its various forms, realizes the radical insufficiency of this changeable world; it teaches a way by which men, in a devout and confident spirit, may be able either to acquire the state of perfect liberation, or attain, by their own efforts or through higher help, supreme illumination.[36]

The problem with these and parallel conciliar texts is twofold: first, they do not seem to address the doctrines professed by these *religions*, which the Council recognizes as legitimate; secondly, the content of these *religions* is clearly opposed to Catholic Doctrine. As happens, for example, with key points of Islam; to name just a few:

Women are inferior to men.[37]

Belief in the crucifixion and resurrection of Jesus Christ is false.[38]

---

[35] *Lumen Gentium*, n. 16.
[36] *Nostra Aetate*, n. 2.
[37] Sura 4:34.
[38] Sura 4: 157–159.

The Great Dinner and the Discourteous Guests 69

It is blasphemy to believe in the divinity of Jesus Christ.[39]

It is a serious error to believe that Jesus Christ is the Son of God.[40]

Muslims are mandated to fight against Christians and against all who oppose Islam.[41]

Difficulties increase because many of the statements contained in the conciliar documents are amphibological and confused, and they do not provide adequate explanations that may help in their clarification; which leads some people to think that those proclamations are mere logomachies. This is the case, for example, of the Declaration *Nostra Aetate*, which states that in Hinduism *the divine mystery is expressed through an inexhaustible abundance of myths and through searching philosophical inquiry.*

However, if one carefully examines the words, one might ask what an *inexhaustible abundance of myths and searching philosophical inquiry* may mean. With regard to the *inexhaustible abundance of myths* it should be noted that the experts have not been able to agree on the origin, meaning, and sociological scope of the myths, as evidenced by the many and varied theories of famous anthropologists such as Mircea Eliade, Levi Strauss, Bronislaw Malinowski, Carl Jung, and others. As for the *searching philosophical inquiry* it must be said that, given the extraordinary multitude of existing currents of thought, it would be useful to know more unequivocally which kind of philosophy the Council is referring to.

Worse yet; the Holy Scriptures do not seem to agree with some of the benevolent conciliar declarations as, for example, when the Council assures that Catholics and Muslims adore the same God:

---

[39] Sura 5:72.
[40] Suras 19:35; 10:68.
[41] Sura 9:26.

Jesus Christ affirms of Himself that *No man cometh to the Father, but by me.*[42]

And in other passages:

He that believeth in the Son, hath life everlasting; but he that believeth not the Son, shall not see life; but the wrath of God abideth on him.[43]

Who is a liar, but he who denieth that Jesus is the Christ? This is Antichrist, who denieth the Father, and the Son. Whosoever denieth the Son, the same hath not the Father. He that confesseth the Son, hath the Father also.[44]

By this is the spirit of God known. Every spirit which confesseth that Jesus Christ is come in the flesh, is of God; and every spirit that dissolveth Jesus, is not of God: and this is Antichrist.[45]

He that believeth in the Son of God, hath the testimony of God in himself. He that believeth not the Son, maketh him a liar: because he believeth not in the testimony which God hath testified of his Son.[46]

For many seducers are gone out into the world, who confess not that Jesus Christ is come in the flesh: this is a seducer and an antichrist.[47] *Whosoever revolteth, and continueth not in the doctrine of Christ, hath not God. He that continueth in the doctrine, the same hath both the Father and the Son. If any man come to you, and bring not this doctrine, receive him not into the house nor say to him, God speed you.*[48]

This seems to open a gap, some kind of doctrinal schizophrenia, between the Council teachings on ecumenism and the data of

---

[42] Jn 14:6.
[43] Jn 3:36.
[44] 1 Jn 2: 22–23.
[45] 1 Jn 4:2.
[46] 1 Jn 5:10.
[47] 2 Jn 7.
[48] 2 Jn 9–10.

Scripture. They tried to solve this problem by resorting to the so-called *hermeneutic of continuity*, almost forgotten nowadays. After this failed attempt they turned to the theories of Karl Rahner and Joseph Ratzinger about the *historicist* interpretation of Revelation, according to which Revelation depends on *human feelings*, which decide the meaning of Revelation according to the *events and circumstances of the historical moment*. The conclusion is obvious: it is not the Holy Scriptures which judge man but man who judges and determines the Scriptures.

Another element that has contributed to the current *General Apostasy* suffered by the Church are the numerous requests for pardon, not easy to explain, on the part of the Hierarchy for the Crusades and the evangelization of America. It is well known that these events have been considered throughout centuries with unanimous and universal consent as true hallmarks of glory for the Church and for the evangelizing Nations. And this is why many Catholics feel confused and bewildered: was the Church of that time wrong or is She making a mistake now?

Indeed times of great turmoil are also times of difficult and perplexing questions. They generally do not find an answer... at least for now. For if *the just man liveth by faith*,[49] he also lives on hope, which is what convinces him that in the end everything will be made clear; when truth will finally overwhelm error and light ends up dispelling the darkness. That will be the day when finally appear the *new heavens and a new earth according to his promises, in which justice dwelleth*.[50]

---

[49] Heb 10:38.
[50] 2 Pet 3:13.

—Go out into the highways and hedges, and compel them to come in, that my house may be filled.

Over the centuries the followers of Jesus Christ obeyed this injunction, fulfilling faithfully the instructions of their Master and making the Church the true Missionary Church that the Catholic, Apostolic, and Roman Church, as founded by Jesus Christ, has always been, and will always be as He also promised with words which nobody will be able to erase.

PENTECOST

The Spirit breatheth where he will;
And thou hearest his voice,
But thou knowest not whence he cometh,
And whither he goeth.[1]

Introduction

Much in accord with the thought of the Fathers of the Church, *The Great Unknown* is one of the names used to refer to the Holy Spirit.

And there have been abundant reasons for using this expression. The Liturgy of the Church, which has some acquaintance with Him, has called Him *Consolator Optimus, Dulcis Hospes Animæ*, or *Dulce Refrigerium*. And even Jesus Christ Himself names Him *Paraclete* (Intercessor or Comforter).[2] All of these names convey the idea of extreme affection or loving effusion, which is no wonder when one

---

[1] Jn 3:8.
[2] Jn 14:26; 15:26; 16:7.

considers that the Holy Spirit is, also according to an expression used by the Fathers, the *Osculum Suavissimum* between the Father and the Son. It is true that the Divine Essence is Love (1 Jn 4:8), but of the three Divine Persons the attribute of Love corresponds to the Holy Spirit.

Therefore, since Love in God is attributed to the Holy Spirit, what is so particular about giving Him those names and ascribing those expressions to Him? Is there in Heaven or on earth a more sublime and loftier reality than Love; or even a more mysterious one, since, as has been said, Love is God?

The Spirit breatheth where He wills

That is, where He wills and only where He pleases, for He is essentially *Freedom*, as the Apostle says: *Ubi Spiritus Domini, ibi libertas.*[3] The Spirit is Love, Who is God, therefore He cannot be *determined* by anything outside Himself. Consequently, He gives Himself to whomever He wants, whenever He wants, wherever He wants, and in whatever way He wants, for His Will is one and the same as the Infinite Abyss of Love that He Himself is, and nothing outside Him can compel Him in any way. What infinite reality could influence the Infinite? Love being Infinite Reality, without limits, from where and in which way could He be compelled to move in this or that direction or with a predetermined intensity? Hence, nothing is more opposed to Love than any intent of coercion or determination.

---

[3] 2 Cor 3:17.

By the same token, there is nothing more *personal* than love (with upper or lower case) since it springs from the will of a *person* alone (with upper or lower case).

A logical conclusion of what has been said is the falsity of the gifts and powers that the Catechumenal, Neocatechumenal, and Charismatic Movements within the Church attribute to themselves. They claim the power to invoke the Holy Spirit, and they allege that they have access to those graces whenever they wish and in any way pleasing to them. Even more outlandish is the way in which they celebrate their *liturgies* and the manner in which the Spirit, always according to them, responds to their invocations, which He always and necessarily does through charisma, inspirations, locutions, and even miracles; so much so that His actions remind us of how an auto service works.

But these *invocations* are more along the line of the *spells* attributed to witches and warlocks, and the only spirit —if any— that may be present in them cannot be other than an evil spirit; as corresponds to Spiritual Movements whose doctrines are entirely outside the authentic and traditional Doctrine of the Church.

What determines the excellence of Infinite Love is that He exclusively *depends* on Himself. God loves because He wants, when He wants, and whom He wants; consequently, no creature can ever glorify itself or consider that it possesses any grace which has not been received: *What hast thou that thou hast not received?*[4] said Saint Paul.

Consequently, the act of God granting love to His creature (participated love) is something absolutely free and *unpredictable*. This is why Jesus Christ said, referring to the Holy Spirit: *thou knowest not whence he cometh, and whither he goeth*; which explains that

---

[4] 1 Cor 4:7.

once the creature has been *wounded* by the impact of this ardent fire, he cannot know whence this flame comes or how it was kindled in him. The mystery of created or uncreated Love goes beyond any cognitive, imaginative, or foreseeing power of man. Jesus Christ expresses this reality using the succinct and suggestive language of Poetry, undoubtedly the most appropriate verbal communication, in order to infuse in the soul feelings which cannot receive adequate expression within the scope of normal language. Thus, it is not happenstance that already in the first verses of the *Song of Songs* the bride tries to find out from the Bridegroom where she can find Him:

> *Shew me, O thou whom my soul loveth,*
> *Where thou feedest, where thou liest in the midday,*
> *Lest I begin to wander*
> *After the flocks of thy companions.*[5]

Since Uncreated Love is the cause of the fruit brought about in man by the presence of the Holy Spirit, and since this fruit is known as created love, given the absolutely unpredictable and free nature of both loves, it is not surprising that God often demands an effort on the part of the soul in searching for and cooperating with Him. How could it be otherwise when we are dealing with what is supremely free and impossible to predict or even imagine? On the other hand, created love is the greatest grace man can receive; hence God wants His creature to be aware that love is something *received*, that is, *freely* given; this is why love is a grace.

Love establishes a line of communication between the lover, he who gives, and the beloved, who receives, thus creating a *relationship of reciprocity* between these two persons, an *I* and a *Thou* in which

---

[5] Sg 1:6.

both give and, in turn, receive. As a result, there must be a *cooperation* or answer on the part of man without which no relationship can even exist.

The soul, therefore, must carry out a laborious and often arduous search for the beloved Person, as the *Song of Song* says in its description of what can be termed as a first stage at the beginning of the relationship of love, or perhaps the second if one considers that the search initiated by the bride has been preceded by the call of the Bridegroom:

> *In my bed by night*
> *I sought him whom my soul loveth:*
> *I sought him, and found him not.*
> *I will rise, and will go about the city:*
> *In the streets and the broad ways*
> *I will seek him whom my soul loveth.*[6]

Mystic human poetry cannot fail to bear witness to this; numerous examples of saints and spiritual authors could be quoted:

> *To the distant stars I climbed*
> *Thinking in those jewels white*
> *Some small vestige of your footprints I would find.*
> *While walking toward the Sun, from the Moon at night.*

The bride's search for the Bridegroom (*Song of Songs*), the way through *The Mansions* to find Him (Saint Teresa), the tiresome *Ascent of Mount Carmel* to where the Bridegroom awaits us (Saint John of the Cross), the *Journey of the Mind into God* (Saint

---

[6] Sg 3: 1–2.

Bonaventure), and many others are constant themes in the History of Spirituality.

And thou hearest his voice,
"But thou knowest not whence he cometh, and whither he goeth"

Love being an Infinite and Mysterious Reality (for Love is God), man on his own cannot know either His origin or whither He goes. Love is *Alpha and Omega*, the Beginning and the End (Rev 21:6). In other words, it is impossible for man to comprehend the reason behind the designs of the Divine Will when God gives him His Love or all the implications of the final End God wants. The grace received is too wonderful; what God has in store for man is extremely lofty and sublime is: *Eye hath not seen, nor ear heard, neither hath it entered into the heart of man, what things God hath prepared for them that love him.*[7] Since it is then impossible to fix any limits to love (no beginning and no end), it is also impossible to define it or explain it completely; one can only speak about it. And this is precisely what man has done throughout the centuries without ever exhausting this mystery and only after overcoming many difficulties and even falling into a number of errors.

Man can know God though reason and, mostly, through Revelation. Since God is Love, any further knowledge about God implies a deeper knowledge about love. By the same token, any attempt to delve into the knowledge of love without the help of the works of the

---

[7] 1 Cor 2:9.

Spirit in the human soul leads to merely natural fabrication that has nothing to do with true love. On the other hand, the knowledge that man can obtain about God, and therefore about love, is incomplete, frequently analogical, and always subject to error when the data of Revelation are not taken into account. Although the knowledge of Jesus Christ which the soul achieves in this life through faith and under the influence of the Spirit (Jn 14:26) is never complete, it is eminently personal and can be communicated to others; not so much the knowledge acquired through mystical experience.[8]

No wonder the uneasiness of the bride of the *Song of Songs* when the maidens of the choir who accompany her try to inquire of her what the Bridegroom looks like. The bride can do nothing other than try to respond through a series of detours: difficult question and more difficult answer yet. Saint Augustine said, regarding the impossibility of achieving an exhaustive knowledge of God even with the help of Revelation, *si comprehendis non est Deus*.[9] And since God is Love, it follows that it is difficult to explain even the notion of created love, as the infinite digressions used by many thinkers since Plato until present day to explain this reality demonstrate.

It goes without saying that Revelation is the only setting where one can *delve* into the knowledge of this mysterious Reality —the greatest and most sublime of all mysteries; a knowledge which, despite help from Revelation and the grace given by God, can never transcend the intellectual powers of man. As expected, the *Song of Songs* deals with this issue which man has never been able to completely answer; it does so through the questions the choir of maidens ask the bride:

---

[8] Saint Teresa begins her *Way of Perfection* by saying that she is going to explain what contemplative life is, but the rest of the book is a reflection on the Our Father. The same thing happens with Origen and his treatise *On Prayer*.

[9] Saint Augustine, Sermon 52, 16.

> *What makes your lover better than other lovers,*
> *O loveliest of women?*
> *What makes your lover better than other lovers,*
> *That thou hast so adjured us?*[10]

The bride answers by resorting to various descriptions, merely beautiful metaphors. But the language of metaphors is limited and can only go so far; impossible for them to describe the Bridegroom:

> *My love is fresh and ruddy,*
> *Chosen among ten thousand.*
> *His head is golden, purest gold,*
> *His locks are palm fronds and black as the raven.*
> *His eyes are like doves beside the water–courses,*
> *Bathing themselves in milk, perching on a fountain–rim.*[11]

In her writings, Saint Teresa strives to communicate her personal experiences about the Person of Jesus Christ. She distinguishes the various types of visions she experienced: real, intellectual, imaginary, etc. However, while her narrations leave us with the feeling that her experiences are genuine and sincere, they cannot help but also cause in us the sensation that, in any case, they are unable to provide an entirely satisfying knowledge.

Saint John of the Cross, on the other hand, is a staunch enemy of any sort of visions, images, or perceptions regarding Jesus Christ in contemplative prayer, defending the need for abstraction and of the

---

[10] Sg 5:9.
[11] Sg 5: 10–12.

total denial of all ideas (including notions concerning Jesus Christ) in the consummate and highest degrees of mystical prayer.[12]

This is not the place to make even a perfunctory analysis of this question. Let it suffice to note some difficulties imbedded in the doctrine of Saint John. It is the Spirit Who causes love with His presence in the soul through His fruits, the first and most important of which is love, and the illumination of His gifts. Moreover, the main task of the Spirit is to give testimony of Jesus Christ (Jn 15:26) and bring His words to our minds (Jn 14:26); consequently, He never speaks about Himself (Jn 16:13), for His mission is to teach us about Jesus Christ and lead us to Him. Therefore, it is difficult to imagine any supernatural love of God in its highest degrees, as happens in contemplative prayer, dispensing with Jesus Christ in any way or form (purely imaginative or intellectual form). It is not possible to think about the Spirit leading us to true love if this guidance is not done through Jesus Christ; neither can the soul get to know and love Jesus Christ if it is not through His Human Nature, wherein the soul finds His Divine Person and Nature, and all of this within the same and one act of love and with the mediation, once again, of the Holy Spirit. Let us finally point out two texts which contain the words of Jesus Christ addressed to His disciples: *I and the Father are one*;[13] *And if I shall go, and prepare a place for you, I will come again, and will take you to myself; that where I am, you also may be.*[14]

It is the Holy Spirit Who, through the love He causes in the soul, impels her to search passionately for the Bridegroom, which does not

---

[12]Von Balthasar already pointed out the different spiritualities of these two giants of Spanish mysticism, an issue which all subsequent Spirituality treatises have avoided.
[13]Jn 10:30.
[14]Jn 14:3.

exclude a continuous, tiresome, and painful effort that sometimes even seems fruitless; nevertheless, this effort is a normal element of the great adventure of love during our earthly pilgrimage.

It is true that weariness, effort, and pain do not belong to the essence of love —at least in the beginning. But ever since the fall of man, and because love is a relationship of total reciprocity, the sufferings of the Passion of Jesus Christ always accompany divine–human love, which is tinged by His Blood poured out on Calvary. This is one of the elements of true love: each lover shares the life and final destiny of the other:

> *Where hast Thou hidden Thyself,*
> *And abandoned me in my groaning, O my Beloved?*
> *Thou hast fled like the hart,*
> *Having wounded me.*
> *I ran after Thee, crying; but Thou wert gone.*[15]

> *In search of my Love*
> *I will go over mountains and strands;*
> *I will gather no flowers,*
> *I will fear no wild beasts;*
> *And pass by the mighty and the frontiers.*[16]

> *In your orchard a small bird,*
> *In grief at your absence, sang with a sad sound;*
> *And, when your soft voice she heard,*
> *Quickly rose up from the ground,*
> *To search in her swift flight where you could be found.*

---

[15] Saint John of the Cross, *Spiritual Canticle*.

[16] Saint John of the Cross, *Spiritual Canticle*.

Hearing the voice of the Spirit poses a special but quite interesting challenge because of its extraordinary importance and numerous implications. Do we really hear the voice of the Spirit? Can one be sure that what he is hearing is indeed the true voice of the Spirit? These questions are especially relevant in a time like ours in which prophets and visionaries (particularly female visionaries) proliferate, along with followers of Catechumenal sects, in a world so filled with lies and prone to self–deception or being deceived by others.

...And thou hearest his voice

It is absolutely true that the Sprit speaks to His Church and also to individual, personal souls. Otherwise, how could He be the Soul of the Church, the One Who leads the disciples of Jesus Christ to the complete truth, Who brings to their mind what He said and makes them understand His words (Jn 14:26), Who reveals to them the things which are to come (Jn 16:13)?

And His language is first and foremost a language of love, for He is Love Himself, *Consolator Optimus, Dulcis Hospes Animae*, and *Dulcis Refrigerium* of souls. Jesus Christ being the Word used by God to express His Love for man, and the Spirit being the only One Who speaks with authoritative and authentic voice about Jesus Christ, the Holy Spirit then only knows how to speak about Love and things concerning love.

It is for this very reason that His language of love can be as sharp and piercing as the *flash of fire* of the *Song of Songs*:

> *The flash of it is a flash of fire,*
> *A flame of Yahweh himself.*[17]

Human mystic poetry echoes this sentiment, resorting to a language in which the intensity of love as well as love being the cause of death of the beloved person are common elements:

> *If you should see me again,*
> *Down in the glen where the singing blackbirds fly,*
> *Do not say you love me then*
> *For, were you ever to repeat that sweet sigh,*
> *On hearing it, I may die.*

But the voice of love is also gentle, delicate; so much so that it can be said about it what is said regarding the voice of the Bridegroom when He speaks to the soul; a voice which is only perceived by the bride and is destined to never leave the scope of the intimacy of both lovers:

> *My Bridegroom's voice is for me,*
> *Like the wake of a ship deeply furrowing*
> *Like winds that stir so lightly*
> *Like a gentle whispering,*
> *Like the solemn moves of a night bird on wing.*

This is why one should be wary of the authenticity of alleged voices of the Spirit publicly aired, with absolute lack of modesty, by the fiery receivers of such *inspirations*. The truth is that the Spirit

---

[17] Sg 8:6.

does not seem to like advertising; and as for His communications being disseminated in the Church, we must say that they are already contained in the official Revelation and endorsed by the Magisterium of the Church herself.[18] On the other hand, when His inspirations are true and authentic they are usually received by the recipient soul with feelings of humility and conditions of silence. The soul to whom such graces are granted never trusts herself; she always subjects herself to the judgment of the Church and is assured by the authority of a serious master of the spiritual life. Lack of humility and desires of being known, on the part of the recipient of the *inspirations*, are infallible signs of falsehood. It is also convenient to analyze the veracity of the voices of the Spirit, regarding both their origin and the consequences to which they may have given rise, paying close and calm examination to the facts. An example of this convenience is what happened with the famous inspiration received, according to him, by Pope John XXIII about the convocation of a Council. And something similar should be said about the spectacular *interventions* of the Spirit in Catechumenal and Neocatechumenal Charismatic worship; taking into account, above all, that no other authentic loud activity of this Divine Person is known except the one carried out through the Apostles and the Virgin Mary on the day of Pentecost. Finally, it must also be taken into account, especially in times of spiritual crisis as the one we are suffering nowadays, that visionaries and false prophets abound everywhere as a ravaging plague; besides, it is a proven fact that there are infinite numbers of Christians who put their trust more in particular revelations than in the official

---

[18]It is amazing how many communications the Spirit forgot to include in the official Revelation. A mistake that He now tries to remedy by means of an infinity of seers (especially female) who are graced with interpretations of current events and prophecies about the immediate future. It is not uncommon that all these communications bring material benefits to those *favored* by the Spirit.

Revelation. The depth to which the naivety of man can reach is unfathomable, and woe to them: *Corona sapientium divitiæ eorum, fatuitas stultorum fatuitas est.*[19]

When the activity of the Spirit is authentic, the sufferings and words it involves have the same characteristics as the sufferings and words that each lover addresses to the other: they take place in silence and away from the eyes of men. After all, it is to the Holy Spirit that the Love of God is attributed:

> *The calm, resplendent deep seas*
> *With peaceful, blue–white waves, rocked and gently stirred,*
> *The soft echoes on the breeze,*
> *Songs of mermaids without word,*
> *A sweet whisper of love that is barely heard.*
>
> *I met with my Beloved*
> *As the wind blew gently across the great plain;*
> *And since He is enamored,*
> *He spoke softly to explain*
> *That my love for him also brings him sweet pain.*

This is the way in which love and the Spirit act, through discreet humility which does not intend to be known by the world: *Caritas non aemulatur, non agit superbe, non inflator.*[20] Hence the mistrust which arises from so many *charities* and so many *charitable* characters whom the world goes to such great lengths to inflate and proclaim as nothing short of heroes. True charity —like true love— is never praised by the world due to the enmity between God (Who

---

[19] Prov 14:24.
[20] 1 Cor 13:4.

is Love) and the world; the approval of the latter infallibly means the disapproval of God. For this reason any glorification can only be justified if one glorifies himself in the Lord (1 Cor 1:31). The *New Church* has enervated the action of the Spirit, turning it into a show *rooted to the spot* with fixed days, predicted hours, and programmed acts of worship to which the Holy Spirit comes when invoked at will by the attendants; at the same time, *Spiritus ubi vult spirat* has been properly shelved to be replaced by the spirituality of the leader of the sect of the moment.

True love of God, contrary to the desire of so many seers to be known, always carries the hallmark of discretion and humility. Longing for mundane noise is an evident sign of falsehood: *Whosoever therefore will be a friend of this world, becometh an enemy of God*,[21] said the Apostle James.

To the Spirit of God is attributed Love; therefore His activity is usually parallel to that of lovers when they flee from people and look for hidden places and solitude. This element of love is much less patent and relevant in purely human love, but it acquires great importance in divine–human love, another feature of love in which once again there is a manifest difference and distance between those two kinds of love. This is why the notes of perfect love suit only divine–human love. We must remember the discretion of the Virgin Mary, who did not communicate even to Saint Joseph the Annunciation of the Angel, running all kinds of risks. *The Song of Songs* makes reference to these features for those who know how to read poetic language. The bride addresses herself to the Bridegroom:

---

[21] Jas 4:4.

> *Come, my love, let us go to the fields.*
> *We will spend the night in the villages,*
> *Let us get up early to the vineyards,*
> *Let us see if the vineyards flourish,*
> *If the flowers be ready to bring forth fruits,*
> *If the pomegranates flourish:*
> *There will I give thee my love.*[22]

And likewise human mystical poetry:

> *Allow me to follow you, my companion,*
> *My dear friend, beloved Husband, my sweet Love,*
> *That we may walk together the paths that run*
> *Through the valley up to the hills far above.*
>
> *And in solitude we shall stay, you and I,*
> *Leaving the World of Men behind, forgotten;*
> *And we will contemplate the blue of the sky,*
> *Surrounded by the breezes of the mountain.*

As Jesus Christ said to His disciples, *The spirit of truth, whom the world cannot receive, because it seeth him not, nor knoweth him: but you shall know him; because he shall abide with you, and shall be in you.*[23] The antinomy between the Spirit and the world and its hullabaloo is once again clear. The discreet way of the Spirit living in the disciples points in the same direction: *at your side and within you*, while the world, on the other hand, cannot see or even know Him. For the Person of the Spirit and His fruits, the first of which is love, are transcendent and sublime Realities which cannot even be

---

[22] Sg 7: 11–12.
[23] Jn 14:17.

expressed by the language of the world. This explains what happens when the world wants to talk or thinks that it is talking about love: it actually *talks about anything but love.*

It is within this climate of solitude and silence, as the most appropriate atmosphere for the main activity of the Spirit to be accomplished —that concerning divine–human love— that are understood the mysterious words with which the Bridegroom of the *Song of Songs* calls upon all things to be silent, with the clear intention of not waking the bride. This strange spell is part of the poetic fabric as one of the pieces that brings about particular beauty. The several repetitions of this text instill in the reader, almost subconsciously and at the same time inexplicably, the feeling that it has an extraordinary importance:

> *I adjure you, daughters of Jerusalem,*
> *By all gazelles and wild does,*
> *Do not rouse, do not wake my beloved*
> *Before she pleases.*[24]

So much so that Saint John of the Cross paraphrases this text with one of his most delicate stanzas in his *Spiritual Canticle*:

> *Light–winged birds,*
> *Lions, fawns, bounding does,*
> *Mountains, valleys, strands,*
> *Waters, winds, heat,*
> *And the terrors that keep watch by night;*

---

[24]Sg 2:7; 3:5; 8:4.

> *By the soft lyres*
> *And the siren strains, I adjure you,*
> *Let your fury cease,*
> *And touch not the wall,*
> *That the bride may sleep in greater security.*

It is difficult to interpret Poetry and it is impossible to exhaust its meaning. However, perhaps these urgent requests —whose repetitions are a clear sign of its importance— want to be an indication of the transcendence of silence, in all the meanings of the term, in divine–human love; and, more specifically, of how decisive the factor that the bride *should disregard the care of all other things* so that they do not distract her from the love of the Bridegroom. Hence, even the very forces of Nature are silent before the sublime beauty of the divine–human relationship of love:

> *Following shepherds and sheep,*
> *I came to where the Loved One awaited me*
> *Hidden in hillsides so deep;*
> *As he spoke to me softly*
> *The whistling sounds of the jungle ceased to be.*

A respectful silence, expressive of the wonder and admiration felt by Creation beholding the reciprocal love between God and His creature which it would not dare to hinder in any way:

> *The sun was peering anew*
> *Thus awaking sleeping flowers with a kiss,*
> *But seeing me hearing you,*
> *Noting my sweet rapturous bliss,*
> *Chose to put off rising for such sight as this.*

The sun would, indeed, break the laws that govern it in order to not disturb the dialogue between the Bridegroom and the bride.

"The Spirit shall give testimony of me"
Consolator Optimus

The Spirit is the *Consolator par excellence* of the soul. His presence brings about peace, consolation, and joy. Saint Paul lists *joy* as one of the fruits of the Spirit, second only to love.

A generally forgotten principle, one quite frequently falsely interpreted, must be taken into account: *supernatural is not contrary to natural, but surpasses and exceeds it.*[25]

Hence, the joy and bliss infused by the Spirit, which bring about consolation in the soul, are of a higher and different degree than natural joy and pleasure. The existence of the latter is not questioned, we are merely stating that they are surpassed and exceeded.

Jesus Christ promised His disciples a joy which clearly does not belong to this world, *His* peace and all that this expression implies: *These things I have spoken to you, that my joy may be in you, and your joy may be filled.*[26] *So also you now indeed have sorrow; but I will see you again, and your heart shall rejoice; and your joy no man shall take from you.*[27] Jesus Christ is giving His followers His joy,

---

[25] *Natural* is understood here in its proper sense, that is, as something that belongs to human nature not corrupted by sin.

[26] Jn 15:11.

[27] Jn 16:22.

complete joy, imperishable joy because *no man or any other thing will take this joy from them.*

These characteristics always are lacking in the natural joys the world and worldly things procure; hence the advice of the Apostle: *Seek the things that are above; mind the things that are above, not the things that are upon the earth.*[28]

So we can see that regarding purely natural joys as authentic happiness is debatable, to say the least. Indeed, on many an occasion those joys can be considered as true, but they will never be perfect since they will never be able to bring *perfect joy.*

It is now appropriate to ask why the Holy Spirit is given the name *Consolator Optimus* —an important question of why the Holy Spirit is the One Who brings true comfort to the soul, along with authentic peace and supreme joy.

True comfort and genuine peace and supreme joy are things which every man desires, whether he admits it or not. Nevertheless, man never achieves them in this life, not completely: *You have made us for Yourself, O Lord, and our hearts are restless until they rest in You,* said Saint Augustine in his *Confessions.*

However, while it is true that complete fulfillment of those three gifts of the Holy Spirit will only take place in the Fatherland of Heaven, a foretaste of them can be obtained even now, in the form of *a pledge* or *first fruits* (2 Cor 1:22, 5:5). The latter do not imply totality, true, but they are a sure guarantee of a future and definitive possession as well as already having a sufficient degree of joy as to overcome essentially purely natural joys.

It must also be taken into account that Christian Spirituality tends to reject the concepts of pledge and first fruits because it regards them as things *partial* which are far from being *complete*;

---

[28] Col 3: 1–2.

in this sense they are not properly valued. While it is true that they cannot claim any equality with the *consummation* that will take place in Heaven, it is impossible, nevertheless, for the man in this world to pinpoint the distance between the natural and the supernatural universe (for it is infinite). So it is not possible for him to know how far the love of a soul for God can go or how deep that love can be in this life: *Unicuique secundum mensuram donationis Christi.*[29] Indeed, but who knows which criteria of measurement will be used in this case?

Let us go back to the fundamental question asked earlier, why is the Holy Spirit the Great Comforter of the soul?

Because it is He Who speaks to her of Jesus Christ; makes Him known to her; makes His words understood by her; and the Holy Spirit is the one Who leads the soul to Jesus Christ: *The Spirit shall give testimony of me* said the Master to His disciples. And Jesus Christ and the love of Jesus Christ are the only things the soul wants and which she sighs for. As Saint Paul said, *He is your life*;[30] the only life that can console our soul and lead her to Perfect Joy. Nevertheless, let us not forget that the Holy Spirit *is not the consolation, but the One Who provides it*; as has been said, He *shall give testimony of me.*

It is not surprising, therefore, that the strength and longings of love caused by the Spirit in the soul impel her to run, overcoming all possible and even impossible obstacles, in the footsteps of the beloved Person Who is Jesus Christ, or the Bridegroom of the bride in the *Song of Songs*:

---

[29] Eph 4:7.
[30] Col 3:4.

> *Draw me in your footsteps, let us run.*
> *The king has brought me into his rooms;*
> *You will be our joy and our gladness.*
> *We shall praise your love more than wine;*
> *How right it is to love you.*[31]

Saint John of the Cross paraphrased these verses in one of the stanzas of his *Spiritual Canticle*:

> *In Thy footsteps*
> *The young ones run Thy way;*
> *At the touch of the fire*
> *And by the spiced wine,*
> *The divine balsam flows.*

In turn, the bride of the *Song of Songs* speaks about her need for consolation and makes reference to the reason for her longings:

> *Feed me with raisin cakes,*
> *Restore me with apples,*
> *For I am sick with love.*[32]

The bride's request for being restored with raisins cakes and comforted with apples is a beautiful metaphor that refers to her need for relief because the strong cravings she experiences are about to make her faint with love.

However, the pains and anguish caused by love are of a different sort than those affecting human nature because of sin. Unlike the

---

[31] Sg 1:4.
[32] Sg 2:5.

latter, the sufferings of love are but a consequence of the *intense joy* also produced by the same love; a joy which, in turn, has nothing to do with, and is even contrary to, the joys of the world. In effect, while physical pain is a sign of a danger that affects the human organism and can bring about its demise, supernatural suffering is a clear manifestation of the presence of something that leads to Life:

> *For love is strong as Death,*
> *Passion as relentless as Sheol.*
> *The flash of it is a flash of fire,*
> *A flame of Yahweh himself.*[33]

A proof of this is that the consolation sought by the bride, far from being a desire for relief or a lessening of her longings is rather the opposite: that is, her desire is rather to have those longings intensified since *they lead her to deeper love.* And as for her saying that she feels faint, she is not warning about a possible fear of death, but rather she is bursting into stammering sighs of love that fill her to the point of exhaustion because of both inexpressible joy and a very deep sense of life. This is what Jesus Christ meant when He said: *I am come that they may have life, and may have it more abundantly;*[34] which would become absolutely real with the outpouring of the Spirit sent by Jesus Christ after His ascension to the Father: *The charity of God is poured forth in our hearts, by the Holy Ghost, who is given to us.*[35] Then takes place that which man would have never dreamed of or imagined: *death out of love* becomes as desirable as fullness of life and a culmination of love:

---

[33] Sg 8:6.
[34] Jn 10:10.
[35] Rom 5:5.

> *If living is to love and to be loved so,*
> *My only longing is to live in Love's glow;*
> *If dying is of love to burn in ardor*
> *That consumes the heart, may I quickly die more.*

In effect, the joy caused by the *Great Consoler* does not exclude physical pain, as happens with the stigmata. But supernatural joy surpasses natural suffering to such a degree of *intensity* that the latter is transformed into a suffering of distinct *quality*, thus becoming bearable, even pleasurable.

On the other hand, joy as a fruit of the Holy Spirit cannot be strange to the Passion of Jesus Christ which the bride necessarily and ardently wants to share. In effect, a bride in love is not indifferent to the sufferings and even death of her Beloved Whose destiny she longs to share totally as love demands. Since this participation is a natural corollary of the personal nature of love, the bride does not want to be supplanted by anybody or to imitate anybody in her sharing; for this sharing derives from the *I–thou* intimate relationship between herself and her Bridegroom: I am *solely and completely* for thee and thou art *solely and completely* for me. Hence, the sentiments of joy and suffering that come along with love are absolutely personal and non–transferable.

> *A small wounded nightingale*
> *I once begged to tell me her sorrows so deep.*
> *She said —but told not her tale—*
> *That I'd be better to keep*
> *My own way of mourning for what makes me weep.*

For love is something eminently *personal*. In Essential Love, the Persons of the Father and the Son express to each other their love through the bond that unites them, which is also a Person, the Holy Spirit. Created love is not a person —it could not be— but is a reality which can only exist between persons in such a way that, when it is true, it consists in the outpouring and presence of the Person of the Holy Spirit in the creature.

When purely human love is completely disconnected from the presence of the Holy Spirit, at that very same instant it ceases to be love and becomes *sex*, or *flesh*; it ceases to be *personal* and is transformed into a mere relationship between a human *I* and another human being who is treated as a *thing* for pleasure.

Thirst or longing for love
Suffered by the bride
And caused by the Spirit

The thirst of which Jesus Christ so ardently speaks, which is a direct reference to the Spirit, is nothing other than the longing for love that touches the heart of man: *If any man thirst, let him come to me, and drink. He that believeth in me, as the scripture saith, Out of his belly shall flow rivers of living water. Now this he said of the Spirit which they should receive, who believed in him.*[36]

The passage of the conversation of Jesus Christ with the Samaritan woman makes a clearer reference to thirst as an expressive metaphor of the unrest caused by the longing for plenitude of love which abides in man's heart:

---

[36] Jn 7: 37–39.

Woman, if thou didst know the gift of God, and who he is that saith to thee, Give me to drink; thou perhaps wouldst have asked of him, and he would have given thee living water... Whosoever drinketh of this water, shall thirst again; but he that shall drink of the water that I will give him, shall not thirst for ever; But the water that I will give him, shall become in him a fountain of water, springing up into life everlasting.[37]

Thirst as a yearning which consumes man's heart is a much stronger and more telling expression than the well–known *restlessness* of the heart which Saint Augustine speaks about in his *Confessions*. Indeed, what torments the human heart and sets it on fire with the desire of loving Jesus Christ is much more than restlessness; it is a longing which can even be considered as anguish. The Holy Spirit is the One Who kindles this fire with which He does not intend to merely encourage the soul to love the Bridegroom but to burn her and urge her to the unfathomable abyss of Infinite Love. Let us say again that infiniteness, by essence, has no limits; like love, which is like *fire which never says, 'Enough!'*[38] Because the soul cannot reach this level of intensity, the Spirit again *adjuvat infirmitatem nostrum*, as Saint Paul said, and helps her by making intercession for her with *gemitibus inenarrabilibus;*[39] a very forceful expression used by Saint Paul. Better words could not be found to describe that what the Spirit does in the soul is not merely infusing breath but a shock as intense as the power of love; a reality that cannot be articulated better than by saying *with groaning which cannot be uttered.*

---

[37] Jn 4: 10.13–14.
[38] Prov 30:16.
[39] Rom 8:26.

It can also be said that this expression is a way of saying that the Spirit acts in union and *in conjunction with the bride*, calling upon the Bridegroom with a passionate display of consuming longing to be united to Him:

> *And the spirit and the bride say: Come.*
> *And he that heareth, let him say: Come.*
> *And he that thirsteth let him come;*
> *And he that will let him take the water of life, freely.*[40]

> *He that giveth testimony of these things, saith,*
> *Surely I come quickly.*[41]

True love means *totality*. The Bridegroom and the bride search for and call upon each other with a mutual longing which is so powerful, it is unable to be expressed in any other way than with *groanings that cannot be uttered.*

1. Importance and transcendence
Of the expression "to thirst"
Referring to the love of God.

The expression *to thirst for the love of God* is the most adequate way of referring to the longing that can consume the heart of someone who truly loves God and wants to be united to Him. As natural

---

[40] Rev 22:17.
[41] Rev 22:20.

thirst torments the body, so in the same way thirst, that is, longing for the love of God, torments the soul. In effect, God cannot be loved except with the greatest and most vehement of all desires; it would not make any sense to love God tepidly: *And thou shalt love the Lord thy God, with thy whole heart, and with thy whole soul, and with thy whole mind, and with thy whole strength.*[42] *If any man come to me, and hate not his father, and mother, and wife, and children, and brethren, and sisters, yea and his own life also, he cannot be my disciple.*[43]

This longing for the love of God which in itself is powerful enough to *torment* the human heart is undoubtedly caused by a situation in which the soul feels that she does not possess God while, at the same time, she desires with all her strength to be united to Him. Whether this absence of God be real or pure sentiment which makes the soul suffer is something totally indifferent to the enamored soul which feels herself separated from God.

But yearning and thirsting for God, for a soul in love who suffers the pain of His *absence*, takes on a double aspect: two different aspects that sometimes appear to be melded and at other times give the impression that they are clearly disconnected. And in the latter case they acquire the note of extreme harshness. The first aspect is of a *hidden or missing God* Who is difficult to find; the second, *an absent God* because He seems to have abandoned the soul; an abandonment that, even in the case of being mere illusion, the soul nevertheless experiences as a difficult and tremendous reality.

As we have said, both aspects appear sometimes apart and sometimes together and almost melded with each other, as can be seen

---

[42] Mk 12:30; Mt 22:37; Lk 10:27.
[43] Lk 14:26.

in this beautiful stanza of the *Spiritual Canticle* of Saint John of the Cross:

> *Where hast Thou hidden Thyself,*
> *And abandoned me in my groaning, O my Beloved?*
> *Thou hast fled like the hart,*
> *Having wounded me.*
> *I ran after Thee, crying; but Thou wert gone.*

The *Song of Songs*, as the true and perfect Poem of love it is, echoes these two aspects. As for the first or the serene and hopeful search, the bride asks the Bridegroom (and the thought of a solitary place of mutual intimacy is contained in her question, as the mention of a rest reveals):

> *Tell me then, O thou whom my soul loveth,*
> *Where will you lead your flock to graze,*
> *Where will you rest it at noon?*
> *That I may no more wander like a vagabond*
> *Beside the flocks of your companions.*[44]

The second, more somber and acute, refers to the search for a Bridegroom Who seems to have fled and is nowhere to be found. This aspect corresponds to the most anguished moments described in the *Nights* of mystical authors.

---

[44] Sg 1:7.

> *On my bed at night*
> *I sought him whom my soul loveth:*
> *I sought but could not find him!*
> *So I shall get up and go through the city;*
> *In the streets and in the squares,*
> *I shall seek him whom my soul loveth.*
> *I sought but could not find him!*
> *I came upon the watchmen*
> *—Those who go on their rounds in the city:*
> *Have you seen him whom my heart loveth?*[45]

Both states of the soul are described extensively by mystical authors, especially by Saint John of the Cross.

The second and most poignant state, which corresponds to those moments when God seems to be gone and is nowhere to be found, is particularly relevant in our times when Christianity has apparently abandoned God —the General Apostasy of the Church. In these very serious circumstances when Christians have *veritably* separated themselves from God there are many confused souls whose feeling of having been abandoned by God are much more than mere sentiments of the soul. Has God, in logical correspondence, *really* abandoned man? An adequate response must take into account that the relationship of love, due to its essential character of reciprocity, demands from one party a response of the same kind as the one provided by the other.

Here we must distinguish the situation of the *official Church*, represented by the majority of the Hierarchy, the governing bodies, Institutions and Associations and, in general, by what we could call the *visible Church*, which is the only one that counts for the world. In this sense, it can be firmly stated that the absence of God

---

[45] Sg 3: 1–3.

with respect to this Church, which is now —according to her own intention— the *New Church* emerged in the post–conciliar times and converted to Modernism, is *absolutely real*. Her Magisterium —to the extent that there is anything of worth to the term—, her Liturgy, her Pastoral activity, and her entire politics with respect to the world, have nothing to do with the teachings of Jesus Christ.

On the other hand, the state of total absence of God concerning the souls as individual persons, experienced as mere sentiment (necessary, nevertheless, for the purification of the soul but which actually is simply an appearance), has already been amply studied by mystic authors and discussed in the treatises on Spirituality.

It should not be surprising in our modern times of serious crises and persecutions that the trials —external and, most particularly, internal ordeals— which the true disciples of Jesus Christ must undergo are especially burdensome and relevant. In this case, we should say that the intensity and strength of the *Nights* of which Saint John speaks have reached their zenith with particular nuances.

Nevertheless, these nuances would be difficult to define. Perhaps the best way to go about it would be to say that there is a *difference of intensity* in the sentiment of the absence of God. But, since the ways of love are as mysterious as love itself, and given also that the final term of this extremely sublime reality is the infinite, speaking here of gradations of intensity would be irrelevant. One must embrace the reality of the mystery of love in connection with the special demands of Divine Justice, applied on this occasion also to the innocent souls according to the demands of the mystery of the Mystical Body; these demands would be concretized in the need to suffer and pay satisfaction even for the sins of others.

Contemporary mystic poetry tries to evoke the asperities and bleakness of the *Nights* of Saint John:

In the dark of night my Beloved left me,
As the sun hides past the hills into the west,
As the broad river flows into the wide sea,
And the swift stag runs into the deep forest.

At night he left for the distant mountain range,
At night he followed the road around the bend,
At night I was left in foreign lands and strange,
At night I was left alone without my friend.

We must consider that our modern socio–religious situation is quite different from that lived by the Spanish mystics of the Golden Age. Although it may seem an unimportant detail, a Christian who sincerely undergoes the crisis of today's Church finds himself without the surroundings of a visible Church whose profound faith would have served as a valuable life–saver. The present Church, despite the promise of her Founder that she would always prevail, has been reduced to a minimum, and her visible structure is so blurred that some consider her as the new Church of the Catacombs. The Christian of the present time is *alone* and is undergoing a *Night* as intense as no Christian of the Golden Age could have ever imagined. Surely the difference in degree of intensity cannot change the quality of the feelings experienced by the soul, but this inequality clearly provides them with a new aspect and other additional characteristics so as to rightly consider them, in a certain way, new.

2. About the groanings of the Spirit
That "cannot be uttered."

If human feelings are difficult to express, those that come from the Heart of God through the Spirit are impossible to describe. The Bible mentions *unspeakable groanings*, employing the most adequate form of human language to refer to a reality that has no name.

The existence and modality of human feelings of deep sorrow can be communicated to others, but their intensity and meaning cannot. And yet, the feelings of God are infinitely deeper than those of His creature, and the *groanings* uttered by the Spirit come from the human Heart of Jesus Christ, Whose Spirit (His human soul substantially united to the Spirit) was not given to the Father until Jesus Christ breathed His last on the Cross (Lk 23:46). Obviously we cannot speak of God being indifferent to the sufferings of His Church as His Body or of souls as individuals. The *silence* of God, undoubtedly more accentuated in times of crisis, is actually an infinite cry —groanings that cannot be uttered— exhaled because of the abyss of sorrow and misery that exists in the world and has been caused by sin; but the very infiniteness of this cry makes it unable to be heard by God's creature.

And something similar can be said of the infinite distance in intensity and manner that there is between the Love that God offers to His creature and the response given by man, not to mention man's ontological smallness, his deficiencies, and defects caused by his concupiscence; all of which would completely disqualify him from accepting the offer received, were he not helped by grace. But even grace cannot eliminate the infinite minuteness of the creature compared to the greatness of his Creator.

This explains why the Spirit has to intercede for us; although not in just any way, but with unspeakable groanings (Rom 8:26). The greater the need, the greater is the help; when necessity is infinite, so is the help. And just as crying is the last resort left to the human being during the most terrible situations, a God *infinitely in love* with His creature cannot do anything but intercede for her with *crying groans* which, as we have said above, when coming from the Heart of God they deserve with all propriety the attribute of *unutterable*: impossible to be expressed by human language or to be understood by man's intellect.

Contrary to popular belief, the nature of weeping, properly speaking, has to do more with a spontaneous deflagration of sentiments of love and joy than with sentiments of sorrow.

The presence of the Spirit in the soul
And difficulties of the notion of love

Created or participated love is but a consequence of the presence of the Spirit in the soul or that presence itself in the sense that the Spirit living in the soul pours out love, His first fruit: *Fructus autem Spiritus est caritas.*[46] And in some other place the Apostle also says: *The charity of God is poured forth in our hearts, by the Holy Ghost, who is given to us.*[47]

But the Spirit is *subtlety* to an infinite degree, corresponding to the very infinitude of this Divine Person. From this derives one of

---

[46] Gal 5:22.
[47] Rom 5:5.

the many difficulties that impede understanding or explaining the reality of love. And this is why Jesus Christ said that the Spirit *breathes* where He wants, alluding to what happens in the bosom of the Trinity with the procession of the Holy Spirit. He proceeds at the same time from the Father and the Son through a mutual and reciprocal *spiratio* (which could be translated as exhalation, breathing, or sigh) of love between them. Hence the procession of the Holy Spirit (exhalation or mutual sigh of love) is immensely more difficult to imagine than that of the Son (Who comes from the Father via intellectual generation). Spirit, exhalation, sigh, wind (and its blowing power) are all notions which evoke, in a very insufficient way, the idea of subtlety or vaporous delicacy whose deep nature the human spirit can never reach, only *intuit*.

That is why the soul is able to hear the soft and delicate voice of the Spirit, but she knows neither *where it comes from nor where it goes*; a reality well reflected in mystical poetry:

> *My Bridegroom's voice is for me,*
> *Like the wake of a ship deeply furrowing*
> *Like winds that stir so lightly*
> *Like a gentle whispering,*
> *Like the solemn moves of a night bird on wing.*

Contrary to popular opinion, the love of the human soul *is not mere feeling*, as if it were one of the many psychological activities of the human spirit; love is an ontological activity, the *presence* of the Holy Spirit in the soul, that is, a true *permanence* or settlement of the Spirit in man: *Know you not, that you are the temple of God, and that the Spirit of God dwelleth in you?*[48] This real presence of the

---

[48] 1 Cor 3:16.

Spirit in the human being becomes more or less intense according to the grace given to each one. *But to every one of us is given grace, according to the measure of the giving of Christ.*[49] Since the Spirit is Love Himself, His presence in the soul becomes love: *The Love of God is poured forth in our hearts, by the Holy Ghost, who is given to us.* There is then a veritable trinomial: Spirit–Presence–Love, in which these three realities come finally into one. God's creature cannot have true *created love* without the true presence in him of *uncreated Love*.

This explains why the human spirit, without excluding Christianity, has maintained during many centuries the idea of love as a mere feeling, without going deeper into the true nature of love.

The Spirit and His special office of Master Within the Church

It would be a difficult task, if not an impossible one, to explain the job of the Spirit as Master of the soul. Already at the beginning we face the first difficulty, since, according to Jesus Christ Himself, there is but only one Master for the Christian: *Be not you called Rabbi. For one is your master; and all you are brethren.*[50] *Neither be ye called masters; for one is your master, Christ.*[51]

However, the Spirit is the true Master of the soul; not by carrying out a secondary function. The problem arises, as it always does

---

[49] Eph 4:7.
[50] Mt 23:8.
[51] Mt 23:10.

in everything relative to the Holy Spirit, when it comes to finding names that reflect appropriately His delicate job which is, in short, as difficult to explain as the question of His origin (*procession*) from the Father and the Son.

Evidently the true Master is Jesus Christ, according to His own confession. But both His teachings as well as His Person *do not come to us but through the Spirit.* And it is in this sense that we might speak of the magisterial or teaching ministry of the Spirit, which is not inferior to that of Jesus Christ; it is simply *different*.

This magisterial teaching consists essentially in the evocation of the Person of Jesus Christ, which mainly is to update in the soul the memory and understanding of Jesus Christ's words.

The very words of Jesus Christ are the foundation of this office of the Spirit: *When he, the Spirit of truth, is come, he will teach you all truth.*[52] *The Paraclete, the Holy Ghost, whom the Father will send in my name, he will teach you all things, and bring all things to your mind, whatsoever I shall have said to you.*[53]

The Church rightly calls the Spirit *Consolator Optimus* which cannot be more appropriate, since He carries out His office as soul comforter by bringing to her the Person and teachings of Jesus Christ. For a true Christian, Jesus Christ is much more than an object of our devotion and a Lord before Whom we are held accountable: Jesus Christ is *the life of the Christian* (Jn 14:6, Col 3:4), which is tantamount to saying that He is Someone without Whom the Christian can no longer live since he has also lost his own life to live only that of his Master (Gal 2:20). Things being so, how could He Who makes possible for the soul to know, love, and identify herself with Christ not be called Consoler?

---

[52] Jn 16:13.
[53] Jn 14:26.

His office as *Consoler* is so essential that without Him the Christian would never remember the Words of Jesus Christ nor understand them or even know Him as a Person. It can very well be said that without His help, *Jesus Christ would not exist for Christians.* Even if the Christian could get to know Jesus Christ, without the Spirit he would never get close to Him: *And no man can say the Lord Jesus, but by the Holy Ghost.*[54]

And since, according to the Words of Jesus Christ, Truth and Life are one thing with Him (Jn 14:6), the Spirit of Truth, as the One Who leads the disciples to the Person of Jesus Christ, is also He who opens the way of Life: *Out of his belly shall flow rivers of living water. Now this he said of the Spirit which they should receive, who believed in him.*[55]

This is why the Spirit is the Master without Whose true and continuous teaching Christian existence goes nowhere.

The same can be said of Pastoral practice which, once it departs from His teachings, becomes the most anodyne thing, if not a useless weight, that leads souls to perdition. Speaking of the ministry of preaching the Word, for example, Saint Paul said that he preached *not in the learned words of human wisdom; but in the doctrine of the Spirit.*[56]

When Modernism invaded the modern Church, she lost faith in the Holy Spirit and turned her back on the Spirit of Truth, opening the door to the spirit of error. The Church has been living a period of more than fifty years in which the Gospel is no longer preached in her.

---

[54] 1 Cor 12:3.
[55] Jn 7: 38–39.
[56] 1 Cor 2:13.

Given the importance of preaching for the life of the Church, preaching *with words learned from the Spirit* is a matter of absolute necessity. However, the Post–conciliar *New Church* has completely lost sight of how transcendent this issue is, which has resulted in the ministers responsible for the Flock hurrying to spread the Word by extracting from their own collection, speaking about themselves and by themselves, and forgetting the condemnation proclaimed by Jesus Christ: *He that speaketh of himself, seeketh his own glory: but he that seeketh the glory of him that sent him, he is true, and there is no injustice in him.*[57]

The Apostles and their successors were sent to evangelize the world according to what they had received and been taught and nothing else: *Going therefore, teach ye all nations; baptizing them in the name of the Father, and of the Son, and of the Holy Ghost. Teaching them to observe all things whatsoever I have commanded you.*[58] Not even the Holy Spirit will speak of Himself but only *of things He hears*, as this important passage states: *But when he, the Spirit of truth, is come, he will teach you all truth. For he shall not speak of himself; but what things soever he shall hear, he shall speak; and the things that are to come, he shall shew you.*[59]

Hence the necessity for a Shepherd of the sheep to *learn the words of the Spirit*, for which he needs to listen to them, which, in turn, is something that can only be done though prayer; for the Spirit speaks only in silence and solitude. Unfortunately, the *New Church* has lost the sense of both and with them the true value of prayer; so much so that this Church has decided to officially do away with consecrated and contemplative life, although cloaked under a false

---

[57] Jn 7:18.
[58] Mt 28: 19–20.
[59] Jn 16:13.

pretense of improving this life. And without prayer, it has become impossible to learn from the words of the Spirit and, consequently, any possibility of true preaching is forfeited. And without the Word that feeds the sheep, they anguish and die by the bushel for lack of food. This is how *general apostasy* and total desolation have invaded the Church.

The Spirit as Judge

And when he is come, he will convince the world of sin, and of justice, and of judgment. Of sin: because they believed not in me. And of justice: because I go to the Father; and you shall see me no longer. And of judgment: because the prince of this world is already judged.[60]

The Spirit continues filling human existence with mysteries and paradoxes. Behold, now the *Optimus Consoler*, the *Sweet Hospes of the soul*, the *Sweet Refrigerium*, as He is called in the Liturgy, is also *The Grand Accuser* referring to one of the functions that Jesus Christ grants Him.

There is infinite logic in everything God does; in this case, it could not be otherwise since the Spirit is the *Sprit of Truth*. Truth always vanquishes lies *because of the very nature of things*. The lie is but an aberrant falsity disguised as truth, which the lie is forced to do since without the appearances of truth the lie cannot even exist: this is how much the lie must humble itself and submit to truth. In

---

[60] Jn 16: 8–11.

turn, vice is but another aberration disguised as good, for there is no other way for evil to be accepted by the human being.

Both the lie and vice, therefore, have no reason to exist. If, in fact, they continue to exist, Justice demands that a moment should arrive when their existence will be *subjected to the mere condition of perpetual curse and eternal damnation.*

Hence the necessity of Judgment as an epilogue of the earthly existence of every man and also of all societies created by him throughout history. If the final intervention of *The Grand Accuser* and the application of Justice delay, this does not mean that they will not occur; this deferral is also part of Divine Providence in the History of Salvation. Saint Peter said in his Second Letter that there will be *new heavens and a new earth according to his promises, in which justice dwelleth*;[61] their delay is but another application of God's Mercy —always united to His Justice— in order to exhaust all opportunities: for the elect, to increase their glory; for the wicked, to the greater intensity of their eternal torments.

Therefore the Spirit will accuse the world of sin because it did not believe in Jesus Christ, and it will be condemned to never see Him again. A sentence about which one does not often reflect sufficiently, for to be deprived of the possession and joy of the love of Jesus Christ *for all eternity* is a punishment whose gravity no created mind can imagine. As for the Prince of this World, his sentence is already pronounced: he will display all his power during a time that will be short, especially if compared with eternity; then, the most terrible aspect of Divine Justice will fall upon him.

Note that these accusations and the Judgment will be leveled *against the world*, as the very words of Jesus Christ assure us, for it has rejected Jesus Christ: *If the world hate you, know ye, that it hath*

---

[61] 2 Pet 3:13.

hated me before you.[62] The status of the elect and the Judgment with which Jesus Christ will receive them will be completely different.

Saint John of the Cross said that *at the evening of life, we shall be judged on our love*; the love of His disciples will be measured. The love for Jesus Christ they always kept, Whose Person they longed to see, Whose Life they wanted to possess and make their own. Love is not judged, only measured, as corresponds to the end of a contest or tournament in which both contenders —God and His creature— have tested their love:

> *He has taken me to his banqueting house,*
> *And his banner over me is love.*[63]

If *there is no law* against the fruits produced by the Spirit in the disciples who loved Jesus Christ (Gal 5:23), much less there will be Judgment for them.

At the end of the trying journey of the disciple of Jesus Christ, through all the vicissitudes which make up this *Valley of Tears*, it is no time to meet a judge, but the Friend —*I shall no longer call you servants*—[64] and the Beloved of the soul.

Nor is it time for any test; it is time to leave behind sufferings and labors, and all other things God created for man which, although good and beautiful, are incapable of satisfying the human heart which, created after all for love and for infinity, is always willing to give up the part to keep the Whole.

Saint John of the Cross beautifully expressed the moment when everything is left behind, as forgotten, before the meeting with the Bridegroom and all that it means.

---

[62] Jn 15:18.
[63] Sg 2:4.
[64] Jn 15:15.

> *I remained, lost in oblivion;*
> *My face I reclined on the Beloved.*
> *All ceased and I abandoned myself,*
> *Leaving my cares forgotten among the lilies.*[65]

Rest is what those who have worked hard deserve. And reaching at long last the goal they have for so long glimpsed and longed for, where they know that He dwells Whom the sentiments of their souls yearned for, is to finally quiet a heart that died for meeting Jesus Christ. Thus said a disciple in love with Jesus Christ upon leaving for the Fatherland and saying goodbye to his soul friend:

> *And although we follow together the way,*
> *Let me precede you, arriving first, I pray,*
> *And there at the end of the road we will find,*
> *Our toils and hard labors are left far behind.*

---

[65] Saint John of the Cross, *Dark Night of the Soul.*

PARABLE OF THE GOOD SAMARITAN[1]

And behold a certain lawyer stood up, tempting him, and saying, Master, what must I do to possess eternal life? But he said to him: What is written in the law? how readest thou? He answering, said: Thou shalt love the Lord thy God with thy whole heart, and with thy whole soul, and with all thy strength, and with all thy mind: and thy neighbor as thyself. And he said to him: Thou hast answered right: this do, and thou shalt live. But he willing to justify himself, said to Jesus: And who is my neighbor?

And Jesus answering, said: A certain man went down from Jerusalem to Jericho, and fell among robbers, who also stripped him, and having wounded him went away, leaving him half dead. And it chanced that a certain priest went down the same way: and seeing him, passed by. In like manner also a Levite, when he was near the place and saw him, passed by. But a certain Samaritan being on his journey, came near him; and seeing him, was moved with compassion. And going up to him, bound up his wounds, pouring in oil and wine: and setting him upon his own beast, brought him to an inn, and took care of him. And the next day he took out two pence, and gave to the host, and said: Take care of him; and whatsoever thou shalt spend over and above, I, at my return, will repay thee. Which of these three, in thy opinion, was neighbor to him that fell among the robbers? But he said: He that shewed mercy to him. And Jesus said to him: Go, and do thou in like manner.

---

[1]Preached on August 16, 2015.

If we examine this passage carefully we find two central ideas shaping the parable as its backbone. The first refers to the exercise of the virtue of mercy, or compassion, as a fundamental virtue of Christian life. The second has to do with the special reactions or diverse behaviors of various human beings in a situation of need or misfortune suffered by their neighbor.

The first idea describes the unfortunate and sorrowful situation of the traveler who had been assaulted, robbed, and wounded by some criminals.

The second recounts the diverse social status of the characters who passed by and reacted so dissimilarly to the misfortune suffered by the unfortunate traveler: a priest, a Levite, and a Samaritan. The first two belonged to the ruling and influential class of the people of Israel; they were indifferent to the blatant misfortune they encountered. The third individual was a poor wretch that belonged to a social class despised by the leaders of the Jews and yet he was the very one who helped the injured traveler.

Let us begin by examining the first idea: compassion or mercy as a fundamental virtue of Christian life. We must then regard what the good Samaritan did, leaving aside for the time being the indifferent behavior of the other two travelers.

The first thing to consider is that the Samaritan summarily disregarded both the causes that gave rise to the situation of the unfortunate who lay by the road and the conduct or circumstances of those who provoked that situation (thieves, in this case). The Samaritan simply focuses his attention on the urgency of the situation: that the wounded man, unable to move, was in great need of assistance. He does not carefully analyze the way the stranger had been mistreated and robbed; much less does the Samaritan examine the mood or possible causes that may have justified the behavior of the criminals: whether they were a wretched lot or possibly were in a situation of extreme duress, etc. He simply acts quickly, given the urgency of the moment, and takes care of the unfortunate suffering man: heals his wounds by pouring on them oil and wine and binding them and, setting him upon his own beast, brings him to an inn. And in an outpouring of goodness and mercy, the Samaritan gives money to the host to take care of the wounded man, assuring him that he will repay on his return whatever he may have spent over and above.

And here we must pay careful attention to the fact that the Samaritan did not stop to examine the causes of the situation of the man who had been assaulted, let alone try to justify in some way the behavior of those who had wronged him. It can be assumed, of course, that the Samaritan would consider the perpetrators of the outrage for what they were: a gang of ruthless outlaws deserving harsh punishment. But he did not address this issue at that time in order to pursue what was truly important.

This attitude of the Samaritan is exceptionally important in the midst of the serious situation of confusion currently affecting a Church plagued by false teachers and doctors who lead her astray with mendacious doctrines that seek to justify even situations and behaviors which are clearly contrary to both Natural and Divine law. And since the faithful who feel confused and bewildered are so numerous, it is important that we analyze and carefully distinguish, without merging them into one, the two different elements that make up the situation described in the parable: the state of necessity in which the victim finds himself, on the one hand, and the causes that led to such a state, on the other.

Compassion or mercy, considered in itself, does not concentrate on the causes that led to the situation which requires this Christian virtue, at least in its first defining moment; it simply hurries to help the needy. Compassion's own object is not to analyze or judge the origins or motives that have led to the situation of necessity; it is concerned only about somebody's needs as such.

The causes that lead to the situation which becomes the object of mercy may be voluntary, caused by the same person who is suffering the painful condition, as in the case of the adulterous woman about to be stoned and who was thrown at the feet of Jesus:[2]

—*They said to him: Master, this woman was even now taken in adultery. Now Moses in the law commanded us to stone such a one. But what sayest thou? And this they said tempting him, that they might accuse him.*

This woman caught in adultery was, nevertheless, *repentant* of her crime; or at least, if she was not at that moment she certainly was induced to repentance by Jesus Christ as the event unfolded; an important fact that should be taken later into account.

Two different elements need to be considered in this episode; first, the condition of the woman: terrified by the imminence of death, sorrowful and repentant of her fault, battered, embarrassed before the crowd of accusers, and bewildered by the unknown character of noble bearing Who looked on her with compassion and at Whose feet she had been thrown mercilessly. Secondly, the sin of adultery in which she had been caught and which had brought about her present plight.

Jesus is concerned above all with the miserable state of this unhappy woman: embarrassed, terrified, and about to be sentenced to death. He, of course, did not fail to take into account the causes that had led her to that situation; He was entirely aware that He

---

[2] Jn 8: 1–11.

was facing an adulteress, but He does not consider, as a priority, making her sin the direct object of His attention; He sees above all the misfortune of this woman and her *need for repentance*. Jesus Christ, least of all, does not try to justify adultery or mitigate it so that the audience is induced to have mercy on her.

There are, therefore, two different elements: first of all, Jesus Christ *pities* the situation of the sinful woman, in order to, immediately after, *forgive and eradicate sin from her*. It should be noted here that if He pardons her it is because He previously recognizes and condemns her sin (otherwise He would have nothing to forgive). That is why Jesus Christ dismisses her, once the situation ended and after having saved her from death and sin, with the familiar words that are both loving and stern: *Go, and now sin no more.*

Something similar happened with the sinful woman who anointed Jesus Christ's feet with ointment and with her tears.[3]

In contrast with the malevolent thoughts that the Pharisee who had invited Jesus Christ to his house was spinning in his mind, considering that an alleged prophet should have known the manner of the woman who was crying ruefully at his feet, Jesus Christ, after giving a lesson to His host, completely forgives the woman once her absolute repentance was recognized: *Many sins are forgiven her, because she hath loved much.*

But Jesus Christ in no way disregards the sinful condition of the woman. Much less does He try to justify her or even allege some attenuating circumstances which could move a person to compassion or to diminish the seriousness of her actions. Jesus Christ assumes that she is entirely repentant, as is shown by the way in which she demonstrates her sorrow, shame, and love of Jesus Christ; since her

---

[3] Lk 7: 36–50.

repentance is great —because *she has loved much*—, much is forgiven her.

And the same could be said of the kind father of the *Prodigal Son* who returns home repentant after having squandered his possessions and leading a life of debauchery.[4] When his father rushed out to meet him the son throws himself to his father's feet:

—*Father, I have sinned against heaven, and before thee, I am not now worthy to be called thy son.*

But the father jubilantly receives him and prepares a great feast to celebrate his return. But this does not mean that the father ceases to recognize the undeniable fact of the crime of his son; nevertheless, he forgives and forgets completely. Thus we again find the reasoning made above: if the father gives his forgiveness it is because of his recognition that there was a sin that he forgives and forgets *in response to the repentance of his son*, but the father never had the intention of justifying or diminishing the importance of the offense. Likewise, the young man, returning to his home ashamed and sorry, also recognized the sin he committed.

But the causes that lead to an unfortunate situation may be entirely unintended by the person in need of help and compassion, as in the case of the injured traveler of this parable. But even in this case, the situation that has arisen is still an effect distinct from the cause which brought it about. One must consider this factor when thinking that compassion or mercy should be shown to a person in need at a given time.

This does not mean that it is necessary to resort to any argument to justify or mitigate the wrong that led to the disaster. It is out of the question to think that Jesus Christ did not know that the

---

[4] Lk 15: 11–32.

adulterous woman, violently thrown at His feet by her accusers, was truly an adulteress; or that the sinful woman who was watering His feet with her tears was really a sinner; or that the prodigal son of the parable had actually grievously sinned against heaven and against his father as the youth himself admitted. When God exercises His attribute of mercy, forgiving a sinner, it is because He recognizes that there was indeed a sin in the first place; otherwise, what would He forgive?

Applying this doctrine —as required by the most basic common sense and logic of any state of affairs— to situations currently under discussion in the Church, we arrive at the conclusion that the divorced who have remarried, and therefore fallen into a situation of adultery, *are actually living in a state of adultery*. And as we have seen in the evangelical examples we have considered here, it would also require *a state of effective and sincere repentance* to admit them to the sacraments. Otherwise one would be justifying adultery and ignoring the teachings of Jesus Christ and all the precepts of Divine Law.

Alleging as a pretext that these situations are concerned with *praxis* but not with *doctrine* (which would continue intact) is an obvious fallacy and an insult to the intelligence of the ordinary faithful.

First, because it is impossible to separate practice from doctrine: *lex orandi, lex credendi*. Practice inevitably leads to doctrine; so much so that if the former is changed the latter is also necessarily altered. The examples to prove this would be innumerable; two should suffice: giving Holy Communion in the hand and the practice of multiplying almost infinitely the number of *extraordinary lay Eucharistic ministers*, both practices which have contributed to destroying the faith of the Christian people in the Real Presence of Jesus Christ in the Eucharist. Something similar has occurred with the new Mass which, contrary to the traditional Mass that is the product of two thousand years of wise practice of the Church, has been prefabricated in liturgical laboratories and *adapted to the needs of the present moment*; it has decimated Sunday attendance to the Holy Sacrifice.

Justifying a sinful situation, or trying to disguise or diminish it in any way, or, which is still worse, not requiring prior repentance, is a mistake and a sin more serious than the originally sinful condition; ultimately it would be an insult and a blasphemy against God, Whom those who act along these lines would try to make an accomplice of error or sin; which could not be classified under a name other than *satanic* abuse.

Trying to justify a sinful situation in which somebody is involved without requiring his prior repentance is tantamount to compelling him to continue permanently in that condition as if it were a legitimate one, putting him in danger of eternal damnation. This would be another terrible offense now conferred to the unfortunate sinner in need of the goodness of divine mercy, which will not be granted without the necessary prior repentance.

Let us now pay particular attention to the second of the two fundamental ideas contained in the parable: the different characters who pass by along the road and their differing ways of reacting before the misfortune of the ill-fated man who had been robbed and beaten.

Three different types of people appear, namely a priest, a Levite, and a Samaritan. The first two belong to the ruling and influential class of the Jewish people; the Levites' role was subordinate to the office of the priests.[5] In contrast, the third character, a Samaritan, seems to have been put intentionally into the parable as the most unfortunate of the group since the Jews traditionally despised the inhabitants of the region of Samaria.

It would be hard not to see in Jesus Christ a deliberate intention to introduce these different classes of people in descending order according to their rank, from the highest to the lowest: a priest, a Levite, and a Samaritan. The first two belonged to the upper class of Jewish society; the third is a stranger, living in a region despised by the rest of the Jews. Clearly, this enumeration corresponded to the expected way in which these three characters should have reacted to someone else's misfortune according to their office and condition: first the priest, as the most suitable person; then the Levite; finally the Samaritan, the individual least expected to respond (according to the social status at that time) to the needs of the injured man.

This deliberate order of enumeration is a clear sign of how undeserving of God's confidence have been throughout history the religious and civil ruling classes of society (the priestly class of the Jewish people covered both areas). Examples of this abound in the Gospel, as shown, for example, in the opinion that Jesus Christ had regarding the rulers of peoples (rulers of peoples in the plural, as shown in the text).

The kings of the Gentiles lord it over them; and they that have power over them are called beneficent [note the phrase *are called*]. *But you not so...*[6] *What went you out into the desert to see? a reed shaken with the wind? But what went you out to see? A man clothed in soft garments? Behold they that are clothed in soft garments are in the houses of kings.*

---

[5]The difference between these two officials and their roles is not clear in the Bible narrative. Their nature seems to have been changed and even mixed up with the passing of time. Both groups usually belonged to the sect of the Pharisees.

[6]Lk 22: 25–26.

But what went you out to see? A prophet? Yea I tell you, and more than a prophet.[7]

As for the religious establishment, one can find diatribes and accusations made constantly by Jesus throughout the gospel against doctors, scribes, and Pharisees.

The explanation is not hard to find if one considers the weakness caused by concupiscence in human nature as well as the danger posed by Power and Wealth to those who wield them (Mt 6:24). In this regard, one must point to the chaotic situation of modern society.

Indeed, throughout the flow of the history of mankind the leaders of nations have never been perfect; the common good of their citizens, which the rulers are obliged to ensure, has not always been their primary concern. Common good has now been entirely forgotten as never before, replaced by the pursuit of private and personal interests; be they the interests of political parties, oligarchies, or other groups of oppression. Moreover, quite common concepts used by all as dogmas, such as freedom, democracy, social justice, equality of all before the law, separation of powers, etc., are nothing more than mere verbal diarrhea that mean nothing, or whose true meaning nobody knows.

The woes of Jesus Christ (Mt 23: 13–16) addressed to the scribes and Pharisees, whom He calls with the common appellate *hypocrites*, are a stern rebuke of a ruling class that embraced both the religious and political spheres. And it would be impossible not to attribute to these woes a universal and generalized sense applied entirely to all types of ruling classes of all time:

---

[7]Mt 11: 7–8. In this text there is an evident contraposition between those *clothed in soft garments*, who live in houses of kings, and the prototype of a true man or prophet personified by John the Baptist.

—*Woe to you scribes and Pharisees, hypocrites; because you shut the kingdom of heaven against men, for you yourselves do not enter in; and those that are going in, you suffer not to enter.*

—*Woe to you scribes and Pharisees, hypocrites; because you tithe mint, and anise, and cumin, and have left the weightier things of the law; judgment, and mercy, and faith. These things you ought to have done, and not to leave those undone. Blind guides, who strain out a gnat, and swallow a camel.*

—*Woe to you scribes and Pharisees, hypocrites; because you make clean the outside of the cup and of the dish, but within you are full of rapine and uncleanness.*

—*Woe to you scribes and Pharisees, hypocrites; because you are like to whited sepulchres, which outwardly appear to men beautiful, but within are full of dead men's bones, and of all filthiness. So you also outwardly indeed appear to men just; but inwardly you are full of hypocrisy and iniquity.*

While all these invectives are equally valid for the religious and socio–political arena, some of them seem to find special application to the religious sector; as can be seen, for example, in the second quote above:

—*Woe to you scribes and Pharisees, hypocrites; because you tithe mint, and anise, and cumin, and have left the weightier things of the law; judgment, and mercy, and faith. These things you ought to have done, and not to leave those undone. Blind guides, who strain out a gnat, and swallow a camel.*

The reference to the abandonment of the essentials of the law in exchange for engaging in *distracting* issues is of great importance. The progressive Theology and Pastoral activity of the Church have indeed falsified concepts such as *mercy*, which has been distorted to the point of being exercised without any regard for justice; or *justice*, which also has been overlooked and exercised without any consideration for the rules derived from the nature of this virtue.

And quite patent is the absolute indifference that the *New Church* displays concerning *fidelity to the Law,* to both Church law (Canon Law and centuries–old Magisterium) and Natural Law or Divine Law.

This absolute indifference before the law, which has even become a mockery of the Established Norm at a superior level, *has become a common feature of civil and ecclesiastical Powers.*

Civil Powers, by not respecting the laws already established in the state, not even those dictated directly by themselves; the vaunted *separation of powers*, so much celebrated and touted with such great fanfare as a triumph of Western society since the Enlightenment are nothing more than mere fiction which serves only one purpose: to be used by politicians at their convenience in order to feed their parliamentary verbal diarrhea. As for ecclesiastical Powers, their mockery of Divine law has even turned into heresy, as they have come to reject the sources of Revelation and to question or deny not only fundamental doctrines of Christianity but the very Person of its Founder.

According to Jesus Christ, those who make up these two ruling classes —religious Power and political Power— suffer the same malady: externally, ostentation of virtue and concern for the governed, shameless demagoguery, talk and speeches that achieve the miracle of speaking without actually saying anything; in reality, this outward appearance is but an exercise in hypocrisy aimed at achieving individual or group ends, or at attaining concealed interests known only to that ruling class.

—*Woe to you scribes and Pharisees, hypocrites; because you make clean the outside of the cup and of the dish, but within you are full of rapine and uncleanness.*[8]

---

[8]Mt 23:25.

When thou dost an almsdeed, sound not a trumpet before thee, as the hypocrites do in the synagogues and in the streets, that they may be honoured by men. Amen I say to you, they have received their reward.[9]

Finally it remains to examine the conduct of the third person who passed along the way: the Samaritan, who was the only one who took pity on the unfortunate man who lay wounded and abandoned.

He does not first stop and analyze the actions of the thieves, let alone does he start looking for reasons that could have justified their behavior. He simply hastens to remedy the only urgent and important thing at the time: the plight suffered by the traveler who had been assaulted, for whom he generously and abundantly makes use of his own means.

True mercy pours itself entirely upon the person in need who is suffering, trying to remedy the situation to every possible extent. The Samaritan was not concerned about procuring the presence of spectators who would applaud his conduct. True charity is discreet and, as the Apostle Paul said, *is not puffed up, is not ambitious, seeketh not her own.*[10] The affliction of so many people in this world who suffer for their sick or unhappy loved ones whose pain they cannot ease as they would like is a huge river whose length is known to God alone, with a flow of water which never worries about any kind of acknowledgement.

The Samaritan succored to the extent of his ability the traveler who had been assaulted and injured, providing help to solve the problem *in a realistic way and as far as it could be solved.* Once the Samaritan healed and bandaged the wounds of the unfortunate traveler, he placed him on his own beast and brought him to an inn, giving the innkeeper enough money to tend the wounded man in his

---

[9] Mt 6:2.
[10] 1 Cor 13: 4–5.

absence, along with the promise of paying at his return whatever the owner may have overspent.

And what is most important of all, the Samaritan did not help the unfortunate man who lay by the wayside by *worsening his condition*. This may seem a platitude only when one forgets that truisms and situations devoid of any logic are relevant in modern society; especially within the Church, where progressive modernist theology is raging.

With regard to the heated debate which will reach it climax in the autumn of 2015, a topic will be discussed which, according to Divine law, should never have been open to debate: the administration of the Holy Eucharist to civilly divorced and remarried people (which implies a situation of adultery) without prior need of repentance or any attempt to abandon their sinful situation. It is alleged that there is justification for the need to have *mercy* on these unfortunates who, after all, have not lost their faith and do not want to feel excluded from full ecclesial communion. But this approach forgets that such a measure permanently *legalizes*, or pretends to legalize, a sinful situation which may lead to eternal damnation.

These claims of the *New Church*, moreover, do not take into account her dependence on the evangelical Law, forgetting something fundamental: in God, mercy and justice *are the same thing*. Thinking, therefore, that God can be merciful without being righteous is a blasphemy and theological nonsense.

The conclusion is obvious: the progressive Church, admitting adulterers to full ecclesial communion and reception of the sacraments, places them *in a worse condition than that in which they were*. Those responsible for this outrage fulfill to the letter the terrible words of Jesus Christ:

—Woe to you scribes and Pharisees, hypocrites; because you go round about the sea and the land to make one proselyte; and when he is made, you make him the child of hell twofold more than yourselves.[11]

---

[11] Mt 23:15.

PRAYER OF PETITION AND THE LOVE OF JESUS CHRIST[1]

And in that day you shall not ask me anything. Amen, amen I say to you: if you ask the Father anything in my name, he will give it you. Hitherto you have not asked anything in my name. Ask, and you shall receive; that your joy may be full.

These things I have spoken to you in proverbs. The hour cometh, when I will no more speak to you in proverbs, but will shew you plainly of the Father. In that day you shall ask in my name; and I say not to you, that I will ask the Father for you: for the Father himself loveth you, because you have loved me, and have believed that I came out from God. I came forth from the Father, and am come into the world: again I leave the world, and I go to the Father.

His disciples say to him:

—Behold, now thou speakest plainly, and speakest no proverb. Now we know that thou knowest all things, and thou needest not that any man should ask thee. By this we believe that thou camest forth from God.

(Jn 16: 23–30)

This is the fifth Sunday of Easter. The Church offers for our consideration a passage of the Gospel of Saint John that contains

---

[1] Preached on May 10, 2015.

part of the farewell discourse of Jesus uttered on the night of the Last Supper and addressed to His Apostles.

These are the exciting moments of a farewell in which the Lord's Heart pours upon His disciples words overflowing with love, filled with generosity, and containing promises never imagined by His disciples... or by anyone. The solemnity of the moment, a few hours before their separation, joins the depth of words that express the incredible greatness of a Heart which, having loved His own *unto the end*,[2] gives Itself completely to them and, acting in divine logic, *promises them everything*:

Amen, amen I say to you: if you ask the Father anything in my name, he will give it you. Hitherto you have not asked anything in my name. Ask, and you shall receive; that your joy may be full.

Moreover:

And I say not to you, that I will ask the Father for you: for the Father himself loveth you, because you have loved me, and have believed that I came out from God.

Jesus Christ makes them a promise as sublime and grand as it is seemingly incredible: ask in my name *what you want* and you shall receive, *that your joy may be full*; consoling words beyond all expectations and any conceivable hope of human imagination.

At the same time, by one of many strange paradoxes of Christian life —but which at closer scrutiny always show their logic— these words almost at all times evoke *some skepticism* in the soul of any Christian who hears them. Perhaps this disbelief is but the fruit of a possibly unconscious outbreak of weakness that has compelled human nature to be more or less reluctant to evangelical slogans.

---

[2] Jn 13:1.

Be that as it may, we should dare ask ourselves sincerely: does any Christian really believe firmly that everything he asks the Father in the name of Jesus Christ, or anything that he requests from the same Jesus Christ, appealing to His love, will be infallibly granted to him? Any Christian, if he thinks and speaks frankly, would probably answer that question in the negative. Indeed, it is one thing to believe the words of the Gospel, while unconsciously leaving reality aside, and quite another to *have the certainty* that those words will be infallibly applied to the particular case of anybody's life.

And yet these words are absolutely true and certain. Not only because they are words of Jesus Christ and therefore cannot fail, but because the very nature of things demands it; that is, because *things are so*, as two plus two equals four and a straight line is the shortest distance between two points. This requires an explanation that will be set forth below, but not without an introductory caveat.

First, we must take into account that there are very few Christians who take seriously the love of Jesus Christ. And since the promises contained in the Sermon of the Last Supper are based and founded on the love between Jesus Christ and His followers, it must be concluded that their effective fulfillment *depends solely on the reality of that love relationship*. It must also be well understood that we are dealing here with a true relationship of love and not with mere affection or superficial devotion. *Being in love* is much more meaningful than what is commonly understood as loving; hence rarely do such promises become actually real.

Second, because a large number of Christians not only have never taken the love of Jesus Christ seriously, but they also have never felt anything but utter indifference toward the Person of Jesus Christ.

It is not possible to tell if we are in the End Times. Nevertheless, it is true that the *General Apostasy*, announced by Prophecies, seems to have already become a reality throughout the entire Church. Society growing increasingly pagan, dissemination of criteria contrary to Divine Law in all areas of social life, widespread rejection of all Christian values, persecution —bloody in Asia and Africa, bloodless in the West— of those who profess the Faith, etc. are normal occurrences in today's society. The Person of Jesus Christ, His doctrine and teachings, His redemptive suffering and death with all that this implies for Christian life, hardly mean anything to the modern Church, including her Hierarchy.

No wonder, therefore, that *things are the way they are*, and that the promises of Christ, far from being words to the wind or mere promises made in the heat of a speech, are realities that cannot be waived: *My words are spirit and life...*[3] *heaven and earth shall pass away, but my words shall not pass.*[4] But in order to be effective His words must be received and accepted by man; he has to meet the necessary conditions that His words require in order to be fulfilled, *according to the demands of their own nature*. And it is well known that a relationship of love –which is the ultimate foundation of such promises—, by the imperative of its own essence, cannot exist without the entire will and full consent of each of the two parts making up this relationship.

To understand this it is necessary to start with the premise that love is the core and crux of Christian life, and then move quickly to try to understand the difficult and complex reality of love, which in turn cannot be explained without analyzing in depth the dynamics of the relationship of love. Moreover, we must add that even though human love and divine–human love are in essence the same thing, they differ in that the latter belongs to a supernatural order. Admit-

---

[3] Jn 6:63.
[4] Mk 13:31.

tedly, purely human love can also operate in a supernatural realm, but it will never reach the lofty character and degree attained by divine-human love.

A real loving relationship is one in which each lover surrenders his or her *total being* to the other. And since here we are talking about true love (whether it be natural or supernatural) this loving relationship assuredly implies, in turn, the concept of *wholeness* in all its aspects; or, put another way, *total being* must be understood in exactly the same sense in which Jesus Christ defined the first commandment: *Thou shalt love the Lord thy God with thy whole heart, and with thy whole soul, and with thy whole mind, and with thy whole strength.*[5]

The real relationship of love, and even more so in the supernatural order of divine-human love which is the type of love primarily being considered here, means an exchange of lives in which everything that belongs to one of the lovers becomes the ownership and possession of the other. The pagan classics, led by Plato, pondered over and over the concept of love without ever hitting what constitutes its main secret and true essence. It would have been impossible for them because they never came to know Christian love contained in Revelation: *God is love* (1 Jn 4:16). But the Revelation of the Old Testament, even before Christianity, understood the mutual and reciprocal possession *of the whole being* of each of the lovers on the part of the Bridegroom and the bride, which is tantamount to saying, in this case, God and the soul, as is clearly seen in the words of the bride in the *Song of Songs*:

---

[5] Mk 12:30.

> *I am my beloved's, and my beloved is mine.*
> *He feedeth among the lilies.*[6]
>
> *I am my beloved's,*
> *And his desire is toward me.*[7]

In the New Testament, the fullness of Revelation and the fulfillment of all Promises, this idea appears much clearer and has much deeper significance: *He that eateth my flesh, and drinketh my blood, abideth in me, and I in him.*[8]

In divine–human love the love relationship is always mutual and reciprocal; therefore, the fact that the soul is in love with Jesus Christ necessarily implies another fact, that Jesus Christ is equally enamored of the soul.

We must consider, however, that merely human love does not always meet the requirements for being *fully equal to authentic love*; therefore, the feelings and the words with which it is expressed cannot always fully correspond to reality. And hence it cannot be said in all instances that the element of *totality*, essential in true love, reaches its full realization in human love.

This is not so in divine–human love. When it says that Jesus Christ has fallen in love with this soul (*falling in love* is much more perfect than simply *loving*), it means exactly that: *Jesus Christ has fallen in love with this human being whose soul is the object of Christ's love.* Also, when divine–human love speaks of mutual and reciprocal self–surrender of lives between Jesus Christ and man, it is stating, indeed, that *each is really living the life of the other*; here words mean exactly what they say and say exactly what they mean.

---

[6] Sg 6:3.
[7] Sg 7:11.
[8] Jn 6:56.

This mutual self–surrender between Jesus Christ and the human being, with the corresponding mutual fusion of lives —which does not at all mean a blend into numerically one and the same life— is beautifully expressed in the verses of Saint John of the Cross:

> *Oh, night that guided me,*
> *Oh, night more lovely than the dawn,*
> *Oh, night that joined Beloved with lover,*
> *Lover transformed in the Beloved!*[9]

Folk poetry says the same, in its own way; this time with the voice of the Bridegroom:

> *I would live your life, it's true,*
> *If you would offer it completely to me,*
> *And I would give mine to you*
> *If you truly do agree,*
> *You wish to exchange them, as I do, freely.*

In this ambiance of true love, the feelings and the will of each lover —God and man— are identified. It is unimaginable that the soul in love may want something not conforming to the will of the Beloved. The soul wants and longs for only what her Beloved wants and desires. It would not be accurate enough to say that both wills are identical since, at least *in a way*, they are the same will, in the sense that both only look for and desire the same things.

And in this context, what will the soul not give to Jesus Christ, with Whom she has fallen in love? And what will Jesus Christ, Who is madly in love with the soul, deny to that soul who is pleading with

---

[9]Saint John of the Cross, *Dark Night of the Soul.*

Him? It is indeed here that the saying *everything I have is yours and all you have is mine* becomes more real than anywhere else. Here also is what Saint Paul describes as his interior life fulfilled most perfectly: *And I live, now not I; but Christ liveth in me.*[10]

It is understood that Jesus' will and man's will are *on a par*, which is but the logical consequence of two lives lived *on a par*. In this case, both wills must coincide since each will has given itself in possession to the other and, therefore, both wills, although different, are one and the same volition. The opposite happens when the lives of two persons who claim to be in love are strange to each other: their wills become divergent and totally at odds. This is why the Apostle James said verily: *you have not, because you ask not. You ask, and receive not; because you ask amiss: that you may consume it on your concupiscences.*[11] Unfortunately, these truths are seldom remembered by Christians.

Nor do those same Christians usually take into account that Jesus Christ loves His own *unto the end.*[12] This expression can be understood as meaning to the last moment of His earthly life or to the ultimate degree of love His human will is able to reach. But even these two meanings do not exclude other more profound and loftier possible interpretations which by and large escape human understanding.

To understand all of this, one must remember that Jesus Christ is true God and equally *true Man.* This latter truth of Faith, as strange as it may sound, is more easily forgotten and more difficult to believe than His divinity. To see how accurate this asseveration is it would suffice to make a self examination: is it not true that when

---

[10] Gal 2:20.
[11] Jas 4: 2–3.
[12] Jn 13:1.

somebody addresses himself to Jesus Christ he is believing that he is addressing God, whereas he is never, or almost never, conscious that *he is also talking to a Man?* And not just to a man who is similar to or like other men, but a man exactly *the same as the rest of men, one of them.* A man who has a human body and soul, with human feelings and thoughts, with specifically human reactions, capable of understanding his brother men, feeling himself one of them, *not one like them.* Believing this is the difficulty that is usually experienced when it comes to accepting something so elementary but which only the saints came to understand: that Jesus Christ can be *actually in love* with a particular human being.

Consequently, prayer is usually understood as a prayer of *petition* only. This type of prayer is useful and even necessary, as Jesus Christ Himself taught in the *Our Father*. But prayer is not generally considered an intimate *loving conversation* with Jesus Christ. As a result, the Christian deprives himself of what should have been the motor empowering his existence and the fundamental reason and meaning of his existence: an intimate, loving friendship with Jesus Christ that would have provided him, in this life, with a foretaste of the Perfect Joy that he will enjoy in his Homeland.

On the other hand, new ideological trends, especially since the Enlightenment, have managed to introduce themselves as elements of Christian thought, diluting the ideal of holiness as it was always rooted among the faithful.

The heroes of the Church, the saints, who were once considered by Christian people as intercessors and also as role models to imitate, were gradually losing this status and were reduced to mere intercessors. Moreover, with the sudden and forceful introduction of the Modernist heresy into the Church, especially after the Second Vatican Council, devotion to the saints completely disappeared from the majority of the faithful, mainly due to the influx of new canonizations, which does not dispel a skeptical attitude among the faithful, otherwise quite understandable.

This had lethal consequences for all the spiritualities based on devotion to the humanity of Jesus Christ; having a close friendship with and love of His person have essentially disappeared. In modern times, the abundant river of spirituality that began with great medieval spiritual men such as Saint Bonaventure and Saint Bernard, continued with the *Devotio Moderna* of Thomas á Kempis, and reached its peak in the classics of the Golden Age, Saint Teresa and Saint John of the Cross, finally became a weak stream destined to be lost in the desolate sea of today's Church. Hence the question: how many Christians today still rely on the loving, intimate prayer with Jesus Christ?

God became man in Jesus Christ for two reasons; first, to be able to give His life for us. This is why He took our human nature, for He could not die in His divine nature. But His human nature implies a true man, and as true man *He is truly Jesus Christ*, for His human nature belongs to a divine Person, and, as is well-known, all operations must be attributed to the Person and not to the nature.

And Jesus Christ being truly man, a man among men, can now love and be loved by man *as a man can and knows how to love*. It is hard to imagine that man can fall directly in love with God as such God because *no man hath seen God at any time*.[13] And no one can feel in love with what he has never seen, since love is in the heart which has been attracted by kindness, by beauty, in one word, by goodness, but *as long as they are perceived*. It is true that man can know, to an extent, the beauty and grandeur of God through creation, but this knowledge is quite imperfect.

---

[13] Jn 1:18.

Man, indeed, loves with his soul, *but through his body and with his body*, for man is a substantial unity of those two elements. Man loves *as man*, not only with his body or only with his soul; and if he is to love with perfection according to his nature, he needs to love another nature like his own. That is why God became Man, so that His creature could love Him to a perfect degree to the extent that he is able and knows how to love. Jesus Christ is true Man, and it is through His human nature that the soul reaches His Person (nobody falls in love with a nature, but with a person); and in that Person man loves His Divine Nature.

The fact that Jesus Christ has a true human nature facilitates man's access to His Person and makes possible the beginning and development of a true relationship of love between them. Man first *comprehends* Jesus Christ *as Man*; he grasps Him as a Man possessing qualities and characteristics, as described in the Gospel, that no human creature has ever dreamed of and which will be enhanced by His divine condition: He calls each one of His sheep by name, goes ahead of them, saves them from all dangers even at the risk of His life, and leads them to good pastures; He goes after the lost one at the greatest risks and with immense love brings it back upon His shoulders to the sheepfold; He puts His life in danger for them when perils arise. On the Mountain of the Beatitudes He promulgates for the entire world a dream doctrine which fulfills all yearnings and longings that for centuries have filled the heart of humanity with desires; then, in the Sermon of the Last Supper, He teaches man how far he can be driven and transformed by a Love that overflows to the infinite for him. He shows man the meaning of his existence and the End for which he has been created; additionally, He teaches him to be free, to love justice and to live honestly, to hate lies and fear sin, to be attracted by goodness and beauty and to enjoy the grandeur of Creation which, after all, had been created out of nothing for him and submitted to his rule. And last but not least, He gives man *everything He has* and *all that He is* when He gives him His own Heart and His own Love to a degree that reaches the *very end*, of course, and also His own Joy with the promise that nobody will be able to take it away from him.

This *first moment* in which man perceives Jesus Christ as man is a *logical*, not temporal, *moment*. We are dealing with *one sole act of love* in which man feels overtaken by the human condition of Jesus Christ; a condition empowered to the highest degree because Jesus Christ is perceived *at the same time* as a Person, and a Divine One.

The human creature, enthralled and overwhelmed by surprise, discovers that this Man, Who has enamored him with a love which penetrates into the deepest recesses of the heart, *is at the same time his God*. But now God does not want to be treated as Lord but as friend; He does not want so much to be worshiped as to share His life, even to interchange it, with the life of His creature. God wishes to have with His creature a relationship of love that can be *compared* to the relationship between spouses —the latter being a mere analogy, although most suitable for human understanding— elevated to a level that expands beyond finitude and reaches the superior world of the supernatural, which defies any description with human language. God Himself tried to draw that world in the best, most accessible way to man; He used the language of Poetry by inspiring the immortal divine Poem, *The Song of Songs*.

The relationship of love is a bilateral and reciprocal relationship; therefore, if Jesus Christ loves man most intimately and affectionately, even *unto the end* in degree (Jn 13:1), it is expected that man requites Him in the same way. And because Jesus Christ has a true Human nature, man can love Him as Man while also perceiving that

that man is his God. These two natures —Human and Divine— belong (without confusion) equally and properly to the one and only divine Person. And hence, when the creature addresses Jesus Christ with the words *I love you* he is saying them to the Man and also to his God in a single act of love. The same thing happens when Jesus says these words to His creature; words which consequently are human and divine at the same time.

The possibility of a true *loving dialogue* between God and man is made possible only in Jesus Christ. In the amorous dialogues as transmitted in the *Song of Songs* between the two characters, the bride and the Bridegroom, it is still difficult to establish a relationship of intimacy and equality between God and His creature.

The authority of the man over the woman within the marital bond has been established since Creation: *The husband is the head of the wife, as Christ is the head of the church*,[14] said Saint Paul. But the words *Henceforth I call you not servants, but I have called you friends*[15] had not yet been pronounced; they made clear that any kind of distance between God and man had been erased though love.[16] The love relationship demands a sincere sentiment of *equality* between the lovers, so much so that each one feels that he/she *belongs*

---

[14]Eph 5:23. Nevertheless, this authority has particular characteristics as pointed out in other passages which explain that this *authority* is an attitude of self–surrender out of love of the man to the woman: *as Christ also loved the church, and delivered Himself up for her* (Eph 5:25).

[15]Jn 15:15.

[16]Even the idea of a combat of love which takes place between the Bridegroom and the bride, already alluded to in the *Song of Songs* (Sg 2:4), cannot help but slip in a trace of condescension on the part of the Bridegroom by allowing the bride to engage in that combat with Him. Only the Gospel makes real the incredible possibility that, in the business of love between the servant and his master, the former can return to the latter double the amount received from Him, as seen in the parables of the talents and the mines.

to the other. In this sense one could also say that each lover would be compelled to feel inferior to the other, although in an improper sense because each lover keeps his or her own personality.

In effect, man would not enjoy the intimacy of the *Humanity* of Jesus Christ, perceiving Him as Man, if at the same time man would not also perceive Him as his God. Otherwise, the whole attractive charm of the Person of Jesus Christ, perceived and enjoyed by His creature through His Humanity, would entirely disappear. As for Jesus Christ, while His love compels Him to be in a situation of intimacy and equality of feelings in regard to His creature, the ensuing and proper joy would increase more, so to speak, when He perceives him as *His creature*, whom He has elevated to be placed and remain always next to Him where He is: *Father, I will that they also, whom thou hast given me, be with me where I am.*[17]

True love for Jesus Christ can only be explained through what Theology calls the *hypostatic union.*

One feels enamored of another person when he perceives in that person qualities and conditions that seduce him. The human soul is irresistibly attracted by the Divine Person of Jesus Christ whom he perceives as *Jesus Christ Man*. It is in this way that Jesus Christ is grasped as Person —since one can only love a person— in Whom there is all the excellence never before imagined in a *human being*: in short, a Man charming beyond words Who can arouse fiery love in the heart of another human being. But it also happens, to cap it all, that this Person, a human being, is also and above all *true God*, the only true God. As Person He is one sole Person (no one would fall in love with a being made up of two persons), but with the double condition of being true God and true Man. The soul indeed perceives Him as Man, and feels herself apprehended and *captured*

---

[17] Jn 17:24.

by Him, by the power of his charm that overflows from that love; although such rapture of love reaches the degree of genuine *ecstasy* of love when man discovers Him to be also *his God*.

When the enamored soul addresses herself to Jesus Christ to tell Him *I love you* —the sweetest expression that can be uttered by a rational being— she is speaking with *Jesus Christ Man* and at the same time and in the same act with *Jesus Christ God*. And yet the soul speaks with and addresses herself to *one and the same Person*, and only one. The same thing happens when it is Jesus Christ Who speaks those same words to the human soul whom He loves, since it is *Jesus Christ as Man* speaking, although He is at the same time and in one sole act *Jesus Christ God*, and it is the *one sole Person* (*divine*) addressing the creature. It could not be otherwise because the mystery of the relationship of love can take place only between one particular person and another particular person, between and an *I* and a *thou*.

Loving a *plurality of people*, which is also true love, is but an elongation of love for others —*Love one another*— which, because it does not possess some of the specific elements of the relationship of love, such as intimacy and totality,[18] does not have the elements of perfect love. This is confirmed by the fact that it is not possible to truly love the others if there is not first a true loving relationship with Jesus Christ, thanks to which one effectively loves the others through his love for Jesus Christ;[19] the fact that *they are loved by Jesus Christ* is the first motivation for our loving them (he who is in love loves everyone and everything the beloved person loves).

---

[18] According to Jesus Christ, one must love God *above all things* but his neighbor *as he loves himself*.

[19] Because of Jesus Christ, they and the lover are part of the same Body, as Saint Paul teaches in his Letter to the Romans and in his First Letter to the Corinthians.

The divine–human relationship of love is an analogy of the relationship that exists in the Holy Trinity: The Person of the Father loves the Person of the Son, and vice versa. The bond of love between both is another Person, the Holy Spirit, due to the simplicity of the Divine Nature.[20] Relations in God cannot be accidents, unlike what happens with creatures where the bond of love between the two lovers has a created nature and, therefore, is not identical to the essence of either of them.

At any rate, as we have seen, love always takes place, both in God and in creatures, *from person to person*, thus giving way to the solitude and intimacy of the *face to face* required by the unfathomable and sublime reality the mystery of love is:

> *In solitude she lived,*
> *And in solitude built her nest;*
> *And in solitude, alone*
> *Hath the Beloved guided her,*
> *In solitude also wounded with love.*[21]

But the identification of wills does not stop at that, since it is founded on something that goes far beyond: the identification of lives, as proclaimed by Jesus Christ Himself: *He who eats my flesh and drinks my blood remains (lives) in me and I in him.*[22] This does

---

[20] Personal relations in God, although *really* different among themselves, are *identical* to the Divine Essence. There are four of them in the Holy Trinity, of which only three are opposite to each other; this is why there are Three Divine Persons. Because the relations in God are identical to the Divine Essence, they cannot be accidents because accidents are not compatible with the Simplicity of the Divine Essence.

[21] Saint John of the Cross, *Spiritual Canticle*.

[22] Jn 6:56.

not mean the merging of two lives into one, but that *each one makes his own the life of the other*; this is how both live the same life.

The mystery of divine love and the great tragedy of man are summarized in this: that God is willing to give everything to the creature He has created in His image and likeness, including Himself; however, He has been rejected by most of those whom He loves: *He came unto his own, and his own received him not.*[23]

---

[23] Jn 1:11.

BORN A DEAF–MUTE vs. DEAF AND DUMB FOR CONVENIENCE[1]

(Mk 7:31-37)

Dear brethren in the Heart of Our Lord and of the Virgin Mary Our Mother:

Today, the Eleventh Sunday after Pentecost according to the so-called Extraordinary Form of the Roman Rite of the Holy Mass, the Church brings to our consideration a passage from the Gospel of Saint Mark which tells us about one of the many events in the Life of the Lord.

The narrative points out that Jesus was, as usual, surrounded by a great crowd and that they brought before Him a deaf-mute and besought Him to lay His hands upon him. The Lord took him apart from the multitude and put His fingers into his ears and touched his tongue with His saliva. Jesus Christ, looking up to heaven, groaned and said to him: *Ephpheta*, which is, *Be thou opened.*

Immediately the ears of the deaf-mute were opened, and the string of his tongue was loosed, and he spoke normally. The crowd was astonished and began to proclaim the wonder they had witnessed despite Jesus charging them that they should tell no man.

---

[1]Homily preached on August 9, 2015.

As we can see, the account tells us about the miraculous cure of a poor wretch who was born deaf and was, consequently, also dumb. Therefore, we could begin our dissertation by saying that there exist two kinds of deaf–mutes: one deaf from birth and a quite different one whose main characteristic is that his deafness is completely voluntary. As strange as it may seem, the first one is rarer, while the second is much more common.

This means, if we now descend to the level of everyday life, that we face the fact that there are some who are deaf because they do not want to hear and there are others who are mute because they refuse to speak; a strange situation, indeed, but one which is in full force in the Church today: pastors who refuse to speak proliferate, and the sheep have acquired the habit of not wanting to hear.

Regarding the Shepherds we are talking about, it seems that the oracle of the prophet Isaiah is fulfilled in them: *The shepherds themselves knew no understanding: all have turned aside into their own way, every one after his own gain, from the first even to the last.*[2] As for the alluded sheep, they make real in themselves the adage *there are none so deaf as those who will not listen.*

The issue here is much more complex and complicated than this simple approach may imply.

There are shepherds who not only never feed their sheep with the pasture of sound doctrine (they always remain silent); other shepherds are worse, they provide them with the poison of ideas and teachings that are lethal for their souls and which lead them to damnation. Both shepherds can be called *mute shepherds*. They are voluntarily mute who never give their sheep the good pastures of the Word of God.

---

[2] Is 56:11.

As for the sheep we have mentioned, because they have been poisoned by the doctrines of the false Shepherds or because they were scandalized by the corruption of the ecclesiastical atmosphere and the scandals of the Hierarchy, they have voluntarily opted to close their ears to the Word of God and live according to the world.

In effect, Shepherds have remained silent as regards the Good Doctrine, either because they did not preach it or because they proclaimed a false Doctrine. The sheep chose the easy way out by not listening to the Good Doctrine and passively accepting without resistance the poison of the false one. And so, with Shepherds maliciously dumb and sheep purposely deaf, the Church has ended up in the present *Great Apostasy* previously announced by the Scriptures. The logical result being the betrayal of the Faith, the option for the World, and the rebellion against God both by most of the Hierarchy and by many of the faithful; which is exactly what is going on at present.

Some prefer, when the sky is filled with huge dark clouds, to stop thinking about storms and close their eyes to reality. They are enemies of problems and not close friends of the truth; nevertheless, they are willing to accuse as soothsayers and doom–mongers those who warn of the danger. And because surely there are those who think that we are painting an overly pessimistic picture of the state of the Church and the world, it is good to recall the words of the Apostle Saint Paul to his disciple Timothy: *For there shall be a time, when they will not endure sound doctrine; but, according to their own desires, they will heap to themselves teachers, having itching ears. And shall indeed turn away their hearing from the truth, but will be turned unto fables.*[3]

---

[3] 2 Tim 4: 3–4.

They will not endure sound doctrine. This reminds us of the reaction of the people after hearing Jesus' Speech at Capharnaum: *This saying is hard, who can hear it?*[4] This phrase expresses feelings which at present have reached full steam as a consequence of the wide-spread hedonism, the exalted materialism which has taken its toll on almost all of humanity, the hatred of the Cross, and the replacement of the supernatural world by the purely natural: all elements which have been advanced by the heresy of Modernism which has invaded the Church.

Post-conciliar Modernism has successfully coined the expressions *enemy of the Council* or *lacking the spirit of the Council* which have been applied to all those who dared to defend the Faith and asked for the application of a Magisterium which *did not begin with the Second Vatican Council but with Jesus Christ Himself* and reaches the present moments. Saint Paul already said in his time that the Cross had become a stumbling block for the Jews and foolishness for the Gentiles (1 Cor 1:23); this rejection of the Cross reaches its culminating point with the elimination of any vestige of the Mass as a sacrifice; it was replaced by the New Mass, the *Novus Ordo* promulgated by Pope Paul VI (1969), which was a death blow for the Church of the twenty-first century as well as the greatest victory of Satan throughout the entire history of the Institution founded by Jesus Christ.

The body of the Christian faithful would never have massively apostatized, as it has done today, had it not been chaired and encouraged by the teaching Church. At this point it would be necessary to speak of the betrayal carried out by the *intelligentsia* of the Church mostly from the nineteenth century onwards, which would not have been possible without the defection of the *Hierarchy*.

---

[4]Jn 6:60.

Much has been written about this issue and about the multiple causes which have slowly led to the present crisis: the abandonment of the *Philosophia Perennis* since the Low Middle Ages, the stream of ideas sprung from the French Revolution, the emergence of Idealism and the doctrines of Immanentism and Historicism which, along with Marxism, gave birth to Modernism, etc. Each and all of them were undoubtedly influential elements to a lesser or greater degree in the present crisis. Their in–depth and meticulous analysis has occasioned the apparition of numerous libraries filled with volumes.

It often happens, however, that the problems affecting the depths of the human being are studied and explained by man in a superficial or, as one would say now, *peripheral* manner. This is a way of confronting crucial issues by beating around the bush over and over but *without ever entering the core of the problem*. This way of addressing and explaining the difficult issues that affect and concern the human being does not seem sufficient. Such problems, which are basically of a supernatural nature, imply the need to be dealt with by using supernatural criteria and methods —*which is exactly what our modern generation is unwilling to do*. In effect, the new man is not willing to face the real problems *because he is afraid of confronting himself.* Fear, in the first place, to affirm his need to rely on God to give meaning to his life. And fear, above all, to recognize in himself *the misery of his current existence*.

The practice of changing the meaning of words reflects this. For example, the covert oppression and tyranny inflicted upon the masses by way of a merciless brainwashing is known as *democracy* and made synonymous with *freedom*, while ruthlessly punishing those who question it. Rejecting any norm of conduct external or superior to the individual, which would prevent each person from doing whatever he or she pleases, is called *liberty of conscience*;

freedom to insult, to slander, or to offend others in any way and with impunity is given the name *freedom of expression*; choosing behaviors that are simply aberrations that degrade man to a level much lower than animals is known as an *attitude that exalts and elevates individual autonomy* to a condition in which humanity has freed itself from old taboos and has found itself; the oligarchic and oppressive groups bent on fattening and enriching themselves by exploiting and cheating the rest of the citizens, are called *political parties* and indispensable tools of democracy; destroying the true Church built by God for the sake of man and replacing it with another, exclusively human and despising God, is acclaimed by using various appellations of triumphalistic hue such as *New Church, New Evangelization, Ecclesiastical Springtime, returning to the early and authentic Church, etc.*

The Church, in particular, has evidently given up her mission of announcing the Gospel to the world following the commandment of Christ for the purpose of pleasing men by speaking about things that *give pleasure to their passions*. As the Apostle Saint John had already announced in his *First Letter, They are of the world: therefore of the world they speak, and the world heareth them*.[5] Left far away are the warnings of the Apostle Saint Paul: *Which things also we speak, not in the learned words of human wisdom; but in the doctrine of the Spirit*.[6] Or in another place: *As we said before, so now I say again: If any one preach to you a gospel, besides that which you have received, let him be anathema. For do I now persuade men, or God? Or do I seek to please men? If I yet pleased men, I should not be the servant of Christ*.[7] Hence it is not surprising that the Church has

---

[5] 1 Jn 4:5.
[6] 1 Cor 2:13.
[7] Gal 1: 9–10.

forgotten the language of the supernatural in order to embrace the chatter of politics: disputes about liberalism, capitalism, or socialism; armament or world peace issues —the latter understood merely in a worldly sense—; the intricate problems of social justice; the legality of the death penalty; the care of the ecosystem and sources of energy; regulation of immigration...; in general, the Church speaks about everything that encourages men to fret about self–sufficiency and forget about God.

This is why men will *turn away their hearing from the truth*, becoming voluntarily deaf, or deaf for the sake of convenience and, consequently, also mute. This attitude has an inbuilt foolishness already pointed out by Saint Paul:

That which Israel sought, he hath not obtained: but the election hath obtained it; and the rest have been blinded, as it is written:

> *God hath given them the spirit of insensibility;*
> *eyes that they should not see;*
> *and ears that they should not hear,*
> *until this present day.*[8]

Insisting on closing one's ears to the truth is the normal attitude of the *Modern Church*, supported by a large number of Catholics, Papolatrists and neo–Catholics, who refuse to admit a reality that is hitting them in the eye; and it is useless, if not impossible, to put in front of them the starkest evidence. Some of them even go to the greatest lengths in trying to present as white what is black and vice versa, thus validating the adage that there is no one more deaf than he who does not want to hear and there is no one more blind than

---

[8]Rom 11: 7–8.

he who does not want to see. Deep down they are Catholics whose faith, generally not very solidly founded, brings about unconscious feelings that compel them to not come to terms with the panic that the truly depressing reality would cause in them. This would lead them to look for *masters* who will *please their ears* by talking only and exclusively about things they want to hear. And, of course, there is no shortage of pretenders willing to offer them the fables mentioned by Saint Paul, for there is quite an abundance of such masters in a *Modern Church* where it is difficult to find an honest Shepherd.

The extremism of some Catholics induces them to defend and justify what cannot be defended or justified (they are usually called neo–catholics, others refer to them as neocons). Other catholics, holding equally extreme views, reject as illegitimate certain ecclesiastical elements (Hierarchy, specifically the Pope, the *Novus Ordo* Mass) because of their doctrine, behaviour or way of worshiping; they themselves, according to their own judgment, decide about the orthodoxy or lack of orthodoxy of those elements. True devotion to the Pope, for example, is at a point equidistant between two opposites: papolatry and refusing one's adherence to the Vicar of Christ, as sedevacantists and others like them do. Both approaches are usually the result of the lack of a solid religious formation or of a sufficiently strong Faith.

> *But I, as a deaf man, heard not;*
> *and as a dumb man not opening his mouth.*[9]

The dumb Shepherds are those who, failing in the fulfillment of their mission, do not proclaim the word of God.

---

[9] Ps 38:14.

They can be divided into two groups. The first group is made up of those Shepherds who speak while saying nothing or, at best, stating banalities, trivialities, frivolities, or touching upon topics which lack any kind of interest and are completely disregarded by the faithful. The second comprises those who preach or write extraneous doctrines contrary, and sometimes even abhorrent, to the Faith of the Church.

And although it would be difficult to determine which of the two groups is more harmful to the faithful, you can be sure that one and the other completely destroy the flock entrusted to them.

Determining the historical limits of the modern Pastoral practice of the Church would require the prior existence of a serious history of the Church covering the twentieth and twenty–first centuries. This would prove to be an extraordinarily difficult task, probably impossible to carry out until several centuries have passed, if it is ever achieved.

However, simplifying the issue to the limit —which is sufficient for a non–historical disquisition as this—, one could arguably say that an era of *mute Shepherds* mainly occupies the second half of the twentieth century, once the *social Shepherds* were no longer fashionable. These Shepherds had devoted infinite time and energy to what they called *the social question*, which they thought to be the only existing problem that could prevent fair relations of coexistence among men.

Nevertheless, mainly preachers and promoters of the *social question* could also be considered —at least in a broad sense— as a subspecies of the *dumb Shepherds*, because in the end, and this may sound scandalous to some ears, their huge, bulky *Social Doctrine* was of no great consequence concerning the proclamation of the Word of God and the salvation of souls.

The *social question* and the pertinent *social Pastoral practice* of the Church reached their peak, with all the signs of a pandemic, about the middle of the last century. It may be impossible to explain why the opinion that the evangelical doctrine could only be proclaimed through and from the viewpoint of the *social question* reached such a wide acceptance within the Church; a *social question* which many maintained for numerous years —and some maintain even today— would be definitively resolved through an ocean of theories grouped under the name *Catholic Social Teaching*. Dogmatic principles came to be reduced to an Ethics which maintained that the only problems Christians were concerned about were those that had to do with social relationships.

Marxism was making inroads into the Church prior to the appearance of *Liberation Theology*, although nobody seemed to perceive the danger. The worker issues, Christian Socialism, oppressive Capitalism, Unions, and the whole conglomerate of related issues, for years occupied the attention and time of theologians, experts in pastoral practice, Bishops, and, as a consequence, thousands of pastors and other priests who were enthusiastically bent on leading souls on the only way that leads to salvation: a humane socialism barely supernatural. The *Documents and Pastoral Letters* of the Hierarchy of the whole Church, with a flurry of studies made by commentators and experts, filled the libraries of the time... as well as the heads of simple priests and of the unfortunate faithful. Catholic Action became Socialist and pro-workers began changing its name to HOAC,[10] JOC,[11] and the like, where the *worker* and *social* nature undoubtedly predominated over *Catholic*. These associations, as anyone might expect, eventually became powerful

---

[10]Spanish acronym for *Workers Brotherhood of Catholic Action*.

[11]Spanish acronym for *Catholic Worker Youth*.

Communist Unions. The standard preaching at Sunday Masses was limited almost exclusively to proclaiming the evils of capitalism and the *oppression* suffered by the Christian people, especially the working class, who were considered exploited by the bourgeois capitalist class. The very expression *bourgeois class* became for many years a kind of logo which encapsulated all the demons and enemies of Christianity and was, for a long time, the *anathema* with which thousands of naive priests, unwitting victims of the Marxist infiltration that was already taking place within the Church, ruthlessly condemned the despised *oppressing* bourgeoisie.

Even a Pope as extraordinary and intelligent as Pius XII (after all a victim of the prevalent atmosphere brought about by the wave of doctrines of his time) authorized the creation of the so-called *Mission of Paris* which included those known as *worker priests*. They, as anyone with some vision might have expected, were eventually suppressed by the same Pontiff in 1954, after almost all of them had become communists.

When, perhaps a long time from now, history calmly analyzes the event, Rome's approval of such a thing may still remain a mystery to be explained. It is difficult to imagine that anyone could think that a priest could better fulfill his mission by *ceasing to be a priest*, at least in the exercise of his ministerial obligations; or that he can give a testimony of his priesthood and of Jesus Christ *without manifesting himself as a priest or as a witness for Jesus Christ*. The Ancient said that those the gods wish to destroy, they first drive mad. Indeed those were times when everything seemed to imply that God had decided to abandon His church, once the Church had already begun to abandon Him.

On this issue of *worker priests* the controversy was served. Both the creators of the institution and its many supporters (the historical truth shows that there were no detractors) were convinced that a priest who abandons his ministry and works as one among other Marxist workers would be better able to bear witness to his priesthood and the truth of Christianity. The results, however, did not respond to any such hopes. The truth is that the Marxist workers considered these priests *as workers working as any other worker*; or, at best, as priests disappointed with their ministry who, consequently, preferred to become workers; which, well examined, seems a logical consequence. In effect, witnessing is but *showing something for all to see* in order to provide clear evidence of that thing; therefore, *what is seen* is really what becomes obvious. If bearing witness to something is to show that thing for all to see, what is seen, and nothing else, is what is perceived by those who are looking.

A large number of studies, Documents, Episcopal Pastoral Letters, papal Encyclicals, conferences, courses and lectures, etc., etc., about the *Social Doctrine of the Church* exhausted the field of Pastoral practice of the Church during the second half of the twentieth century. For a long time the *Social Doctrine of the Church* was seen as the only answer to the social problems of mankind; but today, as in the second decade of the century, it is not given much consideration except for some few references in some places. As, for instance, the Encyclical *Laudato Si* of Pope Francis, based, according to him, on the Social Doctrine of the Church.

But the problem with the *Social Doctrine of the Church* is its excessive meticulousness and immense complexity. Entire seas of books and publications have tried to explain it by countless theories and innumerable documents *ad casum*. Even Episcopal Pastoral practice, perhaps in an attempt to rival papal encyclicals, flooded the church with the contributions in which each Bishop or every expert advisor or theologian believed himself to have found the key to the Philosopher's Stone as the great remedy for social convulsions. Needless to say, the solutions were sometimes contradictory and not always consistent, which is understandable if one takes into account both the immense number of publications and the complexity and variety of contributions. All of which managed to erect the immense edifice of *Catholic Social Teaching* which, when all is said and done, very few have managed to assume in full and even fewer able to understand.

Somebody once begged Jesus Christ to intervene in the partition of his inheritance. Jesus Christ said to him: *Man, who hath appointed me judge, or divider, over you?*[12] In another instance, Jesus Christ uttered a very clear and forceful statement: *Seek ye therefore first the kingdom of God, and his justice, and all these things shall be added unto you.*[13]

And as always happens with the important events in the history of the Church, it will also take many years before this extended period of excessive attention to the *social question* —to the point of making it almost exclusively the center of the Church's Pastoral practice— can be studied calmly. Today it may sound scandalous to asseverate that such attention could perhaps have been too exaggerated.

But sometimes men err by complicating simple questions or by simplifying complicated issues. Regarding the *social question*, it is difficult to imagine that this issue is not sufficiently addressed in the Gospel, for it contains the Doctrine of Jesus Christ addressed to men of all places and all times, and covering, for those who want to read it, all the problems affecting man's behavior and coexistence and their relevant solutions. Possibly, it would only be necessary to

---

[12] Lk 12:14.
[13] Mt 6:33.

read the Scriptures and believe them as the revealed Word of God in order to find the right key for this much–debated question.

Unfortunately, however, there were many who thought that the Gospel was insufficient. So they felt it necessary to complete it and then address the new and complex relationships that arose among men, as the new currents of thought claimed.

History is the teacher of life and *History repeats itself* are expressions that are on everyone's lips but to which nobody pays any attention.

Saint Francis of Assisi, who lived at the crossroads of the twelfth and thirteenth centuries, faced this problem. Earnest man in love with Jesus Christ as he was, he firmly believed in all His Words and tried to translate them to his own life, literally and without further ado. Hence the wording of the *Rule* he made for his Order: he faithfully transcribed the Gospel with almost no elucidation, which he would have considered unnecessary since he was convinced that there was nothing to *add* to or *delete* from the Word of God; as if the Gospel were insufficient to some extent or, on the contrary, contained superfluous, repetitive, or obsolete items.

And, as expected, the whole world came down upon poor Saint Francis. Numerous warnings and notices advising moderation were showered upon him, first from the Pope and then from his own brothers. Monastic life as he had planned it —he was told— was too difficult and practically impossible to adapt to the capabilities of a human being; the tremendous difficulty and excessive austerity that accompanied it made it unsuitable for the weakness and little strength of human nature. As for the copy of the evangelical precepts that Saint Francis had transferred too literally to his *Rule*, they said that everything was the result of an exaggerated and too realistic interpretation of the teachings of Jesus Christ.

The Saint was forced to write several and increasingly mitigated redactions of the first *Rule*, but none of them managed to satisfy the tastes of the complicated ecclesiastical environment that surrounded him. The humility of the Saint patiently endured all the contradictions, but the situation became so difficult that the Pope thought it convenient to appoint Cardinal Hugolino as *Cardinal Protector* of the Order —a euphemism concealing his true functions of monitoring and moderating. History is waiting to find out if the office of the Cardinal was to protect Saint Francis from the course of events... or to protect the events from the dreams of Saint Francis, apparently the only one who had taken seriously the words of the Gospel.

The mystery of this story may never be unraveled. Was the Saint really so radical in his interpretation of the Gospel? And the answer —if any can be known— perhaps can only be found in the light of prayer, where the light of the Spirit leads to the serene meditation on the teachings of Jesus Christ. Only thus will one come to understand that the words of Jesus Christ, which *are spirit and life*,[14] need to be heard in a spirit of faith and with no human additions or subtractions, otherwise the hearing would merely be an interpretation of the voice of God according to the desires of a human nature not always willing to deny itself.

The vast sea of doctrines contained in the gargantuan Body of *Catholic Social Teaching*, even allowing that it was motivated by the best intentions of all at large, became a cumbersome *appendix* to the Words of Jesus Christ. Were those teachings perhaps insufficient? Some would say, of course, and they will provide reasons which may seem more or less convincing, that those doctrines need to be explained, applied to newly presented situations. Nevertheless, there are still Christians who do not cease to be alarmed when they hear

---

[14]Jn 6:63.

about the need for *applying* and *adapting* the words of Revelation to a specific historical moment; and probably with good reason, since everything seems to point out that the winds are blowing in favor of *historicist* doctrines definitely embraced by the modernist heresy to propagate them throughout the Church.

It is always the same, over and over again. When man believes that worrying about *human relationships* is more important than caring about the *relationships of love between God and man*... when that actually happens, then the ghost of Disaster has made its appearance heralding the beginning of woes.

The opening of the windows at the Vatican and the appearance of False Shepherds

The fall of the Berlin Wall and the (relative) commencing decline of Marxism in Europe determined the beginning of the diminishment of the *social question*. A great part in this diminishing was also played by the strong winds, which with a fury unmatched until then, shook the Church from the moment Pope John XXIII *opened the windows of the Vatican*; a personal expression which somehow inevitably showed an attitude of disregard for his predecessors.

But, contrary to what the Pope expected and as Paul VI expressly admitted shortly afterwards, what really entered the Church was the *smoke of Satan*. This *smoke* began to manifest itself when the Church, proclaiming her resignation to denouncing errors and announcing her opening to the World, sang the first notes of the *overture* of the strangest and most tragic symphony ever heard throughout her entire history: the Second Vatican Council which left Catholicism helpless before the declared invasion of the modernist heresy which until then had been contained.

The three encyclicals of John Paul II, *Laborem Exercens* (1981), *Sollicitudo Rei Socialis* (1987) and *Centesimus Annus* (1991), along with *Caritas in Veritate* (2009) of Benedict XVI have been the last of the social encyclicals so far. *Laudato Si* (2015) of Pope Francis, which he claims to be based on the Social Doctrine of the Church, is actually an argument for environmentalism, filled with political connotations and modernist undertones.

If we agree that this intense climate of *social doctrine*, which was the main determinant of the ecclesial environment that prevailed in the Church until Vatican II, was relentlessly swept away by the post-conciliar winds filled with Modernism that have been blowing in the Church until today, we must then admit that these encyclicals can hardly manage not to be termed as *out–of–season*. If we also consider that the *Doctrinal Revolution* carried out by Pope Francis, which seems to be aimed at shaking the firm foundation of the Church, is irreversible, then these encyclicals will probably put an end to the wave of social doctrines which have been flooding the Church for so long.

In The Church, once again and as had already happened on many other occasions throughout her history, knew not how to read it or draw anticipated consequences from the failure of the *Worker Priests*. The *Labor Movements* could not withstand the resurgence of Modernism, nor could they be headed for anything other than being *engulfed* by it. Men persist in their radicalisms and venerate them as their own gods; but, as with all idols of all time, radicalisms always end up being displaced and replaced by the imposing current fashion: the strongest simply replacing and eliminating the weakest; Modernism did just that to Marxism.

It is true that Pope Benedict and Pope Francis tried to resurrect Liberation Theology; the former more intently, for he was always a staunch fan of this kind of Marxist theology (or theologized Marxism). Francis, however, realized that this instrument was useless; so he soon abandoned it and chose another more radical and effective means. Thus Gustavo Gutierrez, Leonardo Boff, and the like, who believed they would be born again and re-sing their song of triumph, were not able to realize that, in fact, they also were history, and not a very dignified one.

But if, as has been established as a working hypothesis, we call *Dumb Shepherds* those who, in one way or another, do not preach the Word of God, we must assume that this group also includes those who merely spread superfluous doctrines or banalities, more particularly those who in a clear and blatant way poison the sheep with doctrines contrary to the Catholic faith or even openly heterodox and aberrant.

The era of the *False Prophets* began with the post–conciliar modernist trends. They continue to spread doctrines at odds with the Faith, usually imbued with modernism, in an atmosphere of complete freedom in which the multi-secular institutions established by the Church to ensure the safeguarding of the Faith —the Holy Office of the Inquisition, presently the Congregation for the Doctrine of the Faith— have became practically nonexistent bureaucratic offices with zero effectiveness.

The sad reality of the present moment is that modernist doctrines are being freely preached from the highest offices of the Church to the most humble parishes of the whole universe, resulting in the *General Apostasy* of the Catholic faithful at large.

This phenomenon is relatively similar to what happened with Arianism in the third and fourth centuries; although there are three major important differences. First, while the Arian heresy denied *some* truths of the Faith, Modernism rejects the very foundations of the Faith (*the sum of all heresies*, as Saint Pius X put it). Second, Arianism was resisted by some members of the hierarchy, championed by the great Saint Athanasius, a veritable hammer to this heresy. Finally, we must emphasize the extraordinary fact that while the Arian errors took their toll on nearly the entire Hierarchy of the Church as well as on the nobility and the army, plain and simple people remained true to the Faith; in short, they contributed more efficiently than the hierarchy to the disappearance of this heresy.

The attacks against the Faith and the Foundations of the Church have reached their climax during the pontificate of Pope Francis. It is under Pope Francis that a *decisive* event, which could very well be fatal and *final* for the life of the Church, has taken place: the assault and conquest of the Vatican by the "gay" lobby.

A society like ours, especially the Catholic world, accustomed to being manipulated by the Powers that handle the *media* and used to living as if it were numb and drugged, deprived of its power to react and even incapable of thinking, is witnessing the most important and serious events apparently without becoming aware of them or, at least, without attributing any importance to them; even when some events are so severe as to lead to its total destruction and extinction. People —generally known as *folks*— have become accustomed to living from day to day, as if nothing were happening, or, as they also say, to *looking the other way*.

However, the conquest of the Vatican by the "gay" lobby, with all the consequences that could logically be derived from this reality, must be admitted as a fundamental fact which in no way can be explained by purely natural causes. Consequently, it would be necessary to be open to the possibility that Evil Powers are right now operating effectively within the Church.

In effect, the conquest of the Government Body of the Church by the lobbying of "gay" groups, given the magnitude and seriousness of this event which could have never been imagined in the history of the Church and which cannot possibly be attributed to merely natural causes, could mean nothing less than the appearance of the False Prophet previously announced by the prophecies that warned of the approach of the End Times.

But the problem is further aggravated when one considers the close relationship between homosexuality and *Satanism*. This relationship cannot be denied. We have already mentioned that the strength deployed by hidden dark *Powers* which through the "gay" lobby and the worldwide domain of the media, they have managed to take over the Government of the Church.

The Church is going through a deep crisis and nobody wants to know anything about it. This situation resembles a suicide about to throw himself down from the highest point of a tall building: he is being witnessed by a crowd frozen in astonishment —because of a shameful hidden horror— which does not even dare to raise a shout and remains silent.

DEATH AS THE END OR AS THE BEGINNING[1]

Shew me, O thou whom my soul loveth,
Where thou feedest, where thou liest in the midday...
(Sg 1:7)

The Resurrection of the Son of the Widow of Nain

It is the evangelist Saint Luke who tells us the moving episode of the resurrection of the son of the widow of Nain by the power of Jesus Christ.

Following the text of the gospel we can imagine the scene. Jesus came to the entrance of a hamlet followed, as always, by a large crowd as the funeral procession was leaving the village on its way to the interment grounds. A few people carried a stretcher on which the dead body of a teenager was lying, probably wrapped, as usual, in a shroud tied with some strings. The young man was the only son of his mother, as the text specifies; and it also adds that she was a widow. The heartbroken woman was weeping bitterly after the corpse, being followed probably by mourners and musicians, according to the customs of the funeral rites of the time. Following the funeral cortège, relatives and acquaintances brought up the rear, as rural communities with few inhabitants are in the habit of doing.

---

[1]Preached on September 6, 2015.

It was at this moment that Jesus Christ and His followers arrived at the village and found themselves face to face with the cortège leaving the place. The text emphasizes that Jesus Christ, noticing immediately the poor woman sobbing after the corpse, had compassion on her.

It is easy to imagine the moment of silence that probably occurred when Jesus walked toward the grieving widow who had just lost her only son. Both processions stopped at once and silence filled with respectful anticipation ran through both crowds. Jesus Christ spoke short but extremely comforting words, as the woman contemplated Him in utter surprise and wonder:

—*Weep not.*

Then He went up to the dead body and the bearers stood still. The very schematic, compendious, and inquisitorial style of the gospel adds nothing more; but clearly this was the solemn moment in which there was a face–to–face confrontation between death and Him Who said of Himself *I am the life.*[2]

The scene depicted here is undoubtedly poignant: On the one hand men, with what little they can do in facing death, which cannot go beyond mourning, sharing the pain of the relatives of the deceased, and taking the corpse to be buried. On the other hand Jesus Christ, Lord of Life and Death, Who uttered words never before or afterwards spoken by any man: *I am the resurrection and the life.*[3] Hence the solemnity of the statements contained in the Prologue to the Gospel of Saint John: *In him was life, and the life was the light of men.*[4]

---

[2] Jn 14:6.
[3] Jn 11:25.
[4] Jn 1:4.

Death, being the unavoidable wall upon which every man stumbles at the end of his earthly existence, is also an event which those who have chosen to do without God have not yet managed to answer or explain after so many centuries of man's existence upon earth. After spending a life which they regard as exclusively their own, self-justified, in need of nothing except itself, and expecting nothing other than the pleasure of being exhausted to the dregs... they happen to find themselves in the end suddenly and unexpectedly with nothing. This is why paganism, which has never come up with a definition of man other than a *being destined for the tomb*, has never wanted to acknowledge *its shocking defeat and absolute failure*.

The Resurrection of Lazarus

There are several occasions, the gospels tell us, in which Jesus Christ takes on Death, the Resurrection of his friend Lazarus being one of the most remarkable.

The Gospel narrative of this event tells us that Jesus Christ was led to the place where Lazarus had been buried for four days. He orders the stone of the entrance to the tomb to be removed to the dismay of the sisters of Lazarus and those who accompanied them who warn Him that the corpse would already stink. Jesus Christ insists, and they finally slide the heavy stone; the entrance to the cave is laid bare; in the dark end one can somehow glimpse the presence of a body wrapped in shrouds and filling the air with the nauseating stench of death. It is at this time that Jesus Christ falls silent and bursts into tears.

It is the deep sorrow of the God–Man in the presence of death. Throughout the many millennia since their creation, countless generations of men have wept before death. Their tears are understandable to a certain extent; after all, death *had been introduced into this world by them*. Men were not aware that weeping because of death would not make as much sense *as to weep because of the causes which brought death into their midst.*

Anyway, this was the moment when, for the first time in history, human weeping in the presence of death *acquired its deep sense and all the characteristics which accompany true sorrow.*

Sorrow takes on a new and unique feature. From now on, man's sorrow because of the death of a loved one would become not so much a feeling of suffering *because of the other*, as a sentiment of *com–passion* with him, namely: suffering and afflictions that *become identical, the same thing, as the sufferings and afflictions of the other.* And because the feelings of *suffering with the other, making one's own the feelings of the other*, are but an overflow of love because one feels himself one with the beloved person whom he has lost. Thus the crying of Jesus Christ confronting Death —and from now on the weeping of all men before death— becomes *weeping out of love.*

And since this crying of Jesus *fully exhausts* all sorrow caused by Death (for Death was a punishment for sin), now the meaning of these tears is changed. The sentiments of dismay, depression, prostration, fainting, anxiety, and despair effected by death are gone forever to make way for others completely different. This weeping of Jesus Christ was the decisive moment when Death —whose total defeat would soon be consummated— definitively changed its meaning.

First and foremost because its nature as punishment was now transformed into a glorious condition.

Besides, the feeling of sorrow which always accompanies Death —for both those who suffer it and their loved ones— now acquired the status of being a *sharing*, in the sorrow of Jesus Christ. In effect, suffering next to and with the beloved Person, notwithstanding the many tears that come along with this suffering, gives rise to *tears of love*. And joy, which is the fruit of weeping out of love —a mysterious and ineffable paradox— overflows and, as it were, makes one forget all sorrow caused by suffering.

Death is also a milestone in Christian existence. It is not until death that the identification of the Christian with Christ, which is his vocation since baptism, *becomes a completed reality*. Even if the life of Christ had already become the life of the Christian, he would still fall short of becoming one with Him until he shared His Death: if similar in Life, then similar in Death, because love implies reciprocity and places the lovers on the same level in every respect. In this way, Death comes to fill up a lifetime of longings and eagerness, the very feelings which kept the soul in an attitude of earnest expectancy before the most joyous moment of its earthly existence: the union and full and definitive identification with Jesus Christ: for so long sought, so long waited for, and for such a long time dreamed of.

Death has become, as of now, *the greatest proof of love*; as Jesus Christ assured us: *Greater love than this no man hath, that a man lay down his life for his friends*;[5] and as Saint John confirmed in his *First Letter*, wherein he hands on to us the key to true knowledge of love: *In this we have known the charity of God, because he hath laid down his life for us.*[6] It is the mystery which, in turn, makes clear another mystery: love can be the cause of Death. The unraveling of this mystery would lead us into the unfathomable depths of love, as the bride of the *Song of Songs* expressed:

---

[5] Jn 15:13.
[6] 1 Jn 3:16.

> *Feed me with raisin cakes,*
> *Restore me with apples,*
> *For I am sick with love.*[7]

John of the Cross beautifully paraphrased this thought in his *Spiritual Canticle:*

> *O shepherds, you who go*
> *Through the sheepcots up the hill,*
> *If you shall see*
> *Him Whom I love the most,*
> *Tell Him I languish, suffer, and die.*

The mystic poet also makes patent in this stanza this mystery: death as the greatest proof of love, which can be chosen and even desired as the entrance door and way to love. Mystic folk poetry admits it plainly:

> *If living is to love and to be loved so,*
> *My only longing is to live in Love's glow;*
> *If dying is of love to burn in ardor*
> *That consumes the heart, may I quickly die more.*

It is the Apostle Paul who, once again, clearly explains the notion of death caused by love as he says *the love of Christ constraineth us; because we thus judge, that if one died for all, then were all dead.*[8] If it was love that led Christ to Death *for everyone*; then it

---

[7] Sg 2:5.
[8] 2 Cor 5:14.

is this same love that leads *everyone* to death for Christ. In the last analysis, death came to one and to the other because of love.

From now on and thanks to Jesus Christ, Death no longer subjects man to the yoke of terror, as the *Letter to the Hebrews* confirms: *Therefore because the children are partakers of flesh and blood, he also himself in like manner hath been partaker of the same: that, through death, he might destroy him who had the empire of death, that is to say, the devil; and might deliver them, who through the fear of death were all their lifetime subject to servitude.*[9]

But most importantly and above all things: what until now was *the end* of an ephemeral and always sorrowful life has become, because of Christ, the *beginning* of an authentic and true Life.

The Daughter of Jairus

The story of the resurrection of the daughter of Jairus, told by the three Synoptics, has two peculiar details which do not appear in the chronicles of similar miracles performed by Jesus Christ. At a closer examination, these particulars, apparently circumstantial and unimportant, are fine points that deserve attention, which usually happens with other passages of the gospel.

The first detail is narrated only by Saint Mark, who calls our attention to the reprimand of Jesus Christ to the people gathered in the house of mourning:

—*Why do you make a tumult and weep?*

As for the second, it is narrated by the three Synoptics who record the strange and unusual words uttered by Jesus Christ and which provoked the laughter and mockery of the gathering crowd:

—*The girl is not dead but sleeping.*

---

[9]Heb 2: 14–15.

(a) An unfortunate tumult

It is evident that the rebuke of Jesus Christ to the people because of the tumult —*Why do you make a tumult and weep?*— contains an implicit warning that what was being done made no sense.

And indeed it did not. It must be borne in mind that man often does meaningless things when he thinks he cannot act differently or supposes that one particular course of action suits him; even if he may never be able to explain such behavior. On this occasion the uproar was produced by abundant weeping (sincere or paid for in the case of the mourners), crying, condolences (more or less sincere), and the accompaniment of musicians along with the concourse of people, friends, and neighbors. It is impossible to know the particular moment, within man's history on Earth, in which deep sorrow because of the loss of a loved one was gradually accompanied by din and even celebrations.

All of which is, after all, the clearest expression of the astonishment and dismay experienced by man when confronting the incomprehensible and inexplicable reality of death and its causes. Why must the life of a human being come to an end? And what is even more frightening: What is beyond death? In this regard, it should be noted that man, whether he admits it or not, even if he persistently denies it, has never been able to drive out the idea that *there is indeed something on the other side of this mystery.*

The admonition of Jesus because of the bustle generated by the death of the girl may seem an insignificant gesture, but it actually is a true rebuke, for it is wrong to assert that it is impossible to find any meaning in death; in fact death has two clear and obvious meanings. On the one hand, throughout centuries, death has had the negative connotation as being a punishment for sin. On the other hand, Jesus Christ provided death with a positive significance: a participation in His own Death, which also becomes a guarantee of our glory and resurrection.

On the other hand, the uproar that men usually organize in the face of Death is just a way of shielding themselves from the disturbing feeling of *helplessness* that comes with such a tremendous event. Probably it did not take too long for them to understand that they *could do nothing* before the end of their existence, once they decided to do without God and to set themselves up as gods believing *they could do it all*.

Finally, funeral dins are also a means of *distraction* organized by men in order to avoid confronting realities that they either do not know how to explain or which are painful or unpleasant despite being critical to their existence. Funeral commotion is yet another way of exercising human stupidity, graphically described by the image of the ostrich hiding its head so as to not see the danger and pretending that it does not exist. This attitude is more frequent than it seems and degenerate modern societies practice it profusely; an overwhelming reality which is driving millions of human beings to perdition.

(b) Death as simply sleep

The words of Jesus Christ at the decease of Jairus' daughter were not only the strangest expression ever heard, apropos of death, they also sounded like thunder altering the mood of the attendees:

—*The damsel is not dead, but sleepeth.*

Consequently the audience reacted with laughter and mockery, which is what men usually do when they witness something unexpected that amazes and baffles them.

Perhaps it would be appropriate to begin this section with the familiar words of Saint Paul: *It is now the hour for you to rise from sleep.*[10] The Apostle, of course, is using figurative speech and not referring to natural sleep. Likewise Jesus Christ was not referring to natural death when He assured that the girl was only sleeping, which is fully consistent with His doctrine of calling Death only that which leads to eternal damnation (Jn 6: 50–51; 6:58).

But then what did Saint Paul mean with his warning to the Romans? And what meaning could be attributed to the words of Jesus Christ regarding the situation of the deceased girl?

Moreover, if this present life can be considered *sleeping* —in whatever sense— a new series of questions necessarily arise: Is this present life perhaps a dream and only future life can be considered true life, or is it rather the other way around? And if this present life is only a dream, in what sense is it a dream and what is its determining projection as regards future life?

Christianity is a supernatural religion whose doctrines, dogmas, and mysteries belong to the supernatural order but whose projections are closely *bound up* with the natural order since man —for whom Religion exists— being a created being of the natural order, is destined to eternal, supernatural life. This is why human life —natural as well as supernatural— is filled with mysteries concerning both orders.

Consequently, we need to ascend to the supernatural order to inquire about the mystery of human life: whether it is a vibrating reality or rather a dream whose meaning must be found. Thus an issue is posed which is extremely important and has difficult implications.

The words of Saint Paul addressed to the Romans are clearly an invective urging them to stop sleeping; which means that, according to the Apostle, his disciples were in a *dormant* situation or state.

---

[10]Rom 13:11.

And while we have said that his words can only be interpreted in a metaphorical sense, we must acknowledge, nevertheless, that they refer to a situation of *unconsciousness* or *outside-of-reality* existence in those whom Saint Paul is addressing.

This question may seem, at least at first glance, a trivial discussion; it is, nevertheless, important to human nature due to its serious implications affecting the natural–supernatural structure that conforms human life, which will be seen later when we study the consequences that this question has for the supernatural existence of man and more specifically for mystical life and their dependence on the contents of Revelation.

Pedro Calderón de la Barca seems to have been the first one who, in his famous play *Life Is a Dream*, clearly presented the issue of the human condition as a dream or as reality. For its main character, Segismundo, life is just a meaningless dream:

> *What is life? 'Tis but a madness.*
> *What is life? A thing that seems,*
> *A mirage that falsely gleams,*
> *Phantom joy, delusive rest,*
> *Since is life a dream at best,*
> *And even dreams themselves are dreams.*[11]

This is certainly a pagan concept of life. But the issue of life as a dream, or perhaps as a reality, actually appears at the dawn of Revelation, even before being resolved by Christianity.

If we now advance a Christian concept of life, we must concede that its primary characteristic is actually that of a *dream*. That is

---

[11]Pedro Calderón de la Barca, *Life Is a Dream*; Segismundo's reflections, close of Act II.

what clearly emerges from the two biblical texts cited above containing respectively the assertion of Jesus Christ and the Apostle Saint Paul. For those who live the spirit of Christianity, life is, therefore, certainly and necessarily a *dream*.

This dreaming state, a characteristic of human life, must be interpreted in two completely different senses, both mentioned in the quoted biblical texts; one of them is *completely negative* and the other *highly positive.*

The negative feature of life as a *dream*, the state of unconsciousness or outside–of–reality existence is denounced by Saint Paul in his recrimination intended for the Romans: *It is now the hour for you to rise from sleep.*

Jesus Christ considers real or true life only that which is informed by grace and has a supernatural character: *I am come that they may have life and may have it more abundantly.*[12] Or more clearly: *Amen, amen I say unto you, that he who heareth my word, and believeth him that sent me, hath life everlasting; and cometh to no judgment, but is passed from death to life.*[13] This agrees with the admonition of Saint Paul to the Colossians reminding them of their past condition: *And you, when you were dead in your sins and the uncircumcision of your flesh, he hath made alive together with him, forgiving you all offences.*[14]

It should be understood, therefore, that the Christian who lives outside the life of grace does not live a real life. Therefore, his current state of unconsciousness or dormancy is for him but a premonition of the true Death, which is Eternal death.

---

[12] Jn 10:10.
[13] Jn 5:24.
[14] Col 2:13.

According to the Christian notion of existence, life is the dream of a night waiting for the dawn of the next day to wake up and meet Christ. Life is, therefore, a dream filled with yearnings, longings, expectations, and hopes which, while deeply wounding the soul, push her harder in search of the Bridegroom and fill her with joy because of the certainty of an awakening that will give place to their meeting. Night would be then the time of sleep, or of absence and pursuit of the Bridegroom:

> *In my bed by night*
> *I sought him whom my soul loveth;*
> *I sought him, and found him not.*[15]

One of the common, although most neglected, features of the three theological virtues, is that of suffering. Faith is believing and trusting in the midst of darkness; Charity is love suffering because of the absences and longings never filled; Hope, meanwhile, has to deal with the vicissitudes of a search that looks to a future always uncertain as to its outcome, which even has to have intervals of apparent failures, many fruitless inquiries leading nowhere.

> *To the distant stars I climbed*
> *Thinking in those jewels white*
> *Some small vestige of your footprints I would find.*
> *But I found no stars or light,*
> *While walking toward the Sun, from the Moon at night.*

It is in this sense that one best understands Death as the *end* and as the *beginning*: the end of a bad dream or a night of anguish and the beginning of the Joyous Day of Eternal Life.

---

[15] Sg 3:1.

On the other hand, life considered as a search for the Bridegroom, Who seems to be lost or hidden, is a topic in the poetry of Saint John of the Cross:

> *Where hast Thou hidden Thyself,*
> *And abandoned me in my groaning, O my Beloved?*
> *Thou hast fled like the hart,*
> *Having wounded me.*
> *I ran after Thee, crying; but Thou wert gone.*[16]

Hence the soul begins a search during the sleep of Night:

> *On a dark Night,*
> *Kindled in love with yearnings,*
> *Oh, happy chance!*
> *I went forth without being observed,*
> *My house being now at rest.*[17]

The real suffering for a Christian is brought about by the virtue of hope: a suffering of the soul caused by the absence of Jesus Christ, the beloved Person or the Bridegroom of the *Song of Songs*. Hence the passionate pursuit undertaken as a laborious task and which is at the center of both sharp torments and unspeakable joys at the same time: one of the many paradoxes of the so-called *mystical life* —actually, true Christian life:

---

[16] Saint John of the Cross, *Spiritual Canticle*.
[17] Saint John of the Cross, *Dark Night*.

> *Shew me, O thou whom my soul loveth,*
> *Where thou feedest*
> *Where thou liest in the midday,*
> *Lest I begin to wander*
> *After the flocks of thy companions.*[18]

Despite men having decided to do without God and banishing the notion of a paradise beyond this earth to build on their own a purely earthly one after the Tower of Babel, the world is still a *Valley of Tears* with the peculiar characteristic that every time one cries with more intensity. Wars, calamities, epidemics, all kinds of crimes, vices, and aberrations of the worst kind have become commonplace among men. And to top it all, death in the end, for which men without God have not yet found any explanation.

Christians, for their part, who are not of the world but are in the world and participate in all its ups and downs, necessarily have to be affected by the miseries that are part of their milieu. However, once they have made real in their lives the saying of Saint Paul impelling them to *mind the things that are above, not the things upon the earth,*[19] and continuously remember his warning that *It remaineth that they who use this world be as if they used it not; for the fashion of the world passeth away,*[20] those Christians look toward Heaven and to the true realities.

Some attitudes of the human soul are better understood when men ignore them or cast them away from their lives. Nowhere can modern man's feelings of hopelessness and utter lack of horizons and total emptiness be appreciated more than in Samuel Beckett's play *Waiting for Godot*.

---

[18] Sg 1:7.
[19] Col 3:2.
[20] 1 Cor 7:31.

Beckett's tragicomedy (cataloged as belonging to the theater of the absurd) opens at the beginning of the fifties of the last century. In the plot two characters, Vladimir and Estragon, wait endlessly and in vain for the arrival of someone named Godot whom they never get to know and who never arrives. Beckett always insisted that Godot was not meant for God, but most critics and popular consensus identified the play as a burlesque caricature of the Christian virtue of hope: to live expecting a Second Coming of a God, final Savior of the World, Who will actually never arrive. In the second and final act of the play there appears a messenger to inform Vladimir and Estragon that Godot will not come today but that he will surely *come tomorrow*. The play ends, as was predictable, with a nihilist finale and a conclusive deduction: nobody will come and we must wait for nobody.

Paganism, which has decided at its own risk that God does not exist and that Christian hope is folly, does not find any end or final destination for man other than despair determined by nothingness and the grave (in the words of the existentialist Sartre). But if that is so, one should always ask: then what is the meaning of life, if there is any? Was it worthwhile undertaking so much effort to eradicate the idea of God from the human heart since, after all, nothing makes any sense?

On the contrary, one must admit that Christians, even if it were true that, according to pagans, they live in error, at least have found meaning for their lives. The virtues of Faith and Hope have assured them that they are right; a certainty which is powerful enough to secure Joy already in this life for them:

> *And the spirit and the bride say: Come.*
> *And he that heareth, let him say: Come...*
> *He that giveth testimony of these things, saith,*
> *Surely I come quickly.*[21]

Two different attitudes concerning Death: the attitude of Jesus Christ and the attitude of man

Unless man is imbued with the spirit of Jesus Christ he cannot help adopting a fatalistic attitude toward Death. Death is for him the inevitable end, the sum of all misfortunes, and the greatest of all calamities. Most of the time man does not know how to react to it except with sorrow and tears, often bordering on despair.

Hardly anyone realizes that death, although at first a punishment for sin, was finally overcome and its status was changed from punishment to glory. Despite this, *pagans still consider death a punishment*, but now as a dual concept: death is not only a punishment, but also a chastisement which refuses to be redeemed or give up its status as the proper object of a curse.

Consequently, while Death before Christ indeed called for sorrow and tears, now, once man has rejected the salvation He came to bring us, Death has acquired and added the element of despair for those who suffer it, whether directly or indirectly.

Man indeed is bent on living in the absurd for, as we have already said, he does not want to hear that Death has been definitively overcome:

—*O death, where is thy victory? O death, where is thy sting?*[22]

When Jesus Christ was on His way to the home of His deceased friend Lazarus, Martha, the sister of Lazarus, came out bathed in

---

[21] Rev 22: 17–20.
[22] 1 Cor 15:55.

tears to meet Him; Martha did not realize that Death, already potentially subjected, was about to be finally defeated. Hence Jesus' admonition to her:

—*Thy brother shall rise again.*

To which she said:

—*I know that he shall rise again, in the resurrection at the last day.*

But Jesus Christ leads her to the way of truth and makes this great revelation to her:

—*Martha, I am the resurrection and the life. Believest thou this?*

As it happens to men who do not want to accept Jesus Christ, death is just the conclusion and the end of everything. But Jesus is the only man in the history of mankind Who has been able to come face to face with death and destroy it.

Therefore, confronting Death, which for men is the end, the conclusion of everything, the grave, corruption, and nothingness, the great and solemn affirmation stands before which Death itself falls back and kneels totally confused:

—*I am the resurrection and the life.*

What happened here was not a change of accidents, of *different* situations, but a substantial transformation of one condition into its *opposite* one. Punishment has become the prize, sorrow is transformed into joy, defeat has been replaced by victory, and Death has been definitively overcome by Life.

Therefore, there is no death for Christians, for they share completely the life and destiny of Jesus Christ; for them there is no boundary line between death and Life. An imperfect and ephemeral life, punctuated by sorrow and losses, is succeeded by Perfect Life which is Eternal Life. Thus Death is but a necessary stage—painful, but just a stage—from one life to the other.[23] No Christian can attribute to himself death in the sense man understands it. Since death does not belong to the Christian, and therefore is not his, in what sense can it be said that a Christian actually dies when his Death comes? As the Apostle says: *if we be dead with Christ, we believe that we shall live also together with Christ;*[24] and he adds a little later in the same *Letter to the Romans*:

> *For none of us liveth to himself;*
> *And no man dieth to himself.*
> *For whether we live, we live unto the Lord;*
> *Or whether we die, we die unto the Lord.*
> *Therefore, whether we live, or whether we die,*
> *We are the Lord's.*[25]

.

Moreover, the Christian no longer lives enslaved by the fear of death: *He delivers them who through fear of death were all their lifetime subject to bondage.*[26] All men are gripped by this fear of death which the Christian turns into peaceful confidence accompanied by the certainty that Death clears the way for true Life.

On the other hand, not only is the Christian no longer a slave subjected to the fear of Death, he is now its owner and lord:

---

[23] In this sense, Death could be seen as the epilogue of sorrow. But sorrow caused by death (for those who suffer it as well as for their relatives) is not merely an epilogue, as we will see.

[24] Rom 6:8.

[25] Rom 14: 7–8.

[26] Heb 2:15.

> *For all things are yours,*
> *Whether it be Paul, or Apollo, or Cephas,*
> *Or the world, or life, or death,*
> *Or things present, or things to come;*
> *for all are yours;*
> *And you are Christ's.*[27]

The Beauty of Christian Death

Devout Christians usually commend themselves daily to Saint Joseph with a beautiful and pious ejaculation begging that through his intercession they be granted a good death. It is a beautiful and powerful supplication worthy of being practiced every day by any member of the Church proud of being a Christian.

But when Christians devoutly address themselves to the Patron Saint of the Universal Church with that prayer, quite confident that through his intercession they will obtain a pious death as the culmination of their earthly existence, it is clear that they think of something much loftier than what is meant by the mere significance of the expression *good death*.

The reason for this is that the content of the short, fervent prayer does not express sufficiently what Christian death means. Far beyond the limits encompassed by the phrase *good death*, Christian death is the beautiful culmination of an existence lived in love which now emerges as the beauty of the greatest act of love given to man to accomplish during his earthly pilgrimage. Thus the beauty of Christian death springs from its being the loftiest act of love; and love is the most sublime and ineffable reality there is in Heaven and on Earth.

---

[27] 1 Cor 3: 21–23.

Of course, one first question comes quickly to the mind of any average person which must be met: *Why is Death precisely an act of love?*

And the answer comes swiftly and decisively: because Death is the greatest and best demonstration of love that anyone can give, as Jesus Christ Himself expressly said: *Greater love than this no man hath, that a man lay down his life for his friends.*[28]

But Death is a *demonstration* of love only because it is itself an *act of love*, even the greatest of all possible acts of love, as has already been said.

But a second question no less important than the first necessarily follows: How come is the Christian death an act of love and even the greatest of all possible acts of love?

The answer is easy for those who know the fabric of Christian existence. However, the most fundamental truths of Christian life have been neglected far too long by the very ones who have been baptized, although they still believe that the teachings of Jesus Christ are part and parcel of their lives. Therefore, Death for them continues to be marked by a fatalistic element, and they expect nothing from it, even in the best case, but a pious end accompanied by the hope of salvation.

But the death of a Christian is an act of love; the most beautiful and perfect of all possible acts of love, precisely because it is a *participation in the death of Jesus Christ Himself*. Christians have too often forgotten or ignored the fact that they have been created and baptized *in order to accomplish that supreme act that is the culmination of their earthly existence*, as expressly stated by Saint

---

[28] Jn 15:13.

Paul: *Know ye not that so many of us as were baptized into Jesus Christ were baptized into his death?*[29]

The greatest expectation of him who is ardently in love is to participate in the life of the beloved, according to a genuine exchange of the two lives that become one with the same destiny. True love leads to a mutual and *total* self–giving of the lovers, including their lives and their deaths, which is another forgotten reality in the current times of apostasy and paganism which have lost any notion of true love. And yet this reality is but an essential feature in the structure of the relationship of divine–human love as it is configured throughout both the Old and the New Testaments:

> *My beloved is mine, and I am his:*
> *He feedeth among the lilies.*
>
> ....
>
> *I am my beloved's*
> *And his desire is for me.*[30]

The poetic and still–veiled language of the *Song of Songs* is outweighed by the realistic, clearly supernatural and transcendent language of the New Testament. *He that eateth my flesh, and drinketh my blood, abideth in me, and I in him.*[31] If the lovers are together in life —forming one life— they are also joined in Death. Therefore the Christian's identification with Christ is not fulfilled until his death: if the life of one has also been the life of the other, the same with Death; the death of the disciple is identical to his Master's, and hence the importance of one's *participation* in the Mass.

---

[29] Rom 6:3.
[30] Sg 2:16; 7:11.
[31] Jn 6:56.

The significance of this *participation* is based on the fact that the Mass is the true Sacrifice of Jesus Christ —not symbolic but made true here and now at the altar, although it is not a repetition over time; therefore, the Christian *also truly partakes in that Sacrifice* with a participation described by Saint Paul as an *announcement* of the Death of the Lord: *For as often as you shall eat this bread, and drink the chalice, you shall proclaim the death of the Lord, until he come.*[32] The Apostle speaks, therefore, of a living testimony of the Lord's Death now come true in the life of the Christian as the foretaste of what is to be his final death. And as the earnest or first fruits already contain a *real* taste of what will be the final fruit, so does the announcement of the Death of his Lord that every Christian accomplishes at Mass and which he then must make true in his ordinary daily life: that announcement is a preview of his death which will finally consummate his total identification with Jesus Christ. Hence the utmost severity of having diluted —if not eliminated altogether— the notion of sacrifice in the *Novus Ordo*.

According to these premises, as the death of the Christian is no longer his own death but *the Death of Christ made his very own*, his life is no longer his own life, as the Apostle said: *Christ died for all; that they also who live, may not now live to themselves, but unto him who died for them, and rose again.*[33] Therefore, the life of the Christian is no longer his own life but that of Christ (which is now properly his, according to Love's law of reciprocity), and his death is no longer his but that of Christ (which is now properly his own, according to the just–mentioned law); where now are the sorrows of life and where the anguish and fear of death? Once the person in love has made his own the whole life and destiny of the beloved while, at

---

[32] 1 Cor 11:26.
[33] 2 Cor 5:15.

the same time, the beloved has made his, in perfect reciprocity, the life and the fate of the lover, what is there that could prevent their full participation in the feeling of Joy? That is why Chesterton said that *joy is the gigantic secret of the Christian*s.

The Christian truly in love with Christ —could there be any Christian who would not feel himself seduced by Him?— not only does not fear death, he even desires it as the last step before meeting his Lord. The life of a Christian, therefore, while going through a *Valley of Tears* and walking on a narrow, rough, and steep path, becomes a journey filled with hope which joyfully looks forward to the end of the road in the certainty that he will find Him Whom he searched for throughout his entire life.

> *At early dawn still rosy*
> *I set out to search, with quick and hurried pace,*
> *The One who enamours me;*
> *And, upon seeing his face,*
> *Freed at last from earthly harms*
> *I wanted to die out of love in his arms.*

The lukewarm Christian has not known true love; hence life has been spent by him *without actually living it*. He has wasted the entire time of its existence seeking happiness without ever finding it; nor has he ever known anything about joy but that which he may have heard about it. At no time has he managed to shake off the yoke of the fear of death; consequently there has been for him nothing but a life of early death. He passed like a gust of wind, in an instant, without a trace, and nobody is going to remember him ever.

The Christian who loves Jesus Christ, by contrast, looks at death with the joy caused by the certainty of the definitive encounter with the One Whom, throughout his life, he has sought and eagerly desired in his heart:

> *If only in my walking through the valley*
> *By the fir tree forest I could meet with you,*
> *And could contemplate you finally anew,*
> *Death from love I would share with you completely...!*

THE GOOD SHEPHERD[1]

(Jn 10: 11–16)

1. Some errors on the division between Shepherds and the Faithful in the Church

Jesus Christ founded His Church by establishing two kinds of believers: Shepherds and simple faithful. Hence Catholic Doctrine has always maintained that the Church, though forming one Body, is divided into two separate classes: the *teaching* Church or the Shepherds, and the *learning* Church, made up of the rest of the faithful.

The mission of the first class, the Shepherds, is *sanctifying*, *teaching*, and *governing* the rest of the faithful. It falls upon the second class to listen to the sound doctrine uttered by their Shepherds, receiving from them the means to attain holiness and obeying their commands.

This constitution of the Church was *divinely established* and therefore cannot be changed, not even by the Church herself, which is a truth of faith the Church has always maintained and which is not subject to discussion. At least this is how it should be; the fact of the matter is that this has not been always the case, especially in recent times.

Although man is a being with a rational nature, it would be false to assume that he always acts *rationally*. Truly speaking, we

---

[1] Preached on April 9, 2015.

must recognize that most of the time man is far from behaving in a manner in keeping with his nature.

It does seem hard to believe, but one must recognize that *fidelity* to Christ is a matter of exception in the Church, on the part of both the Shepherds and the faithful. The most obvious consequence of this is the emergence of Shepherds who have never managed to become Shepherds —a group of people made up of the most diverse set of species, as we shall see. There has also emerged a large number of sheep who believe they are Shepherds because they have not come to understand the charism of the laity and their role in the Church. All this mess is but the result of a variety of confused ideas largely introduced by the Modernist theology of the New Church.

But, before we continue with this issue, we must make a reference to the reasons that have helped make possible the emergence of a phenomenon that has transformed the life of the Church and has turned all her structures upside down. Major changes of ideas in a society do not arise suddenly nor are they improvised; they usually come into being at the convergence of very complex antecedents and causes.

In our particular case, the nearest antecedent is the number of new ideas brought about by the Second Vatican Council. A Council which was manipulated by progressive groups imbued with the heresy of Modernism and which determined the procedures and lines of action to be followed. Modernism's main weapon, which is the most important element of this heresy, is resorting to *confusion*, mainly by using intelligently manipulated language as a means of introducing those ideas it wants to disseminate.

The fact that more than two thousand Bishops of the Church, from all over the world, agreed to sign and proclaim a number of ideas and doctrines often *contrary to the tradition of the Church*

—an unprecedented event, after all, in the life of the Church and in the history of Councils— is a mystery that cannot be explained by referring to historical or sociological reasons which will always be insufficient, despite all one may say. More than fifty years have passed since the closing of this Council; it does not seem very probable that someone will dare to raise this issue now.

Actually, people are not accustomed to accepting facts which, due to their particular characteristics, are difficult and unpleasant to explain; hence they have always been reluctant to delve into the real reasons for certain serious events in history and discover the causes that gave rise to them; perhaps because, when the ultimate reasons for those events are known, men feel horrified at the prospect of admitting that they were the culprits.

The Modernist spirit of some Documents of the Council, along with their deliberately ambiguous language used to give way to doctrines foreign to Revelation and the bimillennial Tradition of the Church, unleashed a *devastating wave of confusion* that affected both Shepherds and the Faithful. The immediate consequence took the shape of an apostasy that led to the desertion of nearly most of the Shepherds and of innumerable thousands upon thousands of faithful; all of whom, in a more or less conscious but always guilty manner, became part of the *New Church*.

This desertion, which can properly be termed as apostasy, has manifested itself, it could not be otherwise, in many and varied ways. Most particularly, the issue of the distinction between Shepherds and the simple faithful has produced extremely peculiar and even curious external manifestations which nobody has dared to recognize. Entirely hybrid and even ridiculous characters have emerged: Shepherds determined to not distinguish themselves from the world or the *secularized cleric* and its opposite, the *clericalized layperson*, are ultimately the result of a shameful though unacknowledged *inferiority complex*, the offspring, in turn, of fear.

When Pope John XXIII solemnly pronounced, at the opening address of Vatican II, the slogan proclaiming that the Church *was finally opened to the world*, he unwittingly gave free entry to a legion of demons that had thus far been waiting impatiently at the doors of an until-then impregnable Enclosure.

Any course of action undertaken in detriment to the nature of things always ends in a disaster whose damages and consequences are difficult to gauge at the moment and impossible to foresee as a more or less near future.

Modernism, which never believed in miracles, got one too important: *that the Church stopped hearing the voice of God*, expressed in Scripture and Tradition, *to listen instead to the voice of the world.*

The Church cannot be opened to the world in any way because it would undermine her nature as created and instituted by Jesus Christ. Unfortunately, however, by the time the Council took place many years of Protestant rationalistic biblical criticism had already made a dent in Catholic theology, which went so far as to barely believe any longer in Revelation. This is why the Council ignored the doctrine concerning this issue contained all too clearly in Revelation: *Adulterers, know you not that the friendship of this world is the enemy of God? Whosoever therefore will be a friend of this world, becometh an enemy of God.*[2] And Jesus Christ Himself, speaking to His disciples in His Priestly Prayer to His Father, stated: *I have given them thy word, and the world hath hated them, because they are not of the world; as I also am not of the world. I pray not that thou shouldst take them out of the world, but that thou shouldst keep them from evil. They are not of the world, as I also am not of the*

---

[2] Jas 4:4.

world.[3] The same apostle John went deeper into this issue, urging in his *First Letter*: *Love not the world, nor the things which are in the world. If any man love the world, the charity of the Father is not in him.*[4]

2. Clergy "adrift"

As sin brought death into the world, the inaugural speech of John XXIII introduced confusion in the Church at all levels.

Bishops, who after the Council were elected among men of weak character and devotees of the new regime, felt compelled to approach the faithful with flaunting gestures of apparent humility which in reality made apparent their lack of intelligence. It is difficult to explain why it became customary for the Bishop who took possession of a Diocese to greet the faithful with the announcement that he had come to them with the intention of *learning*; for he is a successor of the Apostles, Teacher and Father in the Faith, entrusted with the delicate task of guiding the sheep. Anyone can imagine what would happen in a school where the teacher would introduce himself to the children saying that he had come there *to learn*. No wonder, therefore, that all Christendom felt confused by the gesture of the new Pope Francis when he appeared on the balcony to greet the crowds and asked them to bless him. He began to upset and empty the meaning of all Christian virtues: the deposition of the duties *inherent to the office of* Pope was now called humility; voluntary and sought exhibition of a demagogic and alleged indigence was called poverty; arbitrary and unjustified provisions to nullify those who had become a nuisance was then named mercy, etc.

---

[3] Jn 17: 14–16.
[4] 1 Jn 2:15.

The mass havoc wreaked among common clergy and the laity was even worse, if possible. Two major lies, gross as well as extravagant, each disseminated among these two different states causing great damage by the modernist *periti* of the Council, well versed in handling instruments of confusion by using all sorts of necessary deceptions (manipulation of the Scripture, ambiguous language, frequently discrediting the value of Tradition and Authority of previous Councils, continuously mocking Thomism, declaring the entire preconciliar Magisterium obsolete, etc.) were enough to disrupt both states within the Church and achieve their virtual destruction.

The fact that important sectors of society, and sometimes even the whole society, accept without any discussion the most absurd lies would be a difficult mystery were the effectiveness of Lenin's slogan not sufficiently attested by experience: *Lie in the widest possible way, since the acceptance of the lie is directly proportional to its size.*

The fallacy introduced into the common clergy would seem too wild and coarse as to be accepted by any being gifted with understanding. But the fact is that *the fallacy was accepted without the slightest consideration by the clergy as a whole*, with the result being the acceptance of the need to eliminate any difference in appearance between the priest and the layman in order to achieve greater pastoral effectiveness. Since the Church had just opened herself completely to the world, it was necessary that the priest did not appear as different from other men, once it was demonstrated that the best approach to them required him to be just one more in the crowd. Or, in other words, *the most effective way of being a priest was none other than the priest not appearing to be or acting like a priest.* After all, it was a way of turning rationality into something absurd, of sending Logic to the trash can.

The consequence of this hallucination is that Christianity was astonished at the appearance of the character of the *layman priest.* The ecclesial and pastoral world was filled with priests wearing open shirts and jeans; clerics in their sixties adopting the clothing style of fifteen–year–old kids; priests, especially young ones, trying to adopt mannerisms thought to facilitate their getting closer to the youth *(call me Peter, not Father Peter!)*; etc. In short, to the immense and incalculable damage done to all the faithful must be added the *ridiculous* situation generally offered by the clergy of the Church to the world: by both the lower clergy and the high clergy.

3. Eucharistic ministers

It would impossible to unravel the entanglement organized in the Church by the Great Deceiver regarding this issue. In effect, Modernism introduced an even greater hoax within Catholicism, which caused more confusion and greater damage than the previous deception. This new and absurd falsehood was spread by the Modernist heresy in ecclesiastical circles with unprecedented success and was totally unopposed; so much so that even today it is impossible to understand how it was accepted so unanimously by the lay establishment.

The Modernist heresy claimed that *the laity had been oppressed for twenty centuries by the clergy*; it was time, therefore, for those so far vexed to rise up and *demand their rights.* According to the modernists, the laity should regain the level of autonomy and freedom it deserves in its own right; this being the only way in which the laity, finally freed from the yoke with which the clergy had subjugated them for so long, could fulfill its charism.

And as it happens with the spirit of innovation that always accompanies any invention, the assertion was so new and so unheard of among the Christian people that its innovative character would have sufficed to disregard it had it not been for the fact that public opinion was already a breeding ground for accepting any sort of lies; which, as we know, the greater the magnitude of the deception the more unanimous and steadfast is the adherence to it, as dictated by the famous and well–known rule of Lenin.

Truth be told, never before, throughout the entire history of the Church, have the faithful held the slightest notion of feeling themselves oppressed by the clergy. Therefore, one cannot say that this modernist approach could be accepted as the coming–forth of repressed and never expressed sentiments; rather it was something as new and surprising as the discovery of the law of gravity or the invention of the printing press. Despite this, the lie was accepted unanimously by the faithful *as if it had always been latent in the minds of all.*

Thus two realities become evident which, like many others, often go unnoticed. The first refers to the pitiful state to which human nature, despite its restoration by Redemption, has been reduced after the fall: a nature always willing to accept anything, no matter how false and harmful it may be, insofar as it satisfies the desires of human nature's lower appetites. The second reality is another example of the progressive state of degradation affecting the Christian world before the Second Vatican Council and which would definitively emerge in its aftermath, leading eventually to the present situation of *general apostasy* that had already been looming over the Church.

The doctrine of Revelation, along with the constant teaching of the Fathers and the Magisterium throughout the entire history of the Church, has been unanimous in affirming just the opposite to what the modernist deception propagated. The New Testament points out that the priest is *ordained for men in things pertaining to God, that he may offer both gifts and sacrifices for sins.*[5] He is, therefore, *ordained for men* and to offer sacrifices for sins, not only for the sins of the Christian people but also for his own as one among his brothers, *because he himself also is compassed with infirmity.*[6] Moreover, Jesus Christ had already well established that the true shepherd is he who *gives his life for his sheep.*[7] These doctrines in no way seem compatible with the accusation of *oppressor* as leveled by Modernism against the priest.

Nevertheless, once again the Great Embroiler achieved his purposes. The sheep rushed like crazy to become shepherds, forgetting that the status of sheep within the Church does not imply any humiliation since the Shepherds are also sheep in the one Flock of Christ, the only *Supreme Shepherd*[8] of all the sheep.

Thus the Father of all Lies succeeded in making many laymen absurdly believe, as many priests before them believed, that the best way of *fully growing as a lay person was to become a priest*; or, at least, half–priest or almost–a–priest, another hybrid and a worse product.

From this moment on there appeared an innumerable crowd of ministers, Eucharistic ministers, ministers of other pastoral activities, pastoral agents, preachers, lay teachers, avant–garde laity willing to *monitor* any ecclesiastical activity... and a large army of lay people who felt suddenly animated by a spirit of command within the Church. The unfortunate mass of the faithful followers of Jesus Christ were compelled to suffer, perhaps more or less unconsciously,

---

[5] Heb 5:1.
[6] Heb 5:2.
[7] Jn 10:11.
[8] 1 Pet 5:4.

the *evangelizing* outrages carried out by an army of troopers who had suddenly turned into officers. Euphoria spread and diocesan bookstores were filled with volumes about this topic, *The Hour of the Laity, The Laity on Its Way*, and the like; most of the books were written by Jesuits and were as filled with theology as a jar on its way to the fountain can be full of water; as if the laity had never been seen nor had its hour, nor had it ever amounted to anything since the beginning of Christianity, or had it perhaps remained in a state of drowsiness while the clergy continued arranging everything at will and steamrolling the unfortunate clerical establishment.

As said Segismundo referring to kings in Calderón's *Life is a Dream*, using an expression that in this case, extrapolated from the sacramental act, may refer to an imaginary situation of *oppression* on the part of the clergy which, according to the modernist of the New Church, had to be completely uprooted:

> *With this deceit commanding,*
> *Disposing, and governing.*

The first, but not the least serious, devastating effect of all this mischievous lie involved the *loss of identity* on the part of the laity and the neglect of the significance of their own charism, with the resultant abandonment of the important functions of their own state and vocation to which they had been called.

Lay Christians, as baptized members of the Church, share in the priesthood of Jesus Christ —the common priesthood of the Faithful— in the first place. Moreover, by the sacrament of confirmation they have been constituted as soldiers of the Militia of Jesus Christ —*milites Christi*— with the unique and essential task of bearing witness to Him in the midst of the world *sanctifying its structures* in their secular condition. Whereby theirs are the tasks that have to do with the functioning of Society: government and international relationships, law enforcement, administration of justice, education, health, charity, retirement, trade, finance, industry, scientific research, cultural world, entertainment, etc. All these are occupations that belong exclusively to the laity and in no way correspond to the clergy.

And yet, the most important role assigned by God to lay people is that which corresponds to the creation and functioning of the family which is the basic cell of the organization and maintenance of society. It is within the family that the most important task entrusted by God to the laity, as its specific mission, has to be accomplished: *the formation and education of children as men and as Christians*; a function that is primarily the responsibility of the parents and not of the priests, who, in this particular matter, have a secondary role.

We must emphasize here that in this particular area the Great Deceiver caused devastating damage. With the occasion of the new winds blowing within the Church, many lay people felt encouraged to become semi-clergy, willing to perform functions of worship and evangelizing; the outcome being a harrowing effect which has surely led souls to perdition, their number known to God alone.

Eucharistic ministers in particular are the ones who, most probably unintentionally, have caused a serious damage to the Faith of the Faithful, though this affirmation may shock the ears of many who are not willing to calmly examine the facts.

Because the shortage of priest was a real problem, the opinion of many priests, overwhelmed when it came to distributing Communion, seemed reasonable. They reached the conclusion that *Eucharistic ministers* had to be established; which was accomplished by appointing to this ministry many thousands of individuals of all classes and conditions; in a restricted way at first, but with flood gates wide open afterwards. In the beginning, the lists of candidates were strictly made up by selecting people eligible to receive this ministry. But it was not long before the number of persons considered suitable to distribute this Sacrament increased and became too numerous, to the point that it was much easier *to make a list of the people not authorized to receive this ministry*. Thus the show was served: women wearing no stockings or in socks, young women with short skirts, people without faith or questionable conduct distributed the Eucharist, while priests remained seated in their chairs. Consequently and with the occasion of these abuses, in many places, especially at important International Eucharistic Congresses, numerous sacrileges took place.

Before listing the real causes of the occurrence of this phenomenon in the Church, it should be noted that in this case the problem was overestimated. Acknowledging the indisputable reality of the enormous shortage of priests, it is also reasonable to remember that fatigue and exhaustion are conditions ascribed to the ministry of the priesthood, whose hands are the only ones consecrated to touch and distribute the Eucharist: *Unless a grain of wheat falling into the ground die, it abideth alone; but if it die, it bringeth forth much fruit.*[9] Exhaustion has always been the instrument with which true priests accomplished the work of evangelization in the Church. In the same vein, long ago, the famous Carthaginian general, Hamilcar Barca, said that *battles are won only by tired soldiers.*

As for the causes mentioned to justify the existence of *Eucharistic ministers*, the first thing that hits one's eye is the usual attitude, already widespread in the Church, of excising the source of problems or, in any case, of attributing the existence of those problems to reasons that have nothing to do with reality. Regarding the spe-

---

[9] Jn 12: 24–25.

cific issue under discussion, several and very serious were the reasons that gave rise to it.

The identity crisis of the priesthood: an idea born from the interpretations following the so–called *spirit of the Council* and promoted by all subsequent modernist theology. General freedom granted by Paul VI for priests to be secularized played no small part in this crisis. This pope soon repented upon seeing the ensuing general defection. Both reasons fed each other.

The loss of prestige and authority of the hierarchy, together with the idea of the *democratization of the Church*, also introduced by the Council, contributed greatly to diminishing the importance of the role of the priest among the faithful.

The lack of care and attention to clergy in general by the Hierarchy of the Church. In fact, attention and vigilance was abandoned in Seminaries, Theological Faculties, and Training Centers, completely neglecting the education imparted in them. In addition to this, for many years and with total impunity they allowed the infiltration, especially in Seminaries, of Marxist doctrines, theories in favor of homosexuality, and even practicing homosexuals. This grave problem reached its most serious point when the unfortunate and sad phenomenon of pederasty became public; which was used by the ecclesiastical authority to attack the lower clergy by attributing to them the whole burden of guilt.

And to bring this topic to a close, it only remains to mention the main and most serious effect of the appearance in the Church of the *Eucharistic ministers.* In the first place, they have contributed, as one of the main causes, to the present lack of respect for the Eucharist displayed by the vast majority of the faithful; but, above all and foremost, to *the loss of faith in the Real Presence of Jesus*

Christ in the Eucharist suffered by nearly the entirety of Christian People.

Indeed, sometimes, though not too many, men react, willy–nilly, in accordance with the requirements imposed by logic to rational nature. If the Church allows, and even encourages, that the Eucharist be treated thus: by anyone and in any way; if consecrated hands are no longer needed; if the slightest sign of respect or trace of faith has disappeared from those who administer the Eucharist; if even sometimes the faithful are invited to serve themselves the Eucharist as if they were in a self–service restaurant...; how can anybody seriously hope, after all this, that there could be someone who believes in the Real Presence of Christ in the Eucharist?

4. The Ministry of Lay Readers
and other ministries in the Liturgy

The damage caused to the Church by the so-called *promotion of the laity* is incalculable and known to God alone. It seems it was taken for granted that Jesus Christ, Founder of the Church, had not *promoted* the status of the laity enough and, consequently, the faithful had remained in a state of pitiful prostration for twenty centuries.

Indeed, human nature has a virtually unlimited capacity to embrace any humbug, no matter how crazy it actually is.

These mischievous lies we have been talking about, caused in the Church by the Father of Lies, led to massive confusion within the two estates that make up the ecclesial Body: the clergy and the laity. Priests thought that they would be more priestly if they looked less like priests and more like lay people; lay people, in turn, thought that the more they became a type of half–priests the better lay people they could be. Consequently, *both forgot their own charisma and failed to fulfill their specific obligations*. Mentalities change with time when men lose the Faith; thus they forgot that wine is not so good when mixed with water (no one has ever thought that watered wine is true wine).

Another serious devastation brought about by these mischievous lies was that the faithful were misled as to the meaning of *participation in the Mass*. It was a veritable disaster, for the majority of lay people thought —as they were told— that their participation in the Mass was to take part in external, absolutely secondary or circumstantial activities (as distributors of the Eucharist, readers during varied liturgical functions, ministers of hospitality, etc.) that had almost nothing to do with the profound mystery of the Holy Sacrifice.

Once the *sacrificial meaning* of the Mass was lost with the introduction of the *Novus Ordo*, when the Holy Sacrifice ceased to be the re-production, here and now, of the Death of Jesus Christ in order to become a *fellowship meal*, the faithful ceased to realize that the Death of Christ is *made actually present*, although without the shedding of blood, in the Holy Mass. Consequently, they also rejected the realization that to participate in the *Holy Sacrifice* is to become intimately united to the Death of their Lord and to make it their own, such as they had previously made the Life of their Master their own (Col 3:4). This participation will continue being real for them, the necessary graces being granted, throughout their daily life which becomes, ultimately, an extension of the Holy Mass.

Although this statement may prove especially painful, it must be said that the institution of the ministry of *lay readers* at liturgical functions (especially the Holy Mass) was another element that contributed to turning the Holy Sacrifice into a modest *show*.

Some lay people of restless spirit, fond of shocking novelties and eager to be promoted, saw themselves finally elevated and their *status recognized* by participating in the readings of the Mass. It was actually only a minority of people, since the vast generality of the laity kept enough common sense as to be satisfied with a situation which they considered honorable and with its own charism, without resorting to becoming a hybrid product which would only distract them from their natural duty to *sanctify temporal activities*; a duty that is their own and which only they can carry out, and which already provides them with more than enough importance and worries.

As for their participation as actors in what is not purely *sacred* but which is an additional and also ornamental part of the liturgical function, they do cooperate with special dignity when they serve as acolytes to the minister of the Holy Sacrifice or when they sing as members of the choir in solemn functions, etc; without forgetting that the real way to *participate* in the Mass is by being united mystically to the Sacrifice or bloodless Death of Christ that takes place on the altar.

I have personally known *lay readers* who would anxiously await the solemn moment of stepping up to the presbytery to read the appropriate readings of the Mass. I was somehow perplexed at the air of gravity and self-importance with which they read, with pompous voice and the conviction that they were carrying out the essential and most important moment of the Mass. I could see all too often, with no little sadness on my part, that they cared little about anything else of the Mass; they even seemed to believe they were the chief minister of the Holy Sacrifice.

To a certain extent, at least, they may be justified in feeling themselves important, but only when the mentioned *lay ministers* are women, mostly young and pretty. We must recognize that in this case the faithful attending the liturgical function in question tend to be more attentive to the person reading than to the contents of what she reads.

The outcome of all this, once again, is always the same: there is a certain *desacralization* of the liturgical function, as it loses much of its deserved solemn seriousness which contributes to raising the soul to supernatural realities; supernatural realities which suffer some deterioration when mixed, for no reason at all and without any justification, with natural realities; the same happens with good wine when mixed with water.

5. The problem of the new "permanent diaconate"

One of the main weapons used by the modernist heresy to destroy the Church is the indiscriminate spreading of confusion by successfully resorting to all kinds of figures of speech suitable for this purpose, such as ambiguity, amphibology, and double–meaning in everything that concerns the doctrine and worship of the Church, as well as her very institutions. This heresy uses the same words and terms understood by Christians since ancient times, but changes them, emptying them of their traditional meaning and filling them with a disparate and purely human content.

This is the case of the new institution of the *permanent diaconate*.

This institution has given rise to no small number of problems which usually no one addresses. Likewise, nobody mentions the possible intentions of those who pushed for the creation of this new institution; intentions which, if any, apparently had to do with eliminating priestly celibacy. We will deal at length with this issue later.

We have said *new institution* because, although it is true that there have always been permanent deacons in the Church, and more frequently in the primitive community, the permanent diaconate had a *different content and meaning* from its modern counterpart. The former were considered consecrated clergy with the intent of living a life of permanent celibacy that had little to do with the life of a layman. The modern permanent diaconate, on the contrary, mostly made up of married men who continue to fulfill their professional and family duties, does not exclude the possibility of reaching the priesthood while maintaining its marital status. This has turned the modern permanent diaconate into a new institution, different from the one the Church has traditionally admitted. Moreover, this possibility of having easy access to the priesthood, without abandoning a marital relationship, is an important detail that must be taken into account.

This is not the place for telling the story of the duties of permanent deacons in the early Church. Suffice it to say, in summary, that they mainly involved social, charitable, and administrative responsibilities, as shown by the words of Saint Peter at the institution of the first deacons: *It is not reason that we should leave the word of God, and serve tables. Wherefore, brethren, look ye out among you seven men of good reputation, full of the Holy Ghost and wisdom, whom we may appoint over this business. But we will give ourselves continually to prayer, and to the ministry of the word.*[10] Saint Lawrence, for example, a deacon of the Church of Rome (martyred in 258), was charged with the responsibility for the material goods of the Church and the distribution of alms to the poor.

The extraordinary shortage of priests was the main reason given for the institution of the new permanent diaconate. There are, in-

---

[10] Acts 6: 2–4.

deed, vast regions (as in Brazil) that hardly ever see a priest. In many other parts of the world there are but a few priests overwhelmed by the demands of their ministry. Nobody can deny that this is an evident problem that seriously affects the whole Church.

We leave aside the serious issue that the true causes leading to this problem were never addressed and that the remedies which would have solved or at least mitigated it were never applied. The study of such a delicate matter would occupy too much time and space and does not belong to this essay.

Be that as it may, in the face of this urgent and serious need, numerous men, usually obligated to marital and family duties as well as to professional responsibilities, responded to the call of the Church and were generously willing to receive the diaconate. They were men of good will with the loftiest intentions, for the most part. Generally speaking, they have fulfilled their task with dignity and sometimes even with commendable zeal, somehow solving distressing situations.

But it is often the case that institutions that emerge in the Church by disciplinary provisions soon present difficulties that must be considered. Good things are not always free from drawbacks. First of all, it should be noted that it is not easy to define the theological or legal *entity* of these new deacons, given the peculiar nature of the permanent diaconate. On the one hand, they are clerics because they have received the sacrament of Holy Orders (in its lowest degree) and are obligated to pray the Divine Office. On the other hand, for all intents and purposes they live as laymen, performing their family and professional duties; so much so that the average faithful would hardly classify them among the clergy. This seemingly unimportant element has inevitably contributed to diluting in the mind of the faithful the nature of the priesthood and the role of the priest.

Another drawback that has emerged in some places as a consequence of the lack, or shortage, of priests is that the celebration of the Holy Mass has become difficult or impossible; hence the introduction of the *Liturgy of the Word*. Permanent deacons wearing sacred ornaments celebrate a liturgy where they read the readings of the Mass, hold some ceremonies unrelated to the essence of the Holy Sacrifice, and preach the Word. This *Liturgy* thus become a kind of *ersatz* or substitute for the Holy Mass, a pious consolation for the faithful who have nothing better available to them.

Unfortunately, remedies are not always practical and may even cause problems. In fact the average faithful, usually lacking religious education, grow accustomed to the *Liturgy of the Word*, confusing it with the Mass; it is not uncommon to hear ordinary people say that they have attended a *Mass without consecration*. Consequently, the belief that one needs to attend the Holy Sacrifice and take advantage of the treasures it contains disappears; the credence that the Holy Mass is irreplaceable as the center of Christian Worship is thus diluted. Yet removing the Mass, regardless of the reasons or motives for it, given the transcendental importance of the Mass and that it cannot be replaced by anything, necessarily implies the *disappearance of Catholicism* where this substitution has taken place.

There also are other more serious problems; for example, the abuse of the right of permanent deacons to *preach*, which precludes a clear intention to reduce the importance of the ministry and the representative figure of the priest.

This has been made possible because of a twisted interpretation of the Rite of Ordination of Deacons which says that *preaching is the office of the deacon*. The meaning of these words has been manipulated into meaning something like this: *preaching is an office which belongs exclusively to the deacon*; a gross falsehood which intentionally forgets that the three orders of the sacrament of Holy Orders (diaconate, presbyterate, and episcopate, from lowest to highest degrees) are *inclusive* and not at all *exclusive*. This means that the priest, in addition to his own powers, does not lose those he received as deacon. Likewise, the Bishop does not lose the powers he acquired in the diaconate and the priesthood when he acquires his own at his consecration.

As a consequence, many priests have been forced to remain seated during religious ceremonies while the deacon preaches, often believing that he has more right to that function than the presbyter who is celebrating the Mass. All this has resulted in yet another way to depreciate the nature and the role of the ministerial priesthood.[11]

To this we must add another no less serious circumstance: the office of preaching has been entrusted to men seasoned in the secular life, whose kindness and good faith cannot be questioned in most cases, but who are lacking in the training required for such a delicate task; which has led to the discrediting of the sacred function of transmitting the Word of God to the Christian people. On the other hand, arguing —reasonably— that the preaching of priests has declined a great deal is not a serious objection. In effect, it is regrettable that an institution may not work because of *external* or *circumstantial* impeding obstacles; but this is different than an institution not fulfilling its duty because of its very *nature*. The fact that the modern priesthood is in a state of lamentable decline and gradual degradation is not due to the nature of the ministry (there are causes that explain this phenomenon, as the influence of the

---

[11] The Traditional Solemn Masses were celebrated by the Bishop who usually sat down on the throne while another minister preached in his name; which was always preceded by a brief ceremony before the bishop in which he deputized the preacher to preach the Word *by the Bishop's mandate*; hierarchical order of the functions proper to one's office have always been kept and respected in the Church.

modernist heresy and surrender to the world it has motivated). But the permanent deacon, *even if his proper office is preaching*, always lacks the necessary preparation for sacred preaching; which is a function that cannot be acquired in a cursory program —which is about the highest formation received by permanent deacons; it requires years of study, in addition to an intense practice and experience in interior life and prayer, for *it is impossible to speak to men about God if one has not leaned first to speak to God about men.*

In addition to what has been said, we must point out that the true reasons that led to the institution of the permanent diaconate are the most serious problem posed by this institution in its present form; a problem about which nobody usually speaks and which is jealously hidden. There is enough evidence to suspect that those reasons have to do with the *elimination of priestly celibacy* from the Priesthood of the Catholic Church. Yet celibacy is a veritable supernatural treasure that for centuries adorned the sacred ministry and were a constant source of sanctification for both those priests who lived it and the souls assigned to them.

Naturally, this statement cannot be proven with documentary evidence. But there are sufficiently reasonable arguments for anyone thinking dispassionately which lead to this conclusion.

First, because everybody knows about the fierce campaign waged against clerical celibacy from the time the modernist wave broke into the Church. If one wants to be more specific about dates, once again the early sixties of the last century must be mentioned, when the opening of the Second Vatican Council and the rise of progressive doctrines took place.

The arguments then offered by the liberals against celibacy were numerous and are still used today to disorient the faithful who have been the victims of a long period of *indoctrination* that has lasted over fifty years. The shortage of priests and the alleged need for the priest to *empathize* better with the secular world and not look like a strange entity *separated* from the world are the main *reasons* given for spreading the idea of the need to abolish the obligation of celibacy; actually, they are merely a pretext.

But it is clear that long and persistent campaigns to spread an idea, indiscriminately using all available means and without opposition, within the scope of any human society always indicate clearly defined and never overtly confessed purposes.

True, Pope John Paul II insisted strongly on the need of ecclesiastical celibacy in his *Letter to all the Priests on the Occasion of Holy Thursday 1979*. The emphasis with which the Pope expressed himself on this subject in the most important part of the Document thrilled traditionalist groups who went so far as to claim that the Pontiff had spoken *ex cathedra*. But because of the ensuing uproar, the Pope himself quickly denied that claim, stating that he did not have any intention of speaking with infallibility.

One of the most important and effective maneuvers carried out in the post–conciliar Church, with the clear intention of promoting the advantages of abolishing clerical celibacy was *the indiscriminate mass admission of groups of converts from Anglicanism*, shepherds (married, of course) as well as simple faithful. The conditions for their admission within Catholicism, allowing them to keep their personal rites and customs, were sufficiently lax as to doubt whether there ever was in fact a true *conversion*. Given that the Anglican clergy is not true clergy because it had lost the apostolic succession, as Pope Leo XIII declared in his Bull *Apostolicæ Curæ* (1896), they quickly proceeded to ordain the corresponding converted Anglican Pastors and Bishops to the priesthood.

It is difficult to find reasons for such haste in ordaining to the priesthood ministers who obviously lacked sufficient training in Catholic Doctrine. The explanations provided concerning ecumenism, pastoral approach, understanding, etc., clearly lacked any seriousness for taking into account the importance of a situation that so seriously compromised the salvation of the souls of both the Anglicans and those faithful Catholics induced to confusion. The married status of these pastors, now priests, also helped to effectively disseminate and legitimize within the Christian people the existence of sacred ministers living a marital status. One could ask whether there was any deeper reason which justified the strange acceleration of these processes.

Naturally, in a matter of such vital importance as the one we are discussing here, everyone is free to hold the view that seems appropriate to him. However, when this issue is framed within the context of the strong campaign organized in support of the abolition of priestly celibacy, it does not seem an unreasonable guess that the intentions clearly point in one direction.

However, the strongest argument in favor of what we are saying is the announcement already made, although not officially, of the topic to be discussed at the Episcopal Synod of the year 2016: namely the *convenience of maintaining in the Church the obligation of priestly celibacy*. And we already know the result of the *deliberations* held in these Synods, as has been demonstrated by the experience of the Synods conducted so far. In effect, whatever the outcome of the discussions, the final decisions always coincide with the purpose for which the Synod was convened; in a nutshell, the end result of a campaign persistently conducted throughout sixty years.

In this issue, as with many others that today's Church is rethinking, several factors concur which ordinarily are not noticed.

First, there is the undeniable fact that Modernism is active in the Church and using two important tools: one of them is time, wisely and patiently measured out; the other is the lie, always shrouded in false language and with alleged good intentions (ecumenism, charitable understanding, mercy, achieving a Christianity more adapted to the world, etc.).

On the other hand, we must take into account the sad fact that a great number of Christian people has opted for the lie and chosen a sort of Christianity *open to the world*; which is the same as saying more mundane.

Evidently, then, it was urgent for Modernism to do away with the Catholic Priesthood; a first, important, and necessary step to achieve this purpose was to suppress priestly celibacy. It was necessary then —taking into account the whole of Modernism's purposes— to fabricate a web of totally new institutions and customs by emptying or discrediting the former ones, spreading among the faithful the belief that is was necessary to *adapt Christianity to new ambitions*, diluting the Faith in Tradition, discrediting the Hierarchy, etc.

No wonder, therefore, that in this highly artificially created environment many men of good faith and with the best imaginable good will generously volunteered to be part of an institution as good as you want it to be, but whose purposes, after all, are not very clear.

It should be noted, however, that naiveté and good faith do not suffice for justifying the acceptance of a wrong situation or the pretense that something wrong is good. The Christian has an obligation imposed on him at all times: to *discern* and distinguish right from wrong and good from bad. Not everything that apparently falls from the sky is good (sometimes we are struck by lightning or hail); and not everything you hear is true. The Christian should know that there have always been in the Church good Shepherds as well as mercenary Shepherds (as Jesus Christ explained), that the entire New Testament is filled with warnings and caveats about false Shepherds and false Teachers who will abound especially in the End Times and *will deceive many*. Given the abundance of deception and falsehoods that reign in the world, Jesus Christ Himself warned about the need to know and distinguish men *by their fruits*, not merely by their words. The truth is that barely anybody has given any thought to the effects caused by the ease with which married deacons will be admitted to the priesthood. These effects will contribute to blurring among the faithful the idea of the necessity and the appropriateness of priestly celibacy.

Those who are easily led by their impulses without caring about discerning what is appropriate from what is false or about seriously seeking the truth should take into account the urgent warning given by the Apostle Saint Paul in his *Second Letter to the Thessalonians* (2 Thess 2: 11–12). In that warning Saint Paul tell us that God sends a seductive spirit so that those who did not believe the truth would end up believing a lie and finally be condemned for having taken their pleasure in wickedness even when it sometimes presented itself with the label of goodness. Hence, *being mistaken in good faith* in as significant an issue as that of salvation does not suffice in any way to save anyone from the path to eternal perdition.

6. The flock needs a shepherd

Jesus Christ Himself used this metaphor referring to the Church, reflecting what happens in the natural realm: the flock goes nowhere if it is not led by a shepherd.

If the Church is the Great Flock of Jesus Christ, He is, in turn, the *Great Shepherd of the sheep* of that flock.[12] He appointed other

---

[12] Heb 13:20.

men as His successors to continue His mission in the office of leaders of the sheep: *As the Father hath sent me, I also send you,*[13] said Jesus Christ addressing His apostles.

But just as in the natural world not everyone is qualified to exercise the office of pastor, despite the fact that this job does not require special qualifications, *a fortiori* the same can be said about the Church, where he who is responsible for the sheep of the Flock of Christ must face the most difficult and important task any human being can accomplish: the salvation of souls.

Jesus Christ carefully distinguished between good and bad shepherds; He pointed out that He is *The Good Shepherd* and described the proper functions of any true shepherd. Since then, all those who have been appointed Shepherds in the Church have a clear–cut comprehension of the way they must follow: none other than walking after the steps of Jesus Christ.

But this mission, which springs from Jesus Christ Himself and has been entrusted to some men chosen to lead the sheep of His Flock, places upon their shoulders the weight of the loftiest of all responsibilities. From now on their lives do not belong to them but to the sheep alone. This is why the Good Shepherd exerts Himself to save His sheep from the dangers that threaten them, risking even His life: *The good shepherd giveth his life for his sheep. But the hireling, and he that is not the shepherd, whose own the sheep are not, seeth the wolf coming, and leaveth the sheep, and flieth: and the wolf catcheth, and scattereth the sheep: And the hireling flieth, because he is a hireling: and he hath no care for the sheep.*[14]

And any good shepherd will have plenty of opportunities to offer up his life. The Flock constantly walks through a field fraught with

---

[13] Jn 20:21.
[14] Jn 10: 11–13.

danger. Saint Peter urged the sheep to be vigilant because the Devil or Great Adversary is lurking, walking around seeking whom he may devour (1 Pet 5:8); a prudent warning which has become particularly relevant in the modern world, where the power of the Evil One has risen to degrees never before known in the history of the Church. Jesus Christ was quite clear in this regard when He warned the sheep about the World: *If the world hate you, know ye, that it hath hated me before you.*[15] *Wonder not, brethren, if the world hate you;*[16] said the Apostle Saint John.

Unfortunately, if one contrasts the texts of Scripture with the present situation of the Church, invaded by a modernist heresy that has affected the very Hierarchy to the point of having led most of its members to a general apostasy, the resulting view is spine–chilling. The faithful have been pushed by droves into a veritable dispersion once a large number of Pastors, from the highest officials of the Hierarchy to the most humble parish priests, have been seduced by this heresy and have become derelict in the duties entrusted to them.

The examination of the texts and their application to the reality of everyday life —something which is not usually done in the Church today— yields results that would have caused great fear had the Church not lost consciousness of her responsibility and the threat that is looming upon her.

According to Jesus Christ, He is the *Good Shepherd* and the only *door of the sheep.*[17] But He goes on to say: *He that entereth not by the door into the sheepfold, but climbeth up another way, the same*

---

[15] Jn 15:18.
[16] 1 Jn 3:13. Cf Jn 15:19.
[17] Jn 10:7.

is a thief and a robber;[18] and *the thief cometh not, but for to steal, and to kill, and to destroy.*[19]

As anybody can see, these words and expressions are quite strong. They clearly accuse the bad Shepherds of being nothing less than thieves and robbers; people who do not care about the sheep and do nothing except steal, kill, and destroy.

Anyone who feels concerned about the present situation of Catholicism as well as of the conduct and the ways of many Shepherds who govern the Church (whose coryphaei range from the highest officials to the most humble priests) can reason in conscience whether these condemning words of Jesus Christ have any application to the current situation of the Church. If the answer is in the affirmative, the consequences to be drawn by anybody without prejudice are really frightening.

According to Jesus Christ, the Good Shepherd *always goes before the sheep* (Jn 10:4), which clearly means, as can be deduced from the connotations of this expression, that he is compelled to *set himself as an example* with the testimony of his life.

This task will inevitably lead any good shepherd to give up his life for his sheep. His mission of *setting himself as an example*, which at first sight is important but which in itself should not give rise to opposing attitudes, could derive into seriously committed situations for him; the reason being that the testimony of his example must accompany the preaching of the Word, otherwise the preaching would be a useless labor: both elements go hand in hand and need each other so inescapably. However, the preaching of the Word is as difficult a task as it is a committed business.

---

[18] Jn 10:1.
[19] Jn 10:10.

In effect, Christian life, as Jesus Christ Himself said, is a *narrow and strait way* that leads to life, and hence few there are who find it (Mt 7:14). This is why the Doctrine laying it out is arduous and difficult, often contrary to human nature which, being weak and inclined to evil, is not willing to receive it. The result is easy to appreciate: more often than not, the faithful *will hear the preaching in disgust*. And in today's Church, where the faithful have been bombarded with modernist doctrines for over fifty years, the attitude of criticism and rejection of the preacher of the Word who is sincere and faithful to the mission received will be a habitual and current stance. This attitude is worsened by the same modernist doctrines that have spread the false doctrine of the parity between clergy and laity and have diluted the image and function of the priest. Moreover, as if the prophecies that announced Merciless Times had already been fulfilled and the Church would be standing in the threshold of a veritable *apostasy*, each faithful believes himself to be the arbitrator and judge to judge and decide everything; at the same time, *they will not endure sound doctrine; but, according to their own desires, they will heap to themselves teachers, having itching ears; and will indeed turn away their hearing from the truth, but will be turned unto fables.*[20]

It is especially here where the good Shepherd will feel that the words of Jesus Christ become real in his own flesh: *Except the grain of wheat fall into the ground and die, it abideth alone: but if it die, it bringeth forth much fruit.*[21]

Unfortunately, however, in the modernist Church of the *general defection of the Hierarchy*, from highest ranking officials of the utmost responsibility to the humblest priests, good shepherds willing

---

[20] 2 Tim 4: 3–4.
[21] Jn 12: 24–25.

The Good Shepherd

to die for the good of the souls entrusted to them will be a rare treasure to find.

If it is said that the Good Shepherd is the one who goes before his sheep it is because His life is for any shepherd an example of the fulfillment of a two–facet duty.

The first duty is that all shepherds must strictly confine themselves in their preaching to the received Doctrine. This means to preach the Word of God as contained in Revelation, without removing anything or providing new elements that involve any kind of adulteration: *For we are not as many, adulterating the word of God.*[22] In His farewell to His disciples, Jesus Christ commands them to go and make disciples of all nations *teaching them to observe all things whatsoever I have commanded you.*[23]

The second obligation of the good Shepherd is to adjust his own life to the content of his preaching.

Reality unmistakably demonstrates that both duties are far from been fulfilled.

The obligation to strictly abide by the Teachings received, without subtracting or adding any elements beyond its content, is a duty which involves a loyalty in the Shepherd that may bring him to the point of dying to himself; and we must attribute to this expression all its possible demanding meanings. In effect, *for the word of God is living and effectual, and more piercing than any two edged sword.*[24] It is, therefore, impossible, to preach this word without hurting its listeners, including the very Shepherd who transmits it (as Bernanos said in his *Diary of a Country Priest*), unless the Word is diluted or

---

[22] 2 Cor 2:17.
[23] Mt 28:20.
[24] Heb 4:12.

Its content lowered; that is, to introduce in It the corruptions which Saint Paul spoke of to the Corinthians (2 Cor 2:17).

All this happens because the lives of the listeners, given the weakness of human nature, often preset natural resistance to the teachings of the Gospel: the Doctrine that shows the only road that leads to Life; a veritable narrow, steep, and arduous path (Mt 7:14).

Anyway, the good Shepherd needs to die to himself if he wants to preach the Word fruitfully. This means that he should put aside his own feelings, his own judgments, and his own ideas. Furthermore, he must fight a supremely hostile environment that is willing to crush by all means the Word; for the Word, being contrary to the world and its falsities, is able to discover the *thoughts and intents of the heart*, as the *Letter to the Hebrews* says.

The true preacher of the Word, human after all, can be subject, therefore, to multiple temptations. This is why the Apostle said, referring to his own mission: *I am not ashamed of the gospel.*[25]

The second duty of the good Shepherd, which is even more difficult to bear than the first, is concerned with his obligation to conform his life to the teachings he preaches, which involves a confrontation which can eventually become sorrowful. In effect, on the one hand, the teachings to be disseminated are demanding and lofty; on the other, the life of the Shepherd is usually far from getting even near them. The reason for this is provided by what the *Letter to the Hebrews* tells us about the Shepherd, for *he himself also is compassed with infirmity.*[26]

What has been said, as always happens throughout the History of Salvation, has been foreseen in the Plans of God, Whose ways are inscrutable: *O the depth of the riches of the wisdom and of the*

---

[25] Rom 1:16.
[26] Heb 5:2.

knowledge of God! How incomprehensible are his judgments, and how unsearchable his ways![27]

In this way the Wisdom of God turns the weakness of the good Shepherd into his strength; another mysterious paradox of Christian existence.

The Apostle Saint Paul explains it clearly: *And he said to me: My grace is sufficient for thee; for power is made perfect in infirmity. Gladly therefore will I glory in my infirmities, that the power of Christ may dwell in me. For which cause I please myself in my infirmities, in reproaches, in necessities, in persecutions, in distresses, for Christ. For when I am weak, then am I powerful.*[28]

Thus the knot of this mystery has been untied to end up entering another greater mystery: love; we are back to square one, for now it is clear that love is the beginning and end of everything and the ultimate reality where all things finally converge. As the Apostle beautifully explains, the infirmities and the weaknesses of the minister of Christ —entrusted with the mission of preaching the Word— are the very conditions that allow him to be invaded by the strength of Christ: *Gladly therefore will I glory in my infirmities, that the power of Christ may dwell in me.*

Whereupon we have reached the core of the Christian mystery. The disciple gives everything —and above all his own life— for the sake of the Beloved, Who is Christ. And since love involves mutual correspondence and relationship, Christ also gives Himself up to His disciple. An exchange of life (Jn 6:56) in which the poverty and nakedness of the disciple, accepted voluntarily out of love, is fully filled by the life of Christ: *I live, now not I; but Christ liveth in me.*[29]

---

[27] Rom 11:33.
[28] 2 Cor 12: 9–10.
[29] Gal 2:20.

The implications are exciting. The good Shepherd and preacher of the Word lives his love for Jesus Christ until he becomes indentified with Him, making real the demand inherent to the relationship of love: the lover is for the beloved, and the beloved for the lover. *I am my beloved's, and my beloved is mine*,[30] said the bride of the *Song of Songs*. It is then, and only then, that the preaching of the good Shepherd is no longer his and becomes the Word of Christ speaking through his mouth, as the Master Himself assured us when he said: *He that heareth you, heareth me.*[31]

Finally another mystery has been clarified, this time easier to explain. For now the reason of the futility and banality, if not perversity, of much of the modern preaching is clear: homilies, sermons, exhortations, speeches, documents, and pastoral instruction are but a set of heavy fetid waters that run without course and are useless for all and sunder.

When Jesus Christ describes the characteristics of the Good Shepherd He says that *the sheep hear his voice; and he calleth his own sheep by name, and leadeth them out. And when he hath let out his own sheep, he goeth before them: and the sheep follow him, because they know his voice.* But —Jesus Christ goes on— *a stranger they follow not, but fly from him, because they know not the voice of strangers.*[32]

Traditionally, these words were never difficult to interpret, but they present the current Pastoral activity and the faithful of the modern Church with a *difficult and very serious* problem as regards their interpretation. Given the substantial shift the post–conciliar Church has given to the entire content of Revelation, new events

---

[30] Sg 6:3; 7:11.
[31] Lk 10:16.
[32] Jn 10: 3–5.

ask for an analysis of these words that would take into account the difficulties raised by their interpretation at the present time. On the other hand, the complexity of this sensitive topic needs a thorough step–by–step analysis as the sole means of reaching a satisfactory explanation.

First we must consider the very words of the text. Accordingly, the sheep follow the Shepherd because *they know his voice*; whereas they do not follow the voice of strangers *because they know not the voice of strangers.*

The conclusion is self–evident: when the voice of the Shepherd is *known* by the sheep (which obviously implies that the sheep have heard His voice before and are used to it), then they follow the Shepherd. On the contrary, when the voice of the Shepherd sounds sort of *strange* to the sheep, then they know it not (which means that this voice is different from and at variance with the voice known to them) and, therefore, they follow it not.

Next to determine is what must be understood by *known* voice and *strange* voice. Following elemental logic, those expressions can only refer to a voice *which has always been heard and is already recognized as legitimate,* or, contrariwise, to a voice *which is heard as something new and different, and which, consequently, lacks legitimacy.*

That done, facts must be now analyzed.

First, it should be noted, according to the text and as a necessary corollary, that the sheep fall in behind the Shepherd when they know his voice. Therefore, any sheep who know not the Shepherd's voice and yet still follow him, *these sheep do not belong to the fold.*

Secondly, it is a fact that in the modern Church the *majority of Shepherds* have abandoned the Teaching of Tradition and have accepted instead the ideas of the modernist heresy. Logically, their voice is *unfamiliar* to the voice of Jesus Christ *the Prince of Shepherds*, according to Saint Peter (1 Pet 5:4) and as contained in the Gospels and Tradition.

Thirdly, there is another no less important undeniable fact: *most Catholics today unquestionably follow those Shepherds.*

And the corollary of this reality is that almost the entirety of the Catholic faithful *have ceased to belong to the Flock of Christ*. Nevertheless, this conclusion, despite being well supported by the teachings of the Gospels with compelling logic, will not be accepted and will be unanimously rejected. Why? Because, once again, truth is opposed by several powerful arguments.

Foremost, bad Shepherds are still the legitimate Hierarchy. In fact, *even though they are bad Shepherds they are still legitimate Shepherds*. And a Christian faithful to his Faith cannot openly rebel against the legitimate Hierarchy to whom he owes submission and respect.

On the other hand, any member of the Church, regardless of his place within the ecclesiastical community, can —and even *must*— show his disagreement with error, no matter where it is found, and combat it. This can undoubtedly lead to the plight of maintaining a serene and delicate balance between respect for the Hierarchy and the obligation to denounce error.

In extremely complicated situations, such as the one the Church is going through nowadays, keeping a healthy balance within the Faith is extremely difficult and requires the special assistance of Grace, along with great fidelity to the lights of the Spirit under the guidance of the authentic Magisterium of old. We say the *Magisterium of old* because modern papolaters falsely maintain that the Magisterium of the Church is to be defined by the reigning Pontiff. For example, the difficulty that someone can encounter at present in keeping the Faith between two opposite errors greatly relevant today which affect, in one way or another, the vast majority of Catholics: we are referring to *conciliarism*, on the one hand, and *papolatry*, on the other.

The progressive Church unfairly takes advantage of this situation by demanding obedience to the Hierarchy and to an alleged *spirit of the Council* which no one really knows what it is. In the same way, Progressivism has used this pretext to persecute the few faithful who still keep their fidelity to the Church that follows the Teachings of Tradition; which constitutes an abuse of authority that, ultimately, becomes a manifestation of true *papolatry* if not tyranny.

Another powerful reason that explains why the findings presented here will not be accepted is the fact that for over fifty years Catholicism has been pounded to a pulp by the heresy of Modernism with almost no opposition; consequently, the vast majority of the faithful have determined to surrender to the spirit of the lie and are not willing to offer any resistance.

Modernism offers a sort of Christianity conformed to the world and only for this world which does not know the mystery of the Cross and has thrown out any sense of sin. From a merely naturalistic point of view which has disowned God, it is not surprising that Catholicity has capitulated and surrendered the fort. In such a quandary of opportunistic and cowardly feelings, hardly anyone can be found who is willing to defend the truth.

As a proof of what we have just said, we can consider what happened with the New Mass, the *Novus Ordo*. It was obligatorily imposed by Pope Paul VI to substitute for the Traditional Mass by an illegal disposition which ignored the fact that the Traditional Mass could never be abolished, as Benedict XVI finally acknowledged. The New Mass, despite the fact that it tremendously minimized the essential Sacrificial meaning of the true Mass, making it almost disappear, *was welcomed without resistance by the entire Catholic World*.

The New Mass was, indeed, received without resistance, *but also without acceptance*, as facts are demonstrating. In this regard, somebody has recently said that it is not worth the while to emphasize the values of the Traditional Mass in order to show the damage caused by the imposition of the New Mass since, given its lack of content, it will inevitably end up disappearing, swallowed by the tide of progressivism. Should anyone doubt the stance of this reasoning, just let him pay attention to the fact that almost all of the Catholic churches in the world that champion the Rite of the New Mass have seen a decline in Mass attendance to the point of becoming *steadily deserted*, as statistics can show.

The Shepherd whom Jesus Christ Himself calls a mercenary does not care about the sheep; he comes not but for *to steal*, and *to kill*, and *to destroy*. The result has been a desolate Catholicity of which only a small remnant is left, scattered and persecuted. According to the Gospel of Saint Matthew, Jesus Christ Himself, *seeing the multitudes, had compassion on them: because they were distressed, and lying like sheep that have no shepherd.*[33]

But this small remnant, nevertheless, makes true the Promise which will always be fulfilled: *And the gates of hell shall not prevail against it.*[34] Hence, those who believe in Jesus Christ and love Him continue to comfort their hearts with the virtue of hope, always treasuring those consoling words whose echo is never quenched: *But*

---

[33] Mt 9:36.
[34] Mt 16:18.

when these things begin to come to pass, look up, and lift up your heads, because your redemption is at hand.[35]

---

[35]Lk 21:28.

THE LABORERS SENT TO THE VINEYARD[1]

Dear Brethren in the Hearts of Our Lord Jesus Christ and the Blessed Virgin Mary, Our Mother.

Today, Septuagesima Sunday, as prescribed by the Extraordinary Form of the Roman Rite of the Holy Mass, the Church invites us to consider the Gospel passage of Saint Matthew which narrates one of the parables as part of the Teaching of Our Lord.

The reaction of those who first read or hear this parable, at least as an initial impression, is an odd feeling that makes this a peculiar parable. And yet, the teaching of the parable contains at least two important points that greatly affect the whole of Christian life.

The first point concerns the behavior of Christians as Christians, even as human beings, as they go through their ordinary daily life. Because of the weakness of human nature, as everyone knows from experience, they tend to resist the principles and lessons to be learned from the Gospel.

The second has to do with a serious problem that affects the modern Pastoral activity of the Church, for the Parable contains an important and fundamental teaching which, unfortunately, is alien and even contrary to one of the essential, most widespread, and obligatory impositions of the official Catechesis of the modern Church.

---

[1] Preached on January 24, 2016.

After a cursory exposition of both points, the first conclusion to be drawn is the perennial relevance of the teachings of the Gospel. In the episode we will discuss, there will appear again, described with uncanny precision and absolute realism, the problems of men in general and those affecting the modern Church in particular; the errors and deviations with respect to the revealed Word will be clearly expounded and the true solutions to those errors will be clearly pointed out. But let us go step by step; first, a summary of the content of the parable.

A householder went out early in the morning, at the first hour, to hire laborers in his vineyard. He found some workers and agreed with them to a penny a day for their labor; he went out later about the third, sixth, and ninth hours and found other laborers whom he also hired, promising them wages that would be just. He finally went out about the last hour of the day, the eleventh hour, and saw still others standing idle because, they said, no man had hired them. He also sent these to his vineyard with the promise of paying them what had been agreed.

When the day was over, the lord of the vineyard ordered his steward to pay the laborers, beginning from the last even to the first. The steward did so. Those who came at the last hour received every man a penny; and so on, up to those who had arrived first, who also received every man a penny. This caused unhappiness among the latter, who murmured against the master of the house arguing that they, despite having worked from the very first hour and borne the burden of the day and the heat, earned the same as those hired last. The lord answered one of them that he had done him no wrong since he was paid what had been agreed. As for the other laborers, the lord said that if he decided to give them as much as he gave the first ones, he was just in giving his own money at his own will.

So shall the last be first, and the first last.[2]

---

[2] Mt 20: 1–16.

This is the summary of the parable and the explanation that the Lord Himself provides. Nevertheless, once the meaning has been heard and carefully considered, one might notice, as a curious and peculiar thing, that the narrative continues to cause an odd feeling in the soul. It is true that, once the lord of the vineyard explained his behavior to those laborers who complained, the clarity of his reasoning based on strict justice becomes self evident; therefore, one must agree with it. For, indeed, once the work has been finished and what was agreed upon has been received, there is no room for any claim: after all, once what is owed is paid, one can do with his money what he wants, as the owner said; it is clear that justice has been served.

And yet, he who is well informed about the facts must acknowledge that although the demands of justice were fulfilled, there is always left a feeling that there was somehow no equality to the wages or at least that there was a lack of generosity on the part of the lord of the vineyard; after all, those who had arrived first had worked longer and under more difficult conditions than the rest.

Several explanations are in order here:

God wills the salvation of all men, for which purpose He pours His grace and the abundance of His gifts upon all of them, missing no one. It is also true that to some He gives more generously than to others, as Revelation clearly states.

The Apostle Saint Paul, for example, affirms in his *Letter to the Ephesians* that *to every one of us is given grace, according to the measure of the giving of Christ.*[3]

---

[3] Eph 4:7.

And he adds in his First Letter to the Corinthians: *all these things one and the same Spirit worketh, dividing to every one according as he will.*[4]

It is quite clear, then, that while God grants every man more than abundant gifts for his salvation, He also gives *more generously to some than to others*. His reasoning is sufficient; however it leaves in our hearts a more or less latent feeling that God seems to be in some way acting *arbitrarily*: Why are some people given more than others?

Although we are not always able to reach the depth of God's judgments we know that He always acts with Wisdom. Nevertheless, there exist in the same Scripture certain keys that can provide clues about the issue. In the *Parable of the Talents*, for example, it is said that the man who went off to a far country distributed his property among his servants to each *according to his proper ability*;[5] apropos of which it should be remembered that the infinite Wisdom and infinite Power of God are made manifest in His Creation by producing an almost infinite variety of species and subspecies of creatures, and man was no exception. For God created each man different within the unity of a common nature. And He created them as individuals with immortal souls, each with his own character and his own peculiarities, far from resembling the production of robot machines. The capacity of each man being, therefore, different, it is not surprising that God has distributed His gifts according to criteria which, after all, fit the reality of things.

Such reasoning is indeed reassuring, but only to a point, for there is still in the soul some unconscious feeling of dissatisfaction. After all it is still true that God creates some better gifted than others.

---

[4] 1 Cor 12:11.
[5] Mt 25:15.

But, as we have said, the Judgments of God are inscrutable, and we know with all certainty *they are always good and the fruit of His Love*, even if our limited understanding cannot comprehend them. The Apostle, once again, refers to this issue in his *Letter to the Romans*:

O the depth of the riches of the wisdom and of the knowledge of God! How incomprehensible are his judgments, and how unsearchable his ways![6]

The Attributes of God, indeed, appear to our reasoning as being divergent when they are actually identical with the Simplicity of the Divine Essence. This is why God never operates mercifully without including at the same time the exigencies of His Justice, whether we understand it each time or not. Consequently, it is not right to attribute to God attitudes of mercy independent of His justice.[7]

All of which can lead to the conclusion that under the apparent *arbitrariness* committed against the laborers who worked from the first hour, who undoubtedly endured the worst part of the day, there could be a reason, hidden from our understanding, but in which come together as one the Mercy, the Wisdom, and the Justice of God.

Under these circumstances, anyone can understand how poignant this issue becomes. There are too many times throughout our life when difficult situations arise which do not seem to be compatible with Divine Goodness and Providence: the death of loved ones, painful or incurable illnesses, serious family problems that appear through the years, resounding failures in the daily life of every one, and a long list that sometimes makes us feel somewhat reluctant to admit the Apostle's words: *And we know that to them that love God,*

---

[6]Rom 11:33.

[7]With some nuances, Saint Thomas deals with this issue in *Summa Theologiæ*, I^a, q. 21, a. 3, ad secundum; III^a, q. 46, a. 2, ad tertium; II-II^æ, q. 67, a. 4.

all things work together unto good.[8] Finally later on, perhaps with the passing of time, one understands that the goodness, wisdom, and designs of God are the fruit of His love for us that looks after our own good. As we can see, the problem is always the same: the greatness of God as opposed to our limited understanding.

Apropos the parable we are discussing, Bruce Marshall, in his famous novel *To Every Man a Penny*, suggests an original and daring interpretation of the narrative: the laborers who worked from the first hour *were precisely the most favored.*

Those who arrived early and worked, therefore, all day long, complained of receiving the same payment given to those who had come afterwards, including those who arrived only at the end of the day. And indeed it was so; but can we say that because of this they were treated unfairly?

In reality, says Bruce Marshall —and this statement may seem surprising— these laborers, who apparently had been treated unfavorably, *received more and better than the rest*. True, those who arrived first had to put up with the heaviest work, had borne the burden of the day and the heat, and had to make a greater effort and sacrifice than the rest. But it happens, however, that the core, what is most fundamental of the Christian existence or what justifies it and gives it its full meaning is the *Mystery of the Cross and the virtue of suffering as a participation in the Passion and Death of Christ.*

The most fundamental truths of the Faith preached by Jesus Christ are precisely the truths most neglected and most misunderstood by Christians. To substantiate what we have said, we may make reference, among other tenets, to realities so little estimated and so greatly misunderstood as the glory of being among the small-

---

[8]Rom 8:28.

est and the most humble, the privilege of occupying the last place, the bliss promised exclusively to the poor and to those who mourn, and the glory of the Perfect Joy granted only to those who are persecuted for their fidelity to the Faith. And how many Christians today are willing to believe these words of Jesus Christ which otherwise describe the only Way to follow Him: *How narrow is the gate, and strait is the way that leadeth to life: and few there are that find it!*[9]

Christians, being too intent on following the criteria and ways of thinking of the World, drowned in the infected environment that surrounds them and which they breathe continuously, end up longing for and pursuing the goods of this earth; otherwise always outdated but which they consider as eternal and of absolute value: welfare, the absence of pain and sacrifice, money and material goods, power and fame, and all that leads to what vulgar people unconsciously call *enjoying life*. They forget the saying of Saint Paul: *Seek the things that are above, set your affection on things above, not on things on this earth.*[10] It follows that, if there are things worth *savoring* they are precisely the things above, and only those things. On the other hand, the promise of the *Beatitudes* (Perfect Joy), made by Jesus Christ, does not in any way refer to the set of things that the World understands as being those leading to *enjoying life*.

For brevity's sake we will not bring up here the many texts of Scripture —in fact the entire New Testament— which point to the Cross and the imitation of Jesus Christ as the only way forward for His disciples. One important text of the *Letter to the Romans* would suffice: *Know you not that all we, who are baptized in Christ Jesus, are baptized in his death?*[11] A cursory consideration of this text

---

[9] Mt 7:14.
[10] Col 3: 1–2.
[11] Rom 6:3.

would be enough to realize how fortunate was the destiny allotted to the laborers that arrived at the first hour.

Modern Progressivism has emptied Christian existence and robbed it of its meaning. Being a Catholic in today's world means nothing. That is why it is frequently heard *I am a Catholic, but not a practicing one*, as if an empty term would mean anything. The workers of the first hour of the parable were offered the opportunity to be at the last place (when they had been the first) and carry the greatest sacrifice and the heaviest burden. Heroism is accepting the most strenuous and difficult task —which can even lead to death— and, if possible, to take the load that corresponds to the other: *Bear ye one another's burdens; and so you shall fulfill the law of Christ.*[12] When all is said and done, it is evident that the laborers called at the earliest hour were offered the opportunity of taking for themselves the best of the best.

The clearest sign of the gap between Evangelical Teaching and the mentality of modern man is the barely perceptible feeling of perplexity aroused in today's listener by the fact that some laborers who had worked more were, nevertheless, receiving the same wage as those who had worked less. In other words, modern man, to a greater or lesser degree, is no longer Christian. He may have forgotten Christian Teachings or may have simply ceased to believe them; in one way or another, it is obvious that *the Gospel no longer informs his life.*

An almost unbridgeable gap has been opened between the materialistic hedonistic pagan praxis of the philosophy of well-being and the praxis derived from the Evangelical Doctrine. Christian apologetics, which would have a thousand ways of rationally demonstrating the falsity of paganism, has encountered, however, the serious

---

[12] Gal 6:2.

obstacle that modern man no longer listens to reason; he has laboriously exerted himself to destroy the value of reason and to no longer trust it. Therefore, the *criteria of credibility* and all the evidence that Christian apologetics could offer are devoid of value from the outset.

Apologetics is aware that its task has become increasingly difficult in a world which is not only *pagan* but also totally *antichristian*. In this sense, it is evident that the first Christian apologists faced a much easier undertaking than the one their modern counterparts have to confront. The phrase *have to confront* is most appropriate because, in addition to what has been said, the modern Church has officially proclaimed that all religions are equally true (which is tantamount to saying that none of them is the true religion), and has therefore renounced her mission of evangelization, thus impeding any attempt to proselytize.

Faced with this dilemma, today true believers have a very difficult road ahead; probably the most difficult path to be followed by any disciple of Jesus Christ since the beginning of the Church. This reality, however, would never justify giving up, which would actually amount to a betrayal, because this is a story that only those who resist to the end can recount: *he that shall persevere unto the end, he shall be saved.*[13]

Nevertheless, Christian Apologetics cannot renounce reason to carry out its function; it would be tantamount to assenting to the fallacy woven by those who want to invalidate it. This is particularly true now that modern progresivists contradict themselves by negating the value of reason while, at the same time, placing reason above the Word of God. It was a tenet of Protestant rational Liberalism —a liberalism that has been totally assimilated by modern

---

[13] Mt 10:22; cf Mk 13:13; Mt 24:13.

Catholicism— that human reason must judge Divine Revelation. Next was modern Historicism; both concurred in that Divine Revelation can only be accepted and assessed *from the point of view of human reason*.

Modernism, for its part, has no problem using either approach or, on occasion, both of them, for it appreciates contradictions in the same way as the jargon of politicians is often judged; after all, contradiction implies lying by turns and Modernism feels completely at home with lying.

If Apologetics would not recognize the value of reason, it would betray itself and offend God, Who gave man the power of thinking. A different thing is that Apologetics has not exhausted the arsenal of arguments available to it nor has it made use of exceptionally important ones.

Paganism has decided to do without God, even denying His existence, thus departing from the truth and plunging into the lie. But God is Infinite Truth upon Whom all truth is founded. Moreover, Jesus Christ said of Himself that *He was the truth* and had come *to give testimony to the truth*;[14] He also stated clearly that fidelity to His words is the way to know the truth (Jn 8: 31–32), assuring his disciples that the Holy Spirit would be the one who would teach them *all truth*.[15]

Paganism can deny this, as indeed it has done. It argues that the proofs of the existence of God are not conclusive, which compels it to maintain the belief that the Universe comes from a *first element*; but it cannot explain what that element is, much less *where it could possibly have come from*. Its argumentation, therefore, is left without any argument (an explanation which, in the end, has no

---

[14] Jn 18:37.
[15] Jn 16:13.

The Laborers Sent to the Vineyard 247

explanation), unless paganism stubbornly maintains that the first element *came from nothing*, which is another way of implying that *what is absurd must prevail over what is reasonable*.

It follows that there can be only two starting (and arrival) points of Paganism: either an argumentation *lacking conclusion*, which concludes nothing since it is missing the final conclusion which would bring the argumentation to an end, or an argumentation which maintains that *it is reasonable to accept what is absolutely irrational*.

The issue of Love must be added now.

According to Christianity, man has been created by Love and for Love (uppercase or lowercase) which Doctrine is the only one that can elucidate the insatiable desires of joy and infinitude of the human heart, while Paganism *cannot give any explanation for it*.

Hence, Paganism is deprived of the reality of love, thus condemning man to an agonizing emptiness. Consequently, Paganism has replaced love with sex, leading man to a dead end. For sex being devoid of any sense of true love (which must necessarily be determined by reason) degrades man to a condition lower than that which corresponds to him, the condition of irrational animals; and even lower, for it is infamous for man to be equated to animals. Moreover, man's deliberate renunciation of his condition as superior being inevitably leads him to all sorts of aberrations.

Christian Doctrine has constantly taught that God is Love (1 Jn 4:8; 4:16) and that all created love is but a participation in Infinite Love. Nevertheless, Paganism, because it is deprived of God, has no explanation of a higher order that could provide any reason for love; love, therefore, is confined to the merely natural sphere and it cannot be argued that this sphere is that of a rational animal, for it would be difficult to find an explanation for any rationality which makes no reference to a superior order being thus reduced to *merely animal*. Paganism can defend itself by arguing that spirit comes from matter or is a function of matter; but this view leads to a self–imposed alternative: it is either an argument which lacks argument (for it would be necessary first to demonstrate the possibility that spirit comes from matter) or an absurdity that affirms that matter and spirit are one and the same thing (which is a statement that cannot be demonstrated).

By renouncing the reality of love man has become empty and without a soul. Saint Paul said that man without love becomes as *sounding brass or a tinkling cymbal*:[16] a sound that is heard for some seconds, like a passing gust of air that soon becomes nothing. Indeed man, being created to love (a necessary relation between a *thou* and an *I*), loneliness is the only reality he can know when there is no love.

True, there is purely human love which, even without grace, is absolutely sincere in its varied forms of manifestation such as conjugal love, paternal-filial love, and friendship. But if this love is not firmly rooted in God, Who is the Fountain of all Love, *it will never reach any depth or any high degree*; consequently, it will never become *true love*. Moreover, man has become accustomed to being content *with little bordering on nothing* believing that this is precisely *much* and all that he can hope for; and he lives his whole life long with this tragic ignorance. This is what Jesus Christ meant when He said that he who is not be able to lose his life out of love for Him (the only way of finding it) *would lose his own life*,[17] whatever content (imaginable or unimaginable) one may want to give to the expression *lose one's life* uttered by Jesus Christ Himself.

---

[16] 1 Cor 13:1.
[17] Cf Mt 10:39; 16:25; Mk 8:35; Lk 17:33.

As proof of what we have just said, all one has to do is to check the statistics showing the current state of society: broken families; widespread marriages gone bad and wrecked; divorce as a normal marital status (the Church has stopped believing in unwavering love); civil marriages and civil unions by far outnumbering canonical marriage, which is tending to disappear; parent–child relationships open to crisis if not destroyed; childhood without the warmth of a home and the education of children surrendered to secularist States; courtship reduced to premarital sex; etc.

The loss of love has resulted in the loss of virtually all values which have been replaced by aberrations that have been granted all the considerations which should be accrued to the former. This is how things like divorce, homosexuality, and abortion, to name the most outstanding cases, have become legitimized and recognized as a triumph of the new civilization and as progress of mankind.

Something has occurred recently in the Church and at a level least expected which shows more clearly the corruption of the notion of love. We are referring to the attention afforded to the issue of *mercy*.

Mercy is the attribute of God most consoling to the human being for it has to do with the forgiveness of sins that God offers us out of love. Mercy is indeed an act of love and it necessarily implies, therefore, a *bilateral relationship which is essential to love*. In this case between God and His creature, for there is no love when there is no relationship of equality and correspondence between *thou* and *I*, which essentially demands the identification of both wills.

Nevertheless, current Pastoral activity is presenting mercy —and this is the message that is being delivered to the faithful— as if it were a *unilateral* action on the part of God without asking from the creature any disposition other than receiving it. In doing so, the present modernist Pastoral activity devalues (truly speaking, *rejects*) the notion of guilt and sin on the part of the creature and the ensuing need of his repentance. This is an erroneous idea, a veritable falsification of the notion of mercy because it breaks the bilateral relationship of love, destroying any possibility of the amorous self-giving of God to His creature. In the last analysis, this notion of mercy involves the lowering of man to the level of mere *thing* by depriving him of his power of giving a free and responsible answer to love, which, if it is authentic, demands the previous acknowledgment of one's guilt. God does not deal with man as if he were a puppet but as the responsible being that he is with the power of free will (love is essentially *freedom*). A theoretical relationship of love where man were bent on *keeping* his rebellious attitude against God would manifest clearly an opposition of wills that would become conflicting wills, *which make impossible any relationship of love*; consequently, any possibility of mercy would disappear.

Some might object that the modern Pastoral activity increases the use of confessionals in the convoked religious activities. However, any discerning observer will not miss the fact that they talk of the confessional more insistently than of the proper use of the sacrament of confession. One cannot avoid the feeling that this approach to the apparatus of *mercy* is rather ornamental window–dressing intended to achieve a greater influx of people.

We said at the beginning of this dissertation that this parable contains two important issues which are fully affecting Christian existence. We have examined the first one; now we must turn our attention to the second issue, which holds even greater importance and significance for today's Church than the first.

We are referring to the issue mentioned in the parable of the evangelizing mission of the Church, a mission which Modernism has tried to eliminate, being, actually, almost completely successful.

It must be noted that, as regards this issue, Modernist doctrine, which has lately dispensed with its deceptive attitude and acted more overtly, has decided to operate blatantly and without pretense in this task of *doing away with the evangelizing mission of the Church.* Unfortunately, once again, as is usually happening at the present stage of the history of the Church, no cries of alarm or protest have been raised.

Nevertheless, modernist Pastoral activity is contradicted as usual, although more clearly so in this case, by Revelation and the teachings contained in the Gospel, as we shall shortly see.

The parable begins by telling us that the householder of the vineyard went out several times, from early morning until late in the afternoon, *to hire laborers for his vineyard.* The pressing of time, which urges him to go out at an early hour, and his persistence in the successive times that he went out throughout the day, clearly indicate how desperate he was for getting laborers to work in his field. The meaning of this parable, therefore, clearly conveys Jesus Christ's concern about the scarcity of laborers available to work in His vineyard, the Church, and the ensuing urgency of getting more: *Then he saith to his disciples, 'The harvest indeed is great, but the laborers are few. Pray ye therefore the Lord of the harvest, that he send forth laborers into his harvest.'*[18] Moreover, the command of Jesus Christ is clear and forceful: *Going therefore, teach ye all nations; baptizing them in the name of the Father, and of the Son, and*

---

[18] Mt 9: 37–38.

of the Holy Ghost. Teaching them to observe all things whatsoever I have commanded you.[19]

The final going out of the owner of the vineyard towards the end of day has an important feature. *About the eleventh hour he went out and found others standing, and he saith to them*:

—*Why stand you here all the day idle?*

They say to him:

—*Because no man hath hired us.*

He saith to them:

—*Go you also into my vineyard.*

And it is worth noting the insistence of the parable on showing the *urgency* of the owner of the farm to get workers, for he even hires those he found at the last minute and sends them to work. It is clearly the intention of the parable to point out, on the one hand, that there must be laborers, as an inescapable necessity, to perform the work of Evangelization; and, on the other, that there is an obligation to look for them quickly and persistently by whatever means necessary. Evangelization will fail if there are no laborers in the vineyard because no man has found them, since no man has looked for them.

Moreover, the remark uttered by the idle laborers of the last hour of the day seems intentional and significant: *Because no man hath hired us*. Evidently, therefore, *there is a need to search for laborers*. And this need has a reason; that is: the Evangelization that ought to be done.

In this regard, there is a very telling passage in the *Parable of Great Banquet* in the Gospel of Saint Luke: And the Lord said to

---

[19] Mt 28: 19–20.

the servant: '*Go out into the highways and hedges, and compel them to come in, that my house may be filled.*'[20]

But the new, modernist–tainted Pastoral activity of the Church, ignoring the texts of Scripture and a twenty–centuries–old Tradition, is opposed to any work of evangelization that may result in an effort to make the evangelized a member of the Church; it casts into oblivion the traditional Doctrine of the Church which affirms that *There is no salvation outside the Catholic Church*; and, based on the false principle that all religions are valid and suitable for Salvation, it has eliminated the missionary work carried out by the Church since the times of Jesus Christ Himself —sometimes even expressly prohibiting such work, as in the case of the relationship of the Catholic Church with Judaism.

That Evangelization is necessary can be seen in the very words and commands of Jesus Christ: *Go, therefore, make disciples of all nations... Pray ye therefore the Lord of the harvest, that he send forth laborers into his harvest.* But the Modernism that has infiltrated the Church has a long time ago disregarded the commands of her Founder, hence the unavoidable corollary: no Founder, New Doctrine, *different Church*.

There is also a fundamental text of Saint Paul in his *Letter to the Romans* which is an emphatic denial to the new modernist teachings that oppose Evangelization:

How then shall they call on him, in whom they have not believed? Or how shall they believe in him, of whom they have not heard? And how shall they hear, without a preacher? And how shall they preach unless they be sent?[21]

---

[20] Lk 14:23.
[21] Rom 10: 14–15.

Catholicism has reached a point where all its principles and teachings have been disrupted —actually, counterfeited and turned inside out— resulting in a new doctrine that has nothing to do with Scripture and the Tradition of the Church. Another proof of this statement is the odd feeling left as an aftertaste in so many Christians who consider the laborers who came to work at the first hour unfortunate, forgetting, by doing so, all traditional Teachings which are always so contrary to what the weakened human nature prefers. This is why Jesus Christ ends the parable with a teaching that is another key principle of Christian life: *So shall the last be first, and the first last.*

The drifting of the Church, which started after the Second Vatican Council, has reached its peak and is about to end. The mighty river flowing from pure and abundant sources drifted away from its course and became lost in a desert; a dry river bed is all that is now left. The final, culminating phase of the eclipse is near at hand, but not before it is preceded by the most severe persecution suffered by the Church throughout her history. Saint Pius X already said that those who were determined to open themselves to the world always ended up sunk and dead.

It is true that preceding times have been times of tribulation in which millions who were baptized into the Catholic Faith have perished. But these times were not nearly as hard as those which are still to come, when the elect will have to show great fortitude.

Nevertheless, the Words of Him Who has said *My word shall not pass* will never cease to echo; among them, the most consoling ones: *I will establish my Church, and the Gates of Hell shall not prevail against her.*

THE CROSS AND THE MYSTERY OF SORROW[1]

Today, Sunday of Quinquagesima, the Church offers to our consideration in the gospel of the Holy Mass a passage in the Gospel of Saint Luke that tells how Jesus Christ announces the mystery of His Death on the Cross to His disciples on their way to Jerusalem:

—*Behold, we go up to Jerusalem, and all things shall be accomplished which were written by the prophets concerning the Son of man. For he shall be delivered to the Gentiles, and shall be mocked, and scourged, and spit upon. And after they have scourged him, they will put him to death; and the third day he shall rise again.*[2]

According to the text, the disciples could not understand anything of what He was saying, for the language was incomprehensible to them. In a parallel passage of Saint Mark, Peter calls Jesus aside to rebuke Him regarding this matter. This causes a strong reaction from Jesus Who, turning about and facing His disciples, rebukes Peter in a harsh manner:

—*Go behind me, Satan, because thou savorest not the things that are of God, but that are of men.*[3]

And indeed, because the Mystery of the Cross, which Saint Paul has called *a stumbling block unto the Jews, and unto the Gentiles*

---

[1] Preached on February 7, 2016.
[2] Lk 18: 31–33.
[3] Mk 8:33.

foolishness,[4] was always an incomprehensible abyss for men, and it continues to be so. It is true that for any Christian, a disciple of Jesus Christ, it is difficult to admit that the Son of God ended His mission on earth in the apparent failure of the scaffold of the Cross.

But to not understand the Mystery of the Cross necessarily leads to not understanding the mystery of sorrow and of suffering. This happens when a Christian turns away —in whatever way— from the faithfulness, the love, and ultimately from the Person of Jesus Christ.

And so it happens that the Mystery of the Cross, alongside that of sorrow and of suffering, truly causes scandal and generates fear. Because human nature has been wounded and weakened by sin, experience demonstrates that men instinctively tend to want to escape from suffering and work. The fear of Christians, in particular, can be explained because they have lost their faith in Jesus Christ or because their trust in Him has become somewhat weakened.

Such feelings of fear —of the Cross and of sorrow— have only worsened in the actual crisis of Faith which the Church is undergoing. Pastoral Catechesis usually omits talking about the Cross, the necessity of repentance and penance, or the benefits and Christian meaning of sorrow. In everyday preaching these realities are either left out or doctrines distorting their true meaning are spread. Influential Spiritual Movements within the Church, such as the Neocatechumenal Way, deny the sacrificial character of the Death of Jesus Christ on the Cross, arguing that God the Father cannot possibly allow His Son to undergo such cruelty (according to this Movement, Christ redeemed us by the love He showed us and not by His bloody death). According to Pope John Paul II, Jesus Christ redeemed us by becoming a Man rather than by His death on the Cross, thus

---

[4] 1 Cor 1:23.

spreading a concept that has led to the doctrine of *universal salvation*, which Modernism would then extend throughout the whole Church. Thus, the Mystery of the universal Redemption performed by Jesus Christ through His Death on the Cross was denied.

The new neo–modernist Church proves herself to be a fierce enemy of beliefs such as the Sacrifice of the Cross, original sin and sins in general, the need for penance and sacrifice, and, largely, of everything that would lead to admitting any supernatural element based in Jesus Christ. All of which is but the consequence of a new approach, a new doctrine, according to which Revelation does not judge and define man; rather it is man who judges and decides upon the meaning of Revelation. Thus, the Religion of God has been replaced by the Religion of Man.

These doctrines, supported by Shepherds who propagate them and aided by a powerful propaganda carried out by the *mass media*, have become commonplace in the mentality of the Christian People. *Freedom of conscience* must also be added to these doctrines, which is merely the interpretation of the doctrine of the Second Vatican Council regarding *religious freedom*. These elements lead to a religion based on the worship of man's own will (man is an autonomous, not a heteronomous, being) which has nothing to do with Christianity. This comes as the result of Modernism spreading, throughout the Church, a heresy that has attained far more dissemination than the Arian heresy of the fourth century.

Nevertheless, once the Mystery of the Cross is eliminated, Christianity practically disappears as well.

The fear of suffering for the sake of suffering is indeed a human feeling that can be regarded as something normal and natural. Though it is extremely worsened when it lacks the Christian meaning, which can be clearly noted in the preaching of the highest members of the Hierarchy of the Church who have gone so far as to say that there is *no explanation for the mystery of children's suffering.*

When the ultimate reason and the true explanation of things are overlooked (which are often impossible to attain without resorting to Faith), what follows is a succession of errors that brings about more serious consequences each time.

This is why it is said that there is no explanation for the suffering of children. But neither is there explanation for the suffering of adults when *Faith is lacking* and the teachings of Jesus Christ have been forgotten. In the times that the Church is presently facing, governed as she is by Shepherds who have been seduced by the modernist heresy, what should be a cause of *scandal* to the ears of the faithful has become a *commonplace* that disturbs nobody. And yet, losing the Christian meaning of suffering is tantamount to losing the meaning of the Cross; and losing the meaning of the Cross is losing the meaning of Christianity altogether.

He does not know love who cannot understand the meaning of sorrow. But if it is true that *he that loveth not, knoweth not God,*[5] then whoever admits to not understanding the meaning of sorrow is acknowledging that he does not know God. And if such a person hypocritically calls himself a Christian, then he is just admitting that he has nothing to do with the Person of Jesus Christ.

If Christ set man free from the slavery of the fear of death according to the *Letter to the Hebrews* (2:15), it was on account of His love shown to us on the Cross. Fear of death, embedded in human nature ever since man's first sin, cannot be avoided except through a feeling of a very superior nature: love. Therefore, it can be truly said that love is the only thing, given by Jesus Christ, which frees

---

[5] 1 Jn 4:8.

us from the fear caused by death and turns the sorrow of death into a triumph.

> *If living is to love and to be loved so,*
> *My only longing is to live in Love's glow;*
> *If dying is of love to burn in ardor*
> *That consumes the heart, may I quickly die more.*

The true purpose of Modernism's campaign against the meaning of Christian sorrow (replacing it with the Pharisaical concept of *we do not know what it consists of*) is none other than to efface the Person and the doctrine of Jesus Christ from the conscience of the faithful, thus removing every reference to the Mystery of Salvation given to men by Him. Never before has any heresy launched such a direct attack against the Church.

In order to realize to what extent the fear of the Cross affects the life of a Christian, all one has to do is to regard his personal experience. And yet, what leads us to participate in the sufferings and Death of Christ is essential to a Christian existence. Just as Saint Paul clearly asserts:

Know you not that all we, who are baptized in Christ Jesus, are baptized in his death?[6]

This is, therefore, the end for which Christians are baptized: to participate in the Death of Jesus Christ. Nevertheless, this is a reality that remains forgotten most of the time. Because this essential truth is so important, the Apostle was most insistent upon it:

For the word of the Cross, to them indeed that perish, is foolishness; but to them that are saved, that is, to us, it is the power of

---

[6] Rom 6:3.

God. For it is written: I will destroy the wisdom of the wise, and the prudence of the prudent I will reject.[7]

Isaiah's quote (29:14) demonstrates that the *wisdom* and *prudence* of men often attempt to interfere with God's plans and God's Wisdom, as can be seen (to give an example) in the rejection by the Neocatechumenal Way of Christ's Sacrifice on the Cross. On account of original sin human nature was subjected to an extreme indigence that causes men to think of themselves as being more intelligent than God, and thus able to outline their own destiny and organize the World according to their own understanding. This is due not so much to the weakness of their intelligence as to their sin of *pride*, which is the sin most hated by God and the source of all other sins.

Love or contempt of the Cross causes in the life of every Christian a crucial dilemma that puts his fate on the line: he must decide between love of himself with contempt for God and love of God with contempt for himself. Jesus Christ expressed this very clearly:

He that loveth his life shall lose it, and he that hateth his life in this world, keepeth it unto life eternal.[8]

On the contrary, love of the Cross on the part of a Christian becomes for him not only a hallmark of salvation, it also grants him the necessary *strength* to carry out his journey on earth, which would be impossible without such love, since the Cross is the only path to salvation, first walked by our Lord and upon which every Christian must follow (Jn 14:6), since *the disciple is not above the master, nor the servant above his Lord.*[9]

The life of a Christian is filled with all sorts of obstacles and persecutions:

---

[7] 1 Cor 1: 18–19.
[8] Jn 12:25; Mt 16:25; 10:39; Lk 9:24; 17:33.
[9] Mt 10:24.

If the world hates you, know ye, that it hath hated me before you. If you had been of the world, the world would love its own: but because you are not of the world, but I have chosen you out of the world, therefore the world hateth you. Remember my word that I said to you: The servant is not greater than his master: If they have persecuted me, they will also persecute you.[10]

These obstacles and persecutions cannot be overcome without love for the Cross. And when such love is lacking, men inevitably do without God and become one with the World.

And yet the Cross is not just a painful road through which and with which salvation is attained; it is also, and above all, a *cause of glory,* just as Saint Paul admitted:

But God forbid that I should glory, save in the cross of Our Lord Jesus Christ; by whom the world is crucified to me, and I to the world.[11]

According to which, the mystery of the Cross is not for the Apostle just a way of salvation that is accepted with resignation; rather it is a cause of glory and a reason for joy. This feeling is far from a fear of the Cross and the difficulty in understanding the mystery of sorrow as the Christian experiences them. Once again the gap between the magnificence of the mysteries of Faith and the lukewarmness of the lives of men becomes evident: *He came unto his own, and his own received him not.*[12]

This is how the incredible generosity of God's Heart in offering His love to men becomes evident; as is palpable the equally incredible stinginess of the human heart which, plunged into mediocrity, rejects it. The divine poem, *The Song of Songs,* clearly points this out:

---

[10] Jn 15: 18–20.
[11] Gal 6:14.
[12] Jn 1:11.

> *Open to me, my sister, my darling,*
> *My dove, my perfect one!*
> *For my head is drenched with dew,*
> *My locks with the damp of the night.*[13]

In spite of which men constantly reject this offering by alleging innumerable excuses, as is also noted in the *Song of Songs:*

> *I have put off my garment,*
> *How shall I put it on?*
> *I have washed my feet,*
> *How shall I defile them?*[14]

Not to understand the mystery of the Cross is to not understand the mystery of love. And since man has been created by Love and for love (to love and to be loved on a natural order that is ordained to a supernatural one), to do without the Cross is to do without Love; that is the definitive destruction of man's own destiny.

And this is so because the mystery of the Cross is inexplicable and without meaning if it is not based upon another mystery which justifies it: the mystery of love, which is the reason the Apostle gives for finding in the Cross the grounds for his own glory. The scandal of the Cross becomes a glorious thing when we find out that the Cross is but the result and the final proof of love. And love is the most sublime reality that there is in Heaven as well as on Earth since, ultimately, God Himself is love. And created love, granted to creatures, is a participation in the very Nature and glory of God.

---

[13] Sg 5:2.
[14] Sg 5:3.

As we have said, Love is God (1 Jn 4:8). It has also been established that since it is impossible for man to know God directly in Himself, man has to resort to an indirect manner and through His vestiges. Nevertheless man can know Him in Jesus Christ: *No man has seen God at any time: the only begotten Son who is in the bosom of the Father, he hath declared him.*[15] And it is precisely in Jesus Christ, Who loved us *to the end* (Jn 13:1), where love is fully known by man. And only when love and the Object of that love are known do sorrow and suffering achieve their full meaning.

The fact that suffering now becomes meaningful for man does not imply that he can fully understand it. And yet, a Christian who is *in love* with Jesus Christ is content upon knowing that his love unites him to Jesus Christ, which, ultimately, is what matters most to him. For he who loves Jesus Christ wants above all to live with Him, suffer with Him, and die with Him. And so, for a Christian, understanding the deepest nature of sorrow becomes secondary in the sense that he is satisfied knowing that it is love that gives meaning to his existence.

In order to comprehend the meaning of sorrow in all its depths it would be necessary to know the deepest meaning of sin —bottomless malice and *mysterium iniquitatis*. And in order to understand the former from a Christian point of view it would be necessary to understand the Mystery of Redemption and, above all, the mystery of love. Thus love is the final and most important of all the mysteries; the ultimate explanation of the History of Salvation and of God's Plan for the entire human race.

And so, fully understanding the mystery of love is an impossible task since it would be the same as fully understanding God. Nevertheless, God not only wanted to make Himself somehow known to man —to a degree totally impossible for man to achieve left to

---

[15] Jn 1:18.

his own strength— He also wanted man to share His own Nature, giving him the gift of His own Love. This means, on the one hand, that God has decided to love man in an intimate manner; and, on the other, the possibility for man to correspond to the love of God in the same way, according to the power of his own nature elevated by grace (we must keep in mind that love is always established as a *relationship*).

For the Christian who loves Jesus Christ, *the Mystery of the Cross is definitively explained.* And once the meaning of the Cross is understood, the mystery of sorrow becomes intelligible: the disciple who is in love wants to share the life of his Master until the very end in order to suffer and die with Him. This happens once the disciple no longer belongs to himself; his life is now the life of Jesus Christ and the life of Jesus Christ is his own. This results in a parity of existences, in life as much as in death, in which each one shares in the fate of the other.

Undoubtedly, true love compels one to share the feelings of the beloved person. Saint Paul's words, according to which a Christian must *rejoice with them that rejoice; weep with them that weep*[16] may seem —at least at first sight— as a mere feeling of *solidarity* and even of Christian *charity*. It is true that this apostolic exhortation is nothing but a general principle, clearly exceeded by the deeper and more personal texts of the same Apostle:

For none of us liveth to himself; and no man dieth to himself. For whether we live, we live unto the Lord; or whether we die, we die unto the Lord. Therefore, whether we live, or whether we die, we are the Lord's.[17]

And in another passage:

---

[16] Rom 12:15.
[17] Rom 14: 7–8.

For the charity of Christ presseth us: judging this, that if one died for all, then all were dead. And Christ died for all; that they also who live, may not now live to themselves, but unto him who died for them and rose again.[18]

These texts lead to the paradoxical conclusion —normally forgotten, as usually happens with most truths of our Faith— that a Christian, from the very moment that he belongs to Jesus Christ, no longer is the master of his own life. Therefore, it is not he, but Christ living in him: *And I live, now not I; but Christ liveth in me.*[19] This reality, far from diminishing or removing altogether his own personality —another paradox—, is precisely what ennobles and exalts it: *He that findeth his life, shall lose it: and he that shall lose his life for me, shall find it.*[20]

It cannot be stressed enough that Christianity is a religion of paradoxes; or at least a religion of truth so lofty that its depth and grandeur escape the power of human intelligence. How can anyone say that man is able to truly live his own life only when he loses it...?

Nevertheless, it must be noted that the Christian loses his life in order that Christ may live in him, which, in turn, is an essential condition for man to be able to *live the life of Christ*. This union caused by love, when it is real, brings about the miracle of making the two lovers be only one, *each one keeping, nevertheless, his own identity*. Because love cannot exist if there is not an *each one*: an *I* and a *thou*. To live in Christ is to live in love:

---

[18] 2 Cor 5: 14–15.
[19] Gal 2:20.
[20] Mt 10:39; 16:25; Mk 8:35; Lk 9:24.

Nor height, nor depth, nor any other creature, shall be able to separate us from the love of God, which is in Christ Jesus our Lord.[21]

Man can *be himself* only when he lives in love, since his very nature was created for love. Therefore, he who does not love, not only does not know God (1 Jn 4:8), but he also *remains in death* (1 Jn 3:14). And if the love of Jesus Christ is the only thing that gives meaning to man's life, then it is only natural that whoever is truly in love *cannot live* without the love of the beloved person. And this is not a mere metaphor, since it is Jesus Christ who gives life: *I am come that they may have life, and may have it more abundantly.*[22]

The Mystery of the Cross necessarily implies *totality*. The will of God in redeeming the world was an *excess* of love: *For God so loveth the world, as to give his only begotten Son.*[23] Thus, He wished to carry out the Redemption of the world through the Death of His Son; and not through just any kind of death, but a death carried out in the cruelest, most unimaginable way, undergoing the most painful torture, so infamous then as it was a death reserved only for the worst of criminals. God's reason for doing so can, in a way, be deduced even by the human intellect: because God wanted to offer man the greatest possible proof of love, it was appropriate that He would even undergo death (Jn 15:13), characterized by the note of *totality*, just as the *Letter to the Philippians* states: *He humbled himself becoming obedient unto death, even to the death of the cross.*[24] This is demanded by true love, since absolute *totality* is its nature and essence.

---

[21] Rom 8:39.
[22] Jn 10:10.
[23] Jn 3:16.
[24] Phil 2:8.

One can appreciate now the folly of all those theories which deny not only the bloody Sacrifice of the Cross and, consequently, Love as the essence of Christianity, but even Christianity altogether. These theories have been propagated by the doctrine of *universal salvation*, formulated by Karl Rahner and accepted in the Encyclicals of Pope John Paul II. Nevertheless, the Neocatechumenal Way, oddly approved and blessed by Benedict XVI and confirmed by Pope Francis, has been the main agent responsible for disseminating those theories within the Church. God alone knows the possible devastation and irreparable damage to souls that these errors have caused throughout the Catholic world.

Ostensibly, such profusion of falsehoods and modernist heresies are but the result of human pride, overconfident in its ability to improve God's plans and correct His mistakes. It would seem logical to think that anybody with common sense would rush to reject these falsehoods, for only a blind man would not see the colossal absurdity that stems even from the mere fact of enunciating them. Unfortunately, logic and common sense are not very common among the Christian People as a whole, very much affected by a state of general apostasy which is nourished by the System's efficient and well-organized propaganda bent on putting an end to Catholicism.

Nevertheless, simple explanations regarding the roots of an event, even when true, do not always explain its *deepest cause*. Human pride does not have enough entity to be the reason of a phenomenon so easily and universally accepted and which has caused such a debacle among the Christian People.

The depth and malice of such errors, in addition to their extraordinarily universal acceptance, compel us to look at *Satanism* as their ultimate and only explanation. Unfortunately, in today's Church, where there is a general attitude of rejection of the supernatural, pointing at Satan as the main cause of the current dissolution of the Church is tantamount to causing scandal. Satan's intelligence far exceeds natural human stupidity; hence his great interest in being unnoticed and even ignored which, after all, is the most effective way for him to act freely upon the minds of men.

Saint Paul states that Christ did not send him to baptize but to evangelize; but not in wisdom of words, *lest the cross of Christ should be made void* (1 Cor 1:17). Although these words are not easy to interpret, they surely point to the idea that the Wisdom of God, made manifest on the Cross, infinitely surpasses any claim made by human wisdom and intellect. It is not surprising that Modernism, which so radically rejects the supernatural (and, in so doing, also lowers human nature to degrading levels), and all those who more or less openly follow this heresy, negate so violently the Mystery of the Cross.

THE MYSTERY OF THE PRIESTHOOD[1]

Let a man so account of us as of the ministers of Christ, and the stewards of the mysteries of God. Here now it is required among the dispensers, that a man be found faithful.

(1 Cor 4: 1–2)

1. *Introduction to the theme*

Perhaps never before in the history of the Church have Christians of good will (the *remnant* that still hold fast to the Faith) looked for good Shepherds to guide them as much as modern Christians are searching. Good Shepherds are indeed the ones established by divine institution to lead the People of God along the road to Salvation.

The fact that Jesus Christ Himself determined things so implies that the office and the functions of the ministers of Christ are *essential* for the good progress of the Church, even for her very existence. Without Shepherds, the Flock will go nowhere but to the abyss of perdition.

Nevertheless, not all Shepherds are suited for this office, only those who, according to the words of the Apostle, are true *ministers of Christ and stewards of the mysteries of God*.

---

[1] Preached on December 20, 2015 (a fragment).

It is particularly the priest, since he is the Shepherd most directly in contact with the People of God, who should regard himself, and be regarded by the faithful, in the way Saint Paul describes.[2]

According to the Apostle, therefore, the priest is *the minister of Christ and the steward of the mysteries of God.*

As for being the *minister of Christ*, there seems to be no particular difficulty in understanding the meaning of this expression, at least at first sight. Everybody knows what the role and the function carried out by a minister are. Since the minister depends on the Authority of the one who appointed him —whether he is the King, the President, or the Prime Minister—, he is bound to comply with the rules and must follow faithfully the instructions he has received. His personal initiatives regarding the mission entrusted to him shall be always under the command and control of the Power to whom the minister is subordinated.

One can easily understand that the office of *steward of the mysteries of God* is concerned with the responsibility that this official has regarding those assets entrusted to him (in this case highly valuable goods), which he must administer in order to obtain the best possible yield.

So far everything is apparently clear and the issue at hand seems to be easily comprehended. Nevertheless, we have barely approached the topic in question.

Between the supernatural and the natural world there is an immeasurable distance that cannot be fathomed by the human intellect. Hence, when human language (which is the only available means) tries to express the mysteries of Faith, the words used can

---

[2]Therefore we will focus our attention particularly on the figure of the priest, since he is the Shepherd in the Church who is most in contact with the faithful.

only have a *relative or referential* value. Theologians would agree on the necessity in this case of resorting to analogy.

The priest is indeed a *minister* of the one who appointed him to the office who, in this case, is not a human Ruler but God Himself. Therefore, the rules and issued instructions to be undertaken by the priest, which in themselves are supernatural in origin and endowed with a supernatural content, cannot be considered and measured according to merely human criteria.

Something similar must be said about the priest as a *steward*. He has not been appointed to this office in order to handle and administer just any kind of assets, not even assets considered to be of the highest possible value, but the *mysteries of God*. The mere wording of the expression says it all: to be in charge of the administration of the mysteries of God is not an easy task for the human intellect or the human heart. On the other hand, it is well known that the word *mystery*, when referring to the supernatural, is equivalent to something intractable or inaccessible.

The priesthood is one of the *greatest mysteries* instituted by Jesus Christ in His Church; a mystery for both the sheep entrusted to him and the priest himself.

And this is so because the priest must reproduce in his own life the life of his Master. Hence it would be necessary to understand the mystery of Christ and His office as our Redeemer in order to understand the profound essence of the priesthood. Thus, the *incomprehension*, on the part of the faithful and even of the priest himself, with respect to himself, will be the weight that the priest must bear throughout all his life, as a logical consequence of the task for which he was invested.

According to the *Letter to the Hebrews*, the priest *has been taken from among men;*³ taken from among men or separated from them. This means, if words have indeed any meaning, that the priest is made into a *singular and different* man. This is further confirmed by the text, according to which the priest has been ordained *for the things that appertain to God, that he may offer up gifts and sacrifices for sins.*

And this is exactly how the faithful will always regard the priest. Whether the faithful respect him or look at him with disdain or contempt, they will always consider the priest as *different* from themselves. Loved or hated, the priest will always be a different man; for the satisfaction of some and to the regret of others.⁴

But at the same time the priest is a man *equal to other men*. Hence, the *Letter to the Hebrews* adds that he is especially prepared to understand and have compassion on those who are ignorant and err *because he himself also is compassed with infirmity*.⁵

On the one hand, the fact that the priest sees himself loaded down with misery, compelled to defend himself against the enemies of the soul, and subject to concupiscence is what enables him to understand the infirmities of men, his brethren. On the other hand, he cannot say as his Master did: *Which of you shall convince me of sin?*⁶ for he himself is a sinner. And yet, this twofold condition does not exempt him from the obligation to openly proclaim Christ's

---

³Heb 5:1.

⁴Jesus Christ said about Himself: *He that is not with Me is against Me* (Mt 12:30); therefore nobody can boast of indifference towards Him (this would only mean hatred or contempt). The priest is *another Christ*, and therefore he also takes part in this as his Master did.

⁵Heb 5:2.

⁶Jn 8:46.

Message, and to the best of his abilities, lead souls along the road to salvation. Can there be a greater tragedy?

This singular *dichotomy* of the priest manifests the greatness of God reflected this time in the vulnerable person of a simple man who, invested with the Person of Jesus Christ —this is what men will expect to see in him and nothing else— and overwhelmed with the office of administering the mysteries of God, is obliged to discharge these responsibilities, well aware of his weakness and his sinful condition. This is, once again, another of the loving *jokes* which, in turn, leads to one of the apparent aporias of the Faith: the loftiest, the most exalted thing upon which depends the salvation of souls is placed on the shoulders of a minute and insignificant being: the sublime Wisdom of God Who takes pleasure in showing that He can make possible, through the greatness of His Grace, what seems impossible *because nothing is impossible for God.*[7]

It is not surprising that Modernism has hastened to suppress this dichotomy by precisely eliminating its main element. The enemy of everything supernatural, Modernism has reduced the priest to the condition of a mere man without any other attributes. Using its enormous power of deception, it has convinced him that he *lacks identity* —the well-known *priestly identity* crisis, successfully propagated through significant stress since the early post–conciliar years. Here again appears the abyss of mystery: *Which is greater in this case, the unfathomable wickedness and cunning of the Father of Lies or the terrible credulity of a human nature fraught with weakness?*

And yet, contrary to what some people may think, the priest is not a *divided* man; neither with regards to his person —a mere man invested to administer the mysteries of God— nor with regards to his feelings which he must assume in the existential unity of his

---

[7]Lk 1:37.

personal life, regarding them as the means by which he will share in the mystery of the life and death of Jesus Christ. This constitutes his own cross and his own difficult way to holiness; a way hard, indeed, for any Christian, but still harder for the priest.

The tragedy of his existence has to do with the fact that, even though he sees himself as a mere sinful man, he knows he has been invested with a supernatural ministry which transforms him into *another Christ*. The priest is transformed not just into a follower of the Person and mission of Jesus Christ, or into a mere preacher of His Doctrine, or into a mere administrator, or into a distributor of the means that grant grace, such as the sacraments..., but precisely into *another Christ*.

2. The denial of the mystery and its consequences

One of the greatest tragedies suffered by Catholicism as a major catastrophe happened when the priest *stopped regarding himself as a mystery*. This catastrophe was originated by the Modernist heresy, propagated by strong ideological currents present within the Church after the Second Vatican Council: the priest perceived his existence as completely similar and absolutely identical to that of other men. Hence what usually happens: when something is deprived of an *essential* element belonging to its innermost nature, it no longer is that thing and becomes something else.

As is always the case with Modernism, this deceit came about as a step–by–step approach and, not surprisingly, was propagated everywhere by a gigantic campaign undertaken not only by every available public media but also by the Hierarchy of the Church itself. By then Pope John XXIII had officially proclaimed the openness of the Church to the world by opening the windows of the Vatican.

The first idea to be spread, as an established and unquestionable dogma, was the so-called *crisis of identity of the priest*. In fact, before the Council nobody ever considered that there was such a *crisis*; unfortunately, the fall of human nature was so staggering that man is willing ever since to accept the greatest absurdities as indisputable truths. After twenty centuries, it was now discovered, thanks to the Council, that the nature of the priesthood was unknown, and that there were not enough means to fully explain the role of the priest. This situation coincided with the so-called *promotion of the laity*, another major absurdity, considered then as a fortunate discovery after profound theological studies. At last it was made clear (after centuries of submission and exploitation of the laity by the clergy) that Jesus Christ had forgotten to adequately *promote* the laity as well as to assign them a suitable role within the Church.

Large numbers of priests rushed on to make fools of themselves by striving to appear as laymen, in the futile belief that not showing themselves as priests was the only way to fulfill a ministry... in which they basically did not believe.

The fact that the priest ceased to believe in the *mysterious* nature shrouding his ministerial office entailed a true catastrophe for the Church; a much greater and more terrible catastrophe than what people normally think. As a *supernatural* Society, the Mystical Body of Christ must necessarily be founded and based on the supernatural. But because of Modernism and the desertion of the Hierarchy, the priest ceased to be a *man of God* only to become an *employee*, a member of a New Church that is nothing but another NGO.

The reality known as *priesthood* ceases to exist when it is devoid of its nature as a *mystery*. When the priest is reduced to the condition of being a mere *employee*, he loses that numinous character along with the beauty, attraction, and fascination that always accompany the *supernatural mystery* and which makes man dream of a Salvation beyond this life quite capable of liberating him from the miseries of this world. The priest is a mystery, as is God, of Whom he is a close creature; a mystery that is at the same time *terribly close* and *incommensurably distant*. Just as it happens with poetry when it lacks *charm* (therefore ceasing to be true poetry), the priesthood ceases to exist as a strangely beautiful and fascinating reality the moment it ceases to be a *mystery*. It is then that the former veneration good faithful had for priests is downgraded to a *polite treatment*, and the hatred of the wicked turns into a feeling of absolute *contempt*.

But *mystery* is not just something that comes along with the priesthood as icing on a cake. Mystery belongs to the innermost essence of the priesthood because mystery is the very life of Christ that has been given, in order to be replicated, to a mere man. Ultimately, the priesthood is the result of the love of God for men fulfilled in Jesus Christ. In turn, this bottomless love manifested in Jesus Christ is transferred, as a true copy of His life, to a human being, thus transforming him into *another Christ*. And the Love of Jesus Christ, either considered in the Person of Jesus Christ Himself or in the person of a man chosen to become Him, *cannot be explained without resorting to mystery*.

Therefore, when a priest ceases to regard himself as a supernatural mystery and begins to consider himself as a mere official, the life and Person of Jesus Christ fade away from his life and he no longer keeps any power of loving, becoming a dry tree without fruits. From that very moment, the task he was called to accomplish among men comes to an end, reduced to nothingness. Jesus Christ said it very clearly: *But if the salt lose its savor, wherewith shall it be salted? It is good for nothing anymore but to be cast out, and to be trodden on by men.*[8]

Any speculation about the priesthood, insomuch as it aims to approach truth, must be based on personal experience. For it is only *from within* that we can delve into the knowledge —though a relative one— of its nature. The priesthood can be studied from many different points of view —historically, theologically, sociologically—, but none is sufficiently adequate to grasp the vast depth of its substance. The fact that a mere man lives the identical Life of Christ and carries out His same office cannot be grasped without first acknowledging the mysterious supernatural nature of the priesthood.

The supernatural realities granted to man have such an effect on his nature that from the first moment the priesthood transforms a man into *another Christ*; his entire existence as a human being is wholly transformed; consequently, if concepts and words are indeed meaningful then it is impossible to regard the priest as a man like any other man. Once the Realities from Heaven are bestowed upon him, the priest becomes different from other men to such an extent that neither his fellow men nor he himself could ever understand the nature of his state.

His hands, for example, have been especially *consecrated* to be in contact with the Body of Our Lord in the Sacrament of the Eucharist. If the rite and the ceremony in which this consecration is bestowed are indeed meaningful, then it must be concluded that no other person is authorized to touch the Body of Our Lord. Otherwise, what would be the sense of this solemn ceremony meant for the priest alone and which turns his hands into something *consecrated*? The Old Testament recounts the story of Oza, who was punished

---

[8]Mt 5:13.

by God with instant death for laying his hands on the Ark of the Covenant.[9]

But, once again, Modernism has invaded this topic in its attempt to desacralize what is sacred. The Church herself, incomprehensibly, aided this heretical work of profanation by authorizing the faithful to lay their hands on the Holy Eucharist. By this time, the priest had already abandoned his duties towards the Sacrament and the laity was granted functions that fall outside its competence.[10] Consequences immediately followed; the loss of faith in the Real Presence being not the least of them. The practice of receiving Holy Communion in the hand, treacherously introduced into the post–conciliar Church, has become disastrous for the faith of the Christian People as a whole.

The fact that something as seriously wrong as this practice has been ignored and scarcely denounced by anybody does not diminish its being a collective *profanation* and, ultimately, *scorn* on the part of the Christian People towards something so sublime as the Sacred Eucharist. The universal conspiracy of silence, as though it were the result of an agreement, along with the total indifference toward attitudes that cry out to Heaven, cannot conceal the existence of an offense such as this, about which God is probably not going to remain indifferent.

Therefore, one cannot say that a member of the faithful is exceedingly prudent if, confronted with this practice of laying hands on the Body of Our Lord, he stops and spends some time pondering carefully what he is about to do, and then drops this practice.

---

[9] 2 Sam 6:7.

[10] As always, Modernism specializes in introducing confusion. Here came into play, simultaneously, two intermingled pastoral absurdities meticulously propagated by this heresy: *the secularization of priests* and *the clericalization of the laity*.

Indeed, despite the fact that nobody wants to talk about it, what is happening today in the World, following the path of corruption undertaken by Humanity, is too resounding and obvious. It is an undeniable fact that Humanity has thrust itself on a dizzying slope of *decay* and determined *destruction* of everything that made it survive for ages. Although people fail to admit it, Humanity is devouring itself in a process of self–cannibalism that will soon destroy it. The exaltation and proclamation of Error and Lie as the only possible alternatives; the acknowledgement and legitimization of the most wretched aberrations, which are even being regarded as human triumphs in this *New Age;* the universal hatred toward Christianity; the destruction of every principle that enables man to be regarded as a human being; the appearance of a *New Church* in which the worship of God has been replaced by the worship of man are but a few signs that clearly show that God has forsaken man. Although it might be better and more accurate to say that it was man who first forsook God.

It is absurd to presume that something as serious as the general scorn of the Eucharist, about which nobody talks, dismissing it as unimportant, will remain unpunished: Saint Paul said *Be not deceived, God is not mocked.*[11] In fact, the race that the World has begun at such an accelerated speed towards self–destruction is the most evident proof that divine punishment is *already happening*; and everything suggests that this is just the beginning. Willingly ignoring this fact, along with the attempts made by Society and Governments to conceal and disguise it, will diminish in the least neither its intensity nor the deadline God has planned for it.

It is impossible to fathom the level of stupidity reached by Humanity, as can be demonstrated by establishing a parallelism with

---

[11] Gal 6:7.

the fable of the ostrich. According to this fable, the ostrich buries its head in the ground so as not to see the hunter and thus believes it is avoiding danger. And yet human beings go even further, for they are unwilling to believe that such danger exists: *Likewise as it came to pass, in the days of Lot: they did eat and drink, they bought and sold, they planted and built. And in the day that Lot went out of Sodom, it rained fire and brimstone from heaven, and destroyed them all.*[12]

The World and Modernism claim that the priest is a man like other men, deprived of any supernatural character and of his numinous and sacred state. Nevertheless, against these false pretenses, the Faith in conformity with the divine plan has always regarded the priest as someone *taken from among men for the things that pertain to God.*

Therefore, the priest must not engage in activities concerning human business; not because these activities are in themselves unlawful but rather because they are duties that some may consider as *out of context* for a priest: that is, incompatible with priestly duties and rather belonging to the competence of the laity. The only *testimony*, for example, that a priest working as a plumber may give is that his head and heart have lost their way. The priest *being not totally aware* of the depth and mysterious nature of the priesthood, as we have already said, has become nowadays dreadfully *ignorant* about his person and ministry as a result of a pathological psychopathy that will lead him inevitably to the failure of his existence.

Concerning preaching —one of the main duties of the priest— it is important to note that the topics addressed, the language and the means used to carry out such an arduous task, *must all be supernatural.* Jesus Christ urged his disciples to renounce human means

---

[12]Lk 17: 28–30.

in their work of Evangelization: *Do not possess gold, nor silver, nor money in your purses; nor scrip for your journey, nor two coats, nor shoes, nor a staff; for the workman is worthy of his meat.*[13] The reason is easy to understand, for natural means are not proportionate to supernatural ends; it is, therefore, dangerous to place our trust in the former hoping to obtain the latter.

This explains the catastrophic Pastoral results obtained after the Second Vatican Council. Education systems used in Centers of Formation for the Clergy and Religious (Seminaries, Novitiates, Faculties of Theology), the Pastoral action for Vocations, Systems for imparting Catechesis, etc., seem to place more emphasis in the sciences and in the methods used by human sociology and psychology. Therefore, something as evident as the fact that using merely natural means can only lead to natural results is simply forgotten.

And so, the preaching of a priest must be based neither on human wisdom nor on human reasoning but on the Wisdom and the Word of God that is revealed to men, Whose Wisdom is as distant from the wisdom of man as Heaven is from Earth: *For my thoughts are not your thoughts.*[14] The priest never talks about himself nor does he put forth his own thoughts; since he is another Christ, his words and his Message are the voice of God: *He that heareth you, heareth me.*[15] Hence, human eloquence means nothing to the priest. Saint Paul insisted on this: *And I, brethren, when I came to you, came not in loftiness of speech or of wisdom, declaring unto you the testimony of Christ... And my speech and my preaching was not in the persuasive words of human wisdom, but in showing of the Spirit and power.*[16]

---

[13] Mt 10: 9–10. Cf Mk 6:8; Lk 9:3; 10:4.
[14] Is 55:8.
[15] Lk 10:16.
[16] 1 Cor 2: 1–4.

He went on to stress: *Which things also we speak, not in the learned words of human wisdom; but in the doctrine of the Spirit, expressing spiritual things with spiritual words.*[17]

What is most regrettable is that once the priest of the *New Age* —or of the *New Church*, whatever one wishes to call it— is deprived of the essence of the supernatural and becomes simply an officer, he loses his ability to dream and to open up to the mysterious horizons that transcend him. He resembles an eagle suddenly cast down to Earth which, unable to fly, will surely die of sadness rather than hunger.

For more than half a century now, thousands of priests have been educated in the belief that the Church began with the Second Vatican Council. The immeasurable wealth of Doctrine and Wisdom, together with the heroic lives of thousands of martyrs and saints, and the wonderful effects that grace has worked in millions of Christians for so many centuries, are *unknown to them*. Because of their ignorance about the Person of Jesus Christ —Who in the *New Church* has been demythologized—, they have lost infinite opportunities of knowing and living Love, thus becoming like dried–up fountains or empty wells. They are oblivious to the wonderful world of the interior life and of the *intimacy of love with Jesus Christ* that a life of prayer entails. Post–conciliar theology lacks Life for it has turned away from the fountain of Truth, since both are, ultimately, the same thing: *I am the Way, the Truth, and the Life.*[18]

These priests are like the men Plato describes in his *allegory of the cave*.[19] Because their feet and neck are tied, these prisoners are obliged to look always forward, being able to see only the shadows

---

[17] 1 Cor 2:13.
[18] Jn 14:6.
[19] Plato, *The Republic*, VII.

cast by the light of the fire. These shadows are of animals and men that pass by. The prisoners end up believing that the shadows they see are *the only reality there is*. When one of them is released and goes out and sees the sunlight, and then comes back and explains the truth to the others, none of them is willing to believe him, becoming so irritated that they intend to take his life.

It does not matter that many a priest, mostly belonging to the last generations that have miraculously escaped the influence of modern-day Seminaries, still continue to believe in the supernatural nature of their priesthood, as a proof of the continuity of the Church that the Gates of Hell cannot destroy; they are but an exception in the desolate wasteland that the Land of Catholicism has become. The new priests, and with them almost all Catholics born from the waters that sprouted after the Second Vatican Council, have come to believe, like the men of the Platonic myth, that the mere shadows they contemplate are *the only realities* one may possess or hope for. And yet, the doctrine they have learned, the worship practiced by them, and the pastoral activity for which these priests are being trained are actually *mere shadows* deprived of life and substance. As God lamented through the prophet Jeremiah: *They have forsaken me, the fountain of living water, and have digged to themselves cisterns, broken cisterns, that can hold no water.*[20]

3. "Here now it is required among the ministers, that a man may be found faithful." The importance of "fidelity" in the priestly office

The notion of *fidelity* can be understood as a consent to or an agreement with the consequences of a notion or with the command-

---

[20] Jer 2:13.

ments or instructions received from another person in order to carry them out in perfect conformity to their directives.

But we are dealing here with *fidelity* with respect to the Person of Jesus Christ, which is entirely logical if we consider that a priest as *another Christ* is destined to be the faithful image of the Life of his Master and to propagate His Teachings.

It is evident then that if the priest stops regarding himself as *another Christ* or showing himself as such to the people, the possible fruits of his ministry will vanish as the salt Jesus Christ spoke about which is no longer good for anything; people cast it out and it is trodden on by them (Mt 5:13).

The serious problem of today's Church begins with Modernism, a heresy which has convinced the priest that his ministry lacks supernatural significance and has even severed the bond that joined the priesthood with Jesus Christ, Whom Modernism has tried to *demythologize* by denying His divinity. Herein lies the tragedy of thousands of priests ordained in post–conciliar times, educated in a Modernist–infested Theology that believes the Church began with the Second Vatican Council.

And yet, the fact that many of these priests, mainly those who belong to modern generations, still believe in the supernatural nature of their priesthood is but another proof of the perennity of the Church.

Ultimately, the *mystery* of the priesthood is based on the *mystery* of the Cross and of sacrifice: *Amen, amen I say to you, unless the grain of wheat falling into the ground die, itself remaineth alone. But if it die, it brigheth forth much fruit.*[21] The mysteries of the Cross and death are only meaningful from the point of view of love, which is the ultimate and most important mystery of all mysteries: *I live*

---

[21] Jn 12:24.

in the faith of the Son of God, who loved me, and delivered himself for me.[22]

Obviously, the statement of Jesus Christ quoted before: *Unless the grain of wheat falls into the ground and dies, itself remaineth alone and does not yield fruit*, affects every Christian; but it can be perfectly said that Jesus Christ addressed those words *mainly to the priest*. It is a strong statement that leaves no room for exceptions; so much so that it becomes the only way left for a priest to make his existence abundantly fruitful.

Nevertheless, the priest's decision of accepting sacrifice even to the point of death can only be the result of his love for Jesus Christ, for only He can be the object of his love.

In effect, any merely human love, though real and true, would not only be insufficient, it would also be an obstacle for a priest. It must not be forgotten that, as Saint Paul states, marital love, sanctified as it is by the sacrament of marriage, implies a division in man: *He that is without a wife, is solicitous for the things that belong to the Lord, how he may please God. But he that is with a wife is solicitous for the things of the world, how he may please his wife: and he is divided.*[23] Moreover, we must note that only divine–human love is able to meet the requirements of *perfect love*; that is, totality and absence of conditions: *with thy whole heart, and with thy whole soul, and with thy whole mind.*[24] On the other hand, love for a human person can never be *absolutely exclusive and unconditional*; hence Jesus Christ distinguished between the love of God as the first commandment and the love of neighbor as the second (Mt 22: 37–39).

---

[22] Gal 2:20.
[23] 1 Cor 7: 32–34.
[24] Mk 12:30.

If the grain of wheat, in this case the priest, must fall into the ground and sacrifice himself to the point of death, he must also *love to the point of death*. And this expression has a much deeper connotation than the meaning commonly ascribed to it; it must be understood as the *power of love that surpasses and transcends any other human capability for love*. For it is indeed impossible to love a human person in the same way and to the same degree of intensity as one loves the Person of Jesus Christ.

We must note that love is a reciprocal relationship between an *I* and a *thou* that mutually requite each other's love. But while merely human love is based on a purely human relationship —a human person loving another human person—, divine–human love is based on a divine–human relationship: a divine Person with a human one. And as we have seen, love offered to a human person can never be the same as the love whose object is the Person of Jesus Christ.

The priest cannot but love in a divine–human way, or rather a human–divine way. Indeed, he must be a *man in love*; but so much in love that other men could not match the measure of his love. The priest cannot feel content, as any other Christian may feel, with just *having devotion* toward Jesus Christ or *loving* Jesus Christ; the intensity of his love for his Master must be *to the point of madness*. We must keep in mind that the expression *to the point of madness*, which human love uses in a metaphorical or figurative speech, acquires here its true meaning. *Madness*, indeed, normally refers to a psychological disorder, a pathological state which is an illness in man. But *madness* can also refer to an extreme *exaltation* of the human mind and will, so forceful as to inflame the feelings of man's heart; this is the meaning given by human lovers. This is true for merely human love but not for divine–human love; for in divine–human love the feelings reach such a degree of rapture

—feelings that cannot be measured for they go beyond the threshold of the natural into the supernatural— that they surpass by far the intensity of the feelings accompanying the psychological disorder or even the love between two human persons. When Saint Paul speaks about the Cross as *madness* and a *stumbling block* he is alluding to how the Jews and Gentiles regarded the Cross; but in no way did he mean to say that the Cross was not indeed madness and a stumbling block. Since the Cross is the greatest proof of love ever given (Jn 3:16; 15:13), it identifies with love as its *epiphany*. Hence love (perfect love), which in itself surpasses all the powers of the human intellect and heart, cannot be regarded by men except as being always subject to dimensions such as quantity, temporality, circumstances, etc. (imperfect love); therefore, it can be termed as foolishness in a metaphorical sense only. Nevertheless, love has a natural tendency to exceed all the abilities of human perception and appreciation (imperfection tends towards perfection), and so true love is indeed a *divine* madness that has nothing or little to do with psychological pathologies or merely human love.

In this regard, the priest is destined to fall in love *to the point of madness* with his Master and, consequently, to fulfill the delicate mission entrusted to him.

The choice of giving up his life totally and unconditionally, which the priest is called to do, requires loving *unto the end*, just as Jesus Christ did Who, having loved His own who were in the world, *loved them unto the end.*[25] This expression must also be understood literally and with all the significance that the evangelical text contains: *unto the end*; that is, into an endless dimension. On the other hand, since love is a reciprocal relationship, and Jesus Christ loves man

---

[25] Jn 13:1.

endlessly, the reciprocal human answer in divine–human love cannot be, therefore, of a different nature.

It happens to the supernatural character of the priesthood and its transcending all that is merely human what happens with the loftiest realities about which we cannot speak given the inability of language; in which case one can always resort to Poetry as the last option. Once prose has exhausted its possibilities and little or nothing else can be said, poetic language, by *suggesting* and *evoking*, acquires the magical power of instilling in the human soul sublime realities which seem to wander in mysterious regions, where the soul *senses* the presence of *something* ineffable that cannot explain itself, but which the human soul believes to be the only thing that could fill her emptiness since she has always lived with feelings of longings and yearnings that nothing or nobody satiated. Is it Beauty? Or surely Goodness? Perhaps Truth? Perhaps the three of them, but certainly something else. As it happens, the soul, through the *mystery* of poetry and feelings evoked by poetic language, lives under the impression that something still unknown is missing. Could that something be the presence of a *person*, the only unique and exclusive being able to make *his own* those realities thus leaving room for the mystery of Love? For Beauty, and Goodness, and even all created things, to the extent that they reflect those realities to a greater or lesser degree, can attract with their seductive charms; but only a *person* who possesses them is able to elicit love in another person.

4. Scheduled excursion to the field of Mystical Experience or the last stage of the journey into the Mystery of the Priesthood

What makes the priest different from any other man forces him to live in a peculiar type of solitude. But it happens that man is a social being by nature and so has been created to love; hence the *steward of the mysteries of God* faces two paradoxes that significantly interfere with his life.

First of all, the priest will always be regarded by his fellow men as a strange and peculiar person; and yet, he is required to maintain a full-time dedication to those to whom he has devoted his life and in whose favor he has been appointed: *Taken from among men, is ordained for men.*[26]

Of course, the poor concept that the priest may have of himself turns any relationship with his brethren into something common and fruitless. This is why only *eminently supernatural* friendship with his brethren is licit to a priest, which not only does not negate for him the possibility of maintaining genuine friendship with his brethren, but also gives him special access to the soul and problems of each one of them. Nevertheless, the priest will always be for all of them the *man of God*, they will regard him —with love or with hate— as a different being.

Secondly, his special situation will lead him to consider himself as one living *in solitude*. And it is in this sense that much has been said and written about the *loneliness of the priest*, regarding him as a necessary victim of a singular tragedy and thus making him a sort of *hero by accident.*

But those —whether inside or outside the priesthood— who think like this only show their ignorance as regards the meaning

---

[26] Heb 5:1.

and significance of this sacred ministry. Because the fact that the priest is destined to live detached, or as a stranger among men, in no way means that he is called to live in solitude. It is common among humans that they draw conclusions while using false premises or forgetting to introduce another premise which is precisely essential in the reasoning process.

The truth is that no one is destined to live in solitude because it would go against the demands of human nature. And least of all the priest, called as he is to live and behave according to higher standards of perfection than those of any other man. Do not forget that the priest, although not equal to Christ, True God and Perfect Man, is like *another Christ*; although it is also true that *the disciple is not above his master: but every one shall be perfect, if he be as his master.*[27]

We have stressed the point that the priest is somebody *in love par excellence* and that the object of his love cannot be other than the Person of Jesus Christ. But then, where is the famous solitude of the priest? The idea of someone in love without reference to another person is contradictory; on the other hand, *narcissism* has always been regarded as absurd and aberrant. He who is in love may suffer the *absence* of the beloved person, but he will never be *lacking* the person who is the object of his love.

This is what drives the priest, by strict necessity, to maintain a special relationship of intimacy and love with Jesus Christ. Therefore, when this relationship does not exist, and the priest tries to replace it with another purely human relationship, he is bound for a state of spiritual schizophrenia; it is at this moment that he finds himself not only confronting true *solitude*, which would be less se-

---

[27] Lk 6:40.

rious, but in a situation of *internal tearing* that leads inevitably to personal failure.

Lack of love does not and cannot exist in the ill–named *priestly loneliness*. But the *absence* of the beloved is indeed a frequent reality, sharp and painful. This absence is an ordinary and normal event in any purely human love relationship; it acquires special shades in the spiritual itinerary of any serious Christian; and it finally reaches degrees of high intensity and special peculiarity as one of the phenomena of the so–called *mystical life*: perhaps the very life of a priest...? Let us see, but not before noting that, in reality, mystical life has two special characteristics, among many others, which usually go unnoticed.

Firstly, the *absence* we are talking about here does not produce feelings of *loneliness* in the lover, as one might expect; consequently, we are facing again another paradoxical situation which, in this case, can be promptly explained. In effect, the alleged absence of the beloved brings about in the lover intense feelings of nostalgia and longing which immediately result in strengthening the bond of love. These phenomena are part and parcel of any divine–human relationship of love.

Secondly, reciprocity: one of the essential characteristics of the relationship of love which, applied to the situation of *absence of the beloved person* becomes particularly relevant in the divine–human relationship of love.

What is meant here is that the sense of absence (whether this absence is real or apparent is not relevant for him who is in love) affects not only the human party of this relationship but also, although it may seem surprising, it affects *the divine part*. And it could not be otherwise if we take into consideration the logic of one of the most important properties of any relationship: *reciprocity*. Either there is or there is not a relationship; God never favors situations which resort to mere appearance.

Hence, Saint John of the Cross is the one who masterly expresses these reciprocal sentiments in one of his stanzas:

> *In solitude she lived,*
> *And in solitude built her nest;*
> *And in solitude, alone*
> *Hath the Beloved guided her,*
> *In solitude also wounded with love.*[28]

As far as the divine–human relationship is concerned, this situation of reciprocity, born out of the feelings of longing caused by the absence of the loved one, is not a literary construction invented by the aesthetic convenience of the amatory arts of all times, but a reality required by the same logic of the relationship, and which is endorsed by the most ancient texts describing divine–human love. The Sacred Book of the *Song of Songs* describes the longings of the bride in her search for the Bridegroom:

> *Tell me, O thou whom my soul loveth,*
> *Where thou feedest,*
> *Where thou makest thy flock to rest at noon:*
> *Lest I begin to wander*
> *After the flocks of thy companions?*[29]

And the longings of the Bridegroom to be next to the bride are not less intense, as the *Song of Songs* describes. One must note

---

[28] Saint John of the Cross, *Spiritual Canticle*.
[29] Sg 1:7.

The Mystery of Priesthood

the piling up of amorous compliments with which the Bridegroom addresses Himself to the bride, expressing His ardent desires, so that she may allow Him to be with her.

> *Open to me, my sister, my love,*
> *My dove, my undefiled:*
> *For my head is full of dew,*
> *And my locks of the drops of the nights.*[30]

An important text of the *Song of Songs* expresses in the best possible way this reciprocity of feelings which even results in an equality between the Bridegroom and the bride. The text describes a challenge for a joust or combat of love between the two lovers:

> *He brought me to the banqueting house,*
> *and his banner over me was love.*[31]

Forgetting this point seems to have led to an important failure in classical and traditional Christian spirituality, including Mysticism. The loss of the note of *reciprocity* —or placing it in the background— in the divine–human relationship of love, may have been the occasion of the appearance of a spirituality too unilateral in which God is everything and the soul is nothing more than a passive receptor of God's grace. The very expressions *Contemplation* or *Passive Contemplation* speak for themselves.

---

[30] Sg 5:2.

[31] Sg 2:4. For a tentative explanation of the mystery of the combat between God and man under the guise of a joust, see: Alfonso Gálvez, *The Mystery of Prayer*, pgs. 147 ff. New Jersey, 2015.

The dogma of the universal need of grace, absolutely fundamental, does not negate the also essential dogma in Catholic theology of human freedom; its denial or reduction to nothing would be nothing less than the denial of the value of *merit* on the human part. What would happen then to the reality and the great importance of the divine–human relationship of love?

Some may ask, *What does this mystical speculation have to do with priestly ministry?* And the answer is simple: Nothing and everything.

It has nothing to do with it; or very little if one wants to answer this question in a less radical way; in effect, the priest is called to holiness certainly, but not to a mystical life. It should be noted that holy life and mystical life are not synonymous terms. While it is true that there cannot be an authentic mystical life without holiness, holiness without a mystical life is quite conceivable.

At the same time, this issue has a lot to do with the ministerial priesthood. It is true that mystical life implies special graces from Heaven and also a special generosity on the part of the recipient. To begin with, the priest is not called to be a mystic, at least in its strict sense and as this reality has usually been understood by the Doctrine. But if we consider mystical life as a life of love for Christ *to the very end*, and if we agree that the priest is especially called to be truly *in love with Christ*, in the full meaning of this expression, then we must agree that the priest cannot be thought of as a stranger to whom the highest zenith of a life of intimacy with Christ would be forbidden.

The priesthood is one of the loftiest mysteries ever created by God within His Plan for the History of Salvation. As the mystery the priest is, he cannot understand himself or be understood by his brethren. He is like a work of art that God wants to make for

His own glory and personal enjoyment as well as for the joy and usefulness of men, who are called to benefit extraordinarily from this instrument... although neither they nor the instrument itself will ever understand its internal functioning.

The tragedy of the modern Church, and of many priests as well who belong to this time, is that they no longer believe this mystery. Post–conciliar theology, which draws its sustenance exclusively from the Second Vatican Council and which has lost all contact with the Fountain of Waters that flow from the side of Jesus Christ, is therefore a dead theology which cannot ever offer Life. The priest who has fed exclusively on it no longer is the *man of God* and has become like any other man.

But the words of Jesus Christ concerning the Church: *The Gates of Hell shall not prevail against Her* will go on resounding, as well as His other words addressed to those He elected to continue with His Mission: *As the Father has sent me, so I am sending you.* His elected are sent, therefore, with His same mission, to make His life their own lives and to distribute among men the same innumerable graces; to do in all things as their Master did.

And for the glory of God and to the joy of the Church, it is a fact that there are still men who believe in the Words of Jesus Christ and love Him firmly. Therefore, they have consented to be *taken from among men* and to lose their own lives to become *other Christs*. As the Bible says in the First Book of Kings: *And I have left me seven thousand men in Israel, whose knees have not been bowed before Baal.*[32]

---

[32] 1 Kings 19:18.

EPILOGUE

When I first began writing this book of Sermons I thought to insert in it, as a poor imitation of Ortega y Gasset, a *Prologue for Traditionalists* and an *Epilogue for Progressists*.[1] But I soon desisted after considering that *traditionalists*, on account of *what is happening nowadays*, would most likely not take me seriously and might even believe I was trying to pull their leg. As for *progressists* (a euphemism referring to modernists, or Catholic members of the *New Church*), it would be useless to write anything addressed to them since they would never read it.

It seemed best, therefore, to observe what is customary and discard fancy and, indeed, amusing titles. Writing a book of sermons is in itself something quite daring; I knew I was undertaking an insane task.

Not because this task would be like crying in the wilderness. When John the Baptist referred to himself as the *Voice shouting in the desert*, he was convinced that, despite everything, his preaching would not be altogether useless. Saint John was a true saint, and many centuries would have to pass before the intellectual powers of man would be brought into question. On the other hand, crying in the wilderness does not necessarily imply a waste of time: there is always the chance that a caravan or a Bedouin looking for a lost

---

[1] José Ortega y Gasset, *The Revolt of the Masses*, 1929. In 1937 a *Prologue for the French* and an *Epilogue for the English* was added.

and thirsty explorer may pass by; you never know. Jesus Christ also spoke to His disciples about things hidden, although with the certitude that in time these things would be preached from the rooftops (Mt 10:27).

Laughing to keep from crying. Foolishness is an earmark of those serious situations happening around us that are caused or allowed by human stupidity. After all, sin is the greatest and most unconceivable stupidity that man can commit, although sometimes the intensity of the wickedness conceals the foolishness of the sinner.

Certain things viewed from the outside cannot but give rise to feelings of bewilderment in those who observe them. In some special cases, in which the degree of foolishness can reach extremely high levels, the observer will not know whether to cry or laugh; moved not so much by the ludicrousness of the situation as by the necessity of finding a way of mitigating the feeling of horror at what he is seeing. I think Jacinto Benavente was right when he considered laughter as a gateway similar to what happens *when from his fairground booth Tabarin claimed the attention of every passerby, from the solemn doctor who momentarily reined in his well–trained mount in order to unfurrow for an instant his brow, always laden with grave thoughts, by listening to some witticism of the merry farce, down to the rowdy criminal who spent his leisure time there hour after hour, deluding his hunger with laughter; and the prelate and the lady of quality and the great lord, seated in their carriages, as well as the jolly servant girl, the soldier, the merchant, and the student. There people of all ranks, who wouldn't have forgathered anywhere else, infected one another with their enjoyment, for often the solemn man would laugh not so much at the farce as at the sight of the easily tickled man laughing, and the sage would laugh at the ninny, the poor would laugh seeing the great lords, usually all scowls, laugh, and the grandees would*

Epilogue

laugh at the laughter of the poor, their consciences pacified by the thought: "Poor people laugh, too!" [2]

Therefore, laughter aside, attempting to write a book of sermons during times of darkness and dumbness,

> *God has given them the spirit of insensibility;*
> *eyes that they should not see;*
> *and ears that they should not hear,*
> *until this present day.*[3]

is either a part–mad, part–bold adventure or just a way of taking as a joke what clearly has an obstinate and unyielding character: what has no way out, as some may say. In short, writing this book would be an odd way of choosing laughter over weeping.

I affirm that preaching sermons —talking about the Teachings of Revelation— in today's world is a daring endeavor, since everyone knows that *the Word of God has been silenced*, although nobody has the courage to admit it.

And I say this in spite of the words Saint Paul addressed to his disciple Timothy, which seemingly contradict me: *But the Word of God is not bound.*[4]

Nevertheless, the Word of God, truth in itself and uttered for men of all times and places, stumbles upon unique applications under the various circumstances that will come together at the End of Times. What is the point, for example, of talking about the necessary coexistence of the wheat with the thistle at the time of the *Great Apostasy*, a time when there will be practically no wheat but only thistle in the field?

---

[2] Jacinto Benavente, *The Bonds of Interest*, Prologue.
[3] Rom 11:8.
[4] 2 Tim 2:9.

On the other hand, denying that in the *New Church*, born of modernist trends following the Second Vatican Council, a muzzle of silence has been placed on the Word of God is tantamount to denying what is self–evident. And even though many people do deny this, the facts are irrepressible, unyielding, and unwilling to disappear.

Writing or speaking up in defense of the truths of the Faith, while being aware that there is a sword of Damocles over one's own head, in order to address a People who have chosen the lie and openly reject hearing the truth, is a task that can only be accomplished by an act of obedience to the requirements of God's love.

If we believe that the Bible is indeed the Word of God revealed by the Holy Spirit, and if we admit that the Spirit certainly knows all things contained in the Scriptures, be they past, present, or future, we must conclude that it is necessary to take seriously the words that the Apostle Saint Paul addressed to his disciple Timothy:

I charge thee: —let us play close attention to these solemn opening words— *preach the word, be instant in season, out of season: reprove, entreat, rebuke in all patience and doctrine* —let us notice Saint Paul's exhortation to patience and the insistence on doctrine, no matter what. *For there shall be a time, when they will not endure sound doctrine; but, according to their own desires, they will heap to themselves teachers, having itching ears: And will indeed turn away their hearing from the truth, but will be turned unto fables.* And indeed, this is how things will happen and the apostle or evangelist must be aware of it. Nevertheless, Saint Paul does not encourage resorting either to charism or miracles, or to any other magical method or infallible solution; he rather points to the only way out left to the disciple of Him Who, ultimately, achieved victory

Epilogue

by dying on the Cross: *But be thou vigilant, labor in all things, do the work of an evangelist, fulfill thy ministry.*[5]

He who propagates the Faith cannot put his trust in seeing the fruit of his works. It is enough for him to obey and evangelize, without expecting to obtain any other reward except having obeyed the commandments and requirements of Love. The *Parable of the Sower* tells us that the sower accomplished his task and that the seed was scattered on diverse places with varying results: some fell by the wayside, and the birds of the air came and ate them up. Some others fell upon stony ground, where they could not put roots; they were scorched as soon as the sun was up. Others fell among thorns, and the thorns grew up and choked them. *Only a small portion of seeds fell upon good ground* and they finally brought forth fruit,[6] which would be gathered later by the sower.

Nevertheless, it could happen that he might not have the chance to see the fruit, which is not an obstacle for the fruit to actually exist.

And I have appointed you, that you should go, and should bring forth fruit; and your fruit should remain.[7]

That you should bring forth fruit, says the Lord; the least important thing is whether the sower sees this fruit. What is expected from the sower, what is truly important, is his blind confidence borne of his love for the owner of the field who sent him to work in that field.

To preach the Word of God while being threatened by the sword of Damocles over one's head is an adventure for audacious men. Christians, though, easily forget that:

---

[5] 2 Tim 4: 1–5.
[6] Mk 4: 1–9.
[7] Jn 15:16.

From the days of John the Baptist until now, the kingdom of heaven suffers violence, and the violent bear it away.[8]

Therefore, when the aim is to reach the Kingdom of God, we must count on the possibility that concepts such as violence, visciousness, and snatching enter into play: *I came not to send peace, but the sword.*[9] This is why, in these times of apostasy and persecution (cowardice, in the case of the Spanish Bishops), many have shirked their duty of preaching the Word of God.

But to make a fuss of all this is just idle talk. The duty of preaching the Word of God *is not an option* for him who has received the precept of evangelizing. In effect, our Lord's *commandment* is not a pious counsel but rather a comminatory instruction:

Going therefore, teach ye all nations... Teaching them to observe all things whatsoever I have commanded you.[10]

Saint Paul expressed this same idea with unambiguous words: *For Christ sent me not to baptize, but to preach the gospel.*[11]

On the other hand, the greatest event that centuries have witnessed is the descent of the Word of God in the midst of men:

For while all things were in quiet silence, and the night was in the midst of her course, Thy almighty word leapt down from heaven from thy royal throne, as a fierce conqueror into the midst of the land of destruction. With a sharp sword carrying thy unfeigned commandment and he stood and filled all things with death, and standing on the earth reached even to heaven.[12]

The Word of God will be either heeded or rejected by men, but It will always have decisive and sudden effects, even devastating:

---

[8] Mt 11:12.
[9] Mt 10:34.
[10] Mt 28: 19–20.
[11] 1 Cor 1:17.
[12] Wis 18: 14–16.

For the Word of God is living and effectual, and more piercing than any two-edged sword; and reaching unto the division of the soul and the spirit, of the joints also and the marrow, and is a discerner of the thoughts and intents of the heart.[13]

Jesus' instructions to his disciples are also final:

But into whatsoever city you enter, and they receive you not, going forth into the streets thereof, say: Even the very dust of your city that cleaveth to us, we wipe off against you. Yet know this, that the kingdom of God is at hand. I say to you, it shall be more tolerable at that day for Sodom, than for that city.[14]

And yet, the Word of God did not descend from Heaven to dwell among men with the intention of condemning them, but of saving them and filling them with true Life:

The words that I have spoken to you are spirit and life.[15]

Hence Jesus Christ's sorrowful complaint:

Search the Scriptures, for you think in them to have life everlasting; and the same are they that give testimony of me. And you will not come to me that you may have life.[16]

According to this, the Life of men depends on their listening and receiving the Word of God. The concept *life* must be understood according to the supernatural meaning of true *Life* given in the New Testament, in contrast to its merely natural meaning. Thus the importance of the role of the evangelist who preaches the Word of God: the number of souls that will be eternally saved or damned depends on how he carries out his ministry.

---

[13] Heb 4:12.
[14] Lk 10: 10–12.
[15] Jn 6:64.
[16] Jn 5: 39–40.

Therefore, it is *essential* that the preacher of the Word, as regards the way he carries out his ministry, should abide by the specific instructions received from the One Who entrusted him with and made him responsible for administering and spreading that Word.

These instructions are contained mainly in various passages of the Apostle Saint Paul:

For Christ sent me not to baptize, but to preach the gospel: not in wisdom of speech, lest the cross of Christ should be made void...[17] *And I, brethren, when I came to you, came not in loftiness of speech or of wisdom, declaring unto you the testimony of Christ. For I judged not myself to know anything among you, but Jesus Christ, and him crucified. And I was with you in weakness, and in fear, and in much trembling. And my speech and my preaching was not in the persuasive words of human wisdom, but in showing of the Spirit and power; that your faith might not stand on the wisdom of men, but on the power of God*[18] *...Which things also we speak, not in the learned words of human wisdom; but in the doctrine of the Spirit, comparing spiritual things with spiritual.*[19]

These passages contain the *key to all Christian Preaching* as well as the key to the failure of so many homilies, sermons, exhortations, speeches, teachings, catechesis, pastoral documents, etc., which not only do not teach anything to the faithful, but which quite frequently *lead them along the road to perdition.*

According to the Apostle, his preaching is always carried out *with words learned from the Spirit*, and only with words learned from the Spirit, for what proceeds from the Spirit of God can only be expressed and taught with words learned from the Spirit of God. As

---

[17] 1 Cor 1:17.
[18] 1 Cor 2: 1–5.
[19] 1 Cor 2:13.

the Apostle himself says: *comparing spiritual things with spiritual words*. These two expressions *spiritual things* and *spiritual words* must be understood in their proper sense, that is: as things pertaining to God and words heard and learned from and filled with the Spirit.

Unfortunately, for a long time now Christians have come to regard the Revelation contained in the Scriptures as *pious reading*. In the best–case scenario they even regard it as being comforting and as nourishment for the spiritual life, but not as *the guideline that proceeds from God and must, as such, rule all their thoughts and actions*. And so, it is frequent that in the Centers of formation of candidates to the priesthood they do not refer to the Bible (interpreted by Tradition and the Magisterium) as the true source for the candidates to learn how to preach and its pastoral implications. Ultimately, what happens is that the *New Church* seems to consider the Documents of Vatican II as a sufficient, even exclusive, source for carrying out the task of preaching.

Nevertheless, in order to preach *with words learned from the Spirit* —the only way to achieve fruitful preaching— it is absolutely necessary *to learn to talk with the Spirit*. And the Spirit is a Person, which means that the way of addressing Him is by using words and thoughts which, at the same time as they yearn to be heard they have an equal desire to listen to that Person. In other words, talking to the Person of the Spirit involves the willingness of having with that Person what is commonly known as a *life of prayer* which, insomuch as the Spirit is the expression of the Love of God, cannot be anything other than the loving dialogue that Christian prayer always entails.

The consequence here is also obvious and self–evident: if the preacher of the Word is not a man of prayer, his task will be absolutely fruitless.

We have already seen that the role of the Word —the *Word* of the Father— in the History of the World and in the History of Salvation is essential and fundamental. First of all, everything was made by the Word:

All things were made by Him and without Him was made nothing that was made...[20] *For in Him were all things created in heaven and on earth, visible and invisible... All things were created by Him and in Him.*[21]

Regarding the History of Salvation, there are texts ranging from the Book of Wisdom (Wis 18: 14–15) to the decisive text of Saint John: *And the Word was made flesh and dwelt amongst us.*[22]

Therefore, in the History of Humanity and of Salvation —in fact they are one and the same— the role undertaken by the *Word* of the Father —the Word— is essential, to say the least.

In order to understand this better we need to keep in mind, from the point of view of Creation and Salvation, that the Word of the Father is a twofold reality: ontological, pertaining to *creation*, and propagating, related to *proclamation*, since all things were made by the Word, including the Salvation of men (Creator and Savior) and through the Word of God *communicating* Himself to men, letting them know His Will and Teachings (Preceptor and Teacher).

Saint John of the Cross tied these two roles together when he famously taught that the Father, with only one Word (His Word)

---

[20] Jn 1:3.
[21] Col 1:16.
[22] Jn 1:14.

said all that He had to say.[23] According to this the Word was everything, in Him were all things, and all things came through Him. Nevertheless, this text of the Poet of Fontiveros probably has not been sufficiently studied in connection with the essential didactical characteristic of the *Word —Verbum—* as an instrument of communication:

The Word was the true light, which enlighteneth every man that cometh into this world.[24]

Therefore, the *Word* is simultaneously ontological and didactic.

God created man into His image and likeness, and He made him to share His own divine Nature. It is, therefore, natural that a certain participation in some of the Attributes and Functions of the Divine Essence were bestowed on man through grace *mutatis mutandis* or from an analogical point of view. Unbelievable but true.

And so God has bestowed on men the power to perform actions that are essentially *divine* by using merely human words. Think, for example, of the words *This is my Body*, or *This is the Chalice of my Blood* or *I absolve you from your sins*.

When merely human words are transformed through grace into the *Word of God*, they are endowed with the miraculous power to carry out *institutional* tasks: human lips utter them as if Jesus Christ Himself is the one talking:

He that heareth you, heareth me; and he that despiseth you, despiseth me.[25]

Moreover, when the word of the disciple is founded on faith and trust in his Lord, it acquires miraculous and omnipotent qualities:

---

[23] Saint John of the Cross, *The Ascent of Mount Carmel*, II, 22, 3–4.
[24] Jn 1:9.
[25] Lk 10:16.

For Amen I say to you, if you have faith as a grain of mustard seed, you shall say to this mountain: remove from hence hither, and it shall remove; and nothing shall be impossible to you.[26]

Hence the mysterious, tremendous, and sublime power of the human word when man is *connected* with God. It is impossible, once the gifts of grace are taken into account, not to find a relationship based on analogy between the human word and the *Word* of the Father, on an ontological as well as on a functional level.

Unfortunately, quite often the preacher of the *Word of God* is not aware of the amazing power that God has bestowed upon his lips: *If they have kept my word, they will keep yours also.*[27] And when the word is not heard and does not bear fruit it is because it is not the Word of God that is being preached but a merely human one.

The twofold function, ontological and didactic, of the *Word* cannot but leave an analogical impression even on purely human words. The functional element of the human word is also somehow ontological. In effect, word as a *communication* necessarily implies the task of handing down truth; which means to *translate* or to put into the hands of the brethren part of the being of Him Who speaks, since it is a given that the word entrusts the listener with the true feelings of the heart of the person who utters the word; hence the wickedness of the lie.

Therefore, we must acknowledge the ontological and didactic function of the word. And so, it is impossible to be unaware of the power of the human word when it is enlivened by the divine attribute of love: could such a word cause death out of love?

---

[26] Mt 17:19.
[27] Jn 15:20.

Epilogue

> *If you should see me again,*
> *Down in the glen where the singing blackbirds fly,*
> *Do not say you love me then*
> *For, were you ever to repeat that sweet sigh,*
> *On hearing it, I may die.*

The language of love, where excitement often prevents the word from being more than mere stammering, has the power to arouse such deep feelings that the enamored soul believes she will not be able to overcome them. This is commonplace especially in mystic poetry, as can be clearly noted in this stanza by Saint John of the Cross.

> *All those that haunt the spot*
> *Recount your charm, and wound me worst of all*
> *Babbling I know not what*
> *Strange rapture, they recall,*
> *Which leaves me stretched and dying where I fall.*[28]

In the peculiar and typical language of Poetry, where words acquire their best meaning, the word *babbling* takes on an equivocal or ambiguous sense that is able to raise feelings of *bewilderment* in the mind of the reader: does the impossibility of words to express themselves clearly —or to be understood clearly— come from the feelings of those who utter them or rather from the emotions that overcome the heart of those who hear them? The ambiguity surrounding the words, do they come from the words themselves or exclusively from those who listen to them?

---

[28] Saint John of the Cross, *Spiritual Canticle*.

Words of love have command even over the powers of nature:

> *Burning longings in my breast,*
> *I came where my Love expected me to be.*
> *In his silent hidden nest;*
> *While I spoke to him softly*
> *He silenced the whispers of the wind for me.*

At other times, those words are able to urge someone to undertake daring adventures towards the unknown:

> *In your orchard a small bird,*
> *In grief at your absence, sang with a sad sound;*
> *And, when your soft voice she heard,*
> *Quickly rose up from the ground,*
> *To search in her swift flight where you could be found.*

It is common that the language of love, due to its intimate nature that makes it to be heard and understood only by those who love each other, remains thus as mere whispers to any other person:

> *The calm, resplendent deep seas*
> *With peaceful, blue–white waves, rocked and gently stirred,*
> *The soft echoes on the breeze,*
> *Songs of mermaids without word,*
> *A sweet whisper of love that is barely heard.*

If the human word, enlivened by love, is sacred and powerful, we can only imagine what it is able to become when it is transformed into a *vehicle of the Word of God*. Thus the importance of Christian preaching. And thus the foolishness of those who are unaware of the significance of the mission entrusted to them as preachers of the Word. And hence the seriousness of the sin of those within the Church who are bent on stifling the task of evangelization: when the sower could not go out to sow the seed... because he was forbidden.

Index of Quotations from the New Testament

Matthew

3: 3, **28**
5: 3, **48**
   13, **277**, **284**
6: 2, **129**
   24, **48**, **126**
   33, **12**, **163**
7: 14, **42**, **52**, **226**, **228**, **243**
9: 36, **234**
   37–38, **251**
10: 9–10, **281**
    22, **245**
    24, **260**
    27, **298**
    34, **302**
    37, **61**
    39, **41**, **248**, **260**, **265**
11: 7–8, **126**
    12, **302**
12: 30, **53**, **272**
16: 18, **234**
    25, **43**, **248**, **260**, **265**
17: 19, **308**
19: 23–24, **48**
20: 1–16, **238**
22: 37, **13**, **100**
    37–39, **285**
23: 8, **108**
    10, **108**
    13–16, **126**
    15, **131**
    25, **128**
24: 13, **42**, **245**
25: 15, **240**
    21, **30**
    31–46, **56**
28: 19–20, **65**, **111**, **252**, **302**
    20, **227**

Mark

4: 1–9, **301**
6: 8, **281**
7: 31-37, **151**
8: 33, **255**
   35, **248**, **265**
12: 30, **100**, **137**, **285**
13: 13, **245**
    31, **136**

Luke

1: 37, **273**
2: 52, **10**
6: 20, **47**
   39, **46**
   40, **290**

7: 36–50, **121**
9: 3, **281**
　24, **260, 265**
10: 4, **281**
　10–12, **303**
　16, **230, 281, 307**
　21, **49**
　27, **100**
　41–42, **11**
12: 14, **163**
14: 23, **253**
　26, **61, 100**
　33, **47, 60**
15: 11–32, **122**
17: 28–30, **280**
　33, **248, 260**
18: 31–33, **255**
21: 28, **235**
22: 25–26, **125**
23: 46, **105**

JOHN

1: 3, **306**
　4, **64, 172**
　9, **307**
　10, **34**
　11, **33, 149, 261**
　14, **306**
　18, **142, 263**

3: 8, **73**
　16, **266, 287**
4: 10, **98**
　13–24, **98**
　16, **247**
5: 24, **182**
　39–40, **303**
6: 50–51, **180**
　56, **138, 148, 192, 229**
　58, **180**
　60, **154**
　63, **43, 136, 165**
　64, **303**
7: 18, **111**
　37–39, **97**
　38–39, **110**
8: 1–11, **120**
　31–32, **246**
　46, **28, 272**
10: 1, **225**
　3–5, **230**
　4, **225**
　7, **224**
　10, **44, 64, 95, 182, 225, 266**
　11, **205**
　11–13, **223**
　11–16, **197**
　30, **81**
11: 25, **172**

12: 24, **18, 284**
    24–25, **208, 226**
    25, **260**
13: 1, **12, 13, 134, 140, 144, 263, 287**
14: 3, **81**
    6, **52, 64, 70, 109, 110, 172, 260, 282**
    17, **88**
    26, **73, 79, 81, 83, 109**
15: 11, **91**
    13, **52, 175, 191, 266, 287**
    15, **114, 145**
    16, **19, 37, 301**
    18, **34, 114, 224**
    18–20, **261**
    19, **21, 224**
    20, **28, 308**
    22, **28**
    26, **73, 81**
16: 7, **73**
    8–11, **112**
    13, **81, 83, 109, 111, 246**
    22, **64, 91**
    23–30, **133**
    24, **64**
    33, **34**

17: 13, **64**
    14–16, **201**
    24, **146**
18: 37, **246**
20: 21, **7, 26, 223**

Acts of the Apostles

6: 2–4, **214**

Romans

1: 16, **228**
4: 18, **36**
5: 3–5, **36**
    5, **95, 106**
6: 3, **192, 243, 259**
    8, **189**
8: 24, **36**
    26, **98, 106**
    28, **242**
    39, **266**
10: 14–15, **253**
11: 7–8, **157**
    8, **299**
    33, **229, 241**
12: 15, **264**
13: 11, **180**
14: 7–8, **189, 264**

1 Corinthians

1: 17, **268, 302, 304**
18–19, **260**
23, **57, 154, 256**
26–27, **47**
31, **87**
2: 1–4, **281**
1–5, **304**
9, **78**
13, **110, 156, 282, 304**
3: 16, **107**
21–23, **190**
22–23, **64**
4: 1–2, **269**
7, **75**
7: 31, **185**
32–34, **285**
9: 16, **28**
11: 26, **193**
12: 3, **110**
11, **240**
13: 1, **248**
4, **86**
4–5, **129**
15: 55, **187**

2 Corinthians

1: 22, **92**
2: 17, **227, 228**
3: 17, **74**
5: 5, **92**
14, **176**
14–15, **265**
15, **193**
6: 4–10, **34**
8–10, **62**
12: 9–10, **229**

Galatians

1: 9–10, **156**
2: 20, **109, 140, 229, 265, 285**
5: 22, **64, 106**
23, **114**
6: 2, **244**
7, **279**
14, **20, 35, 261**

Ephesians

4: 7, **93, 108, 239**
5: 23, **145**
25, **145**

Philippians

2: 8, **266**

Colossians

1: 16, **306**
2: 13, **182**
3: 1–2, **41**, **92**, **243**
   2, **185**
   3, **21**, **34**
   4, **41**, **93**, **109**, **211**

2 Thessalonians

2: 11–12, **222**

2 Timothy

2: 9, **299**
4: 1–5, **301**
   3–4, **153**, **226**
   10, **46**

Hebrews

2: 14–15, **177**
   15, **189**, **258**
4: 12, **227**, **303**
5: 1, **11**, **14**, **22**, **205**, **272**, **289**
   2, **205**, **228**, **272**
9: 22, **17**, **26**
10: 38, **71**
13: 20, **222**

James

2: 5, **56**
4: 2–3, **140**
   4, **57**, **87**, **200**
5: 12, **53**

1 Peter

5: 4, **205**, **232**
   8, **224**

2 Peter

3: 13, **71**, **113**

1 John

2: 15, **201**
   22–23, **70**
3: 1, **21**
   13, **224**
   14, **266**
   16, **175**
4: 2–3, **70**
   5, **27**, **44**, **156**

8, **74, 247, 258, 263, 266**
16, **137**
5: 10, **70**

2 John

7, **70**
9–10, **70**

Revelation

2: 7, **42**
11, **42**
17, **42**
21: 6, **78**
22: 17, **99**
17–20, **187**
20, **99**

Books of the Bible

Acts, Acts of the Apostles
Amos, Amos
Bar, Baruch
1 Chron, 1 Chronicles
2 Chron, 2 Chronicles
Col, Colossians
1 Cor, 1 Corinthians
2 Cor, 2 Corinthians
Dan, Daniel
Deut, Deuteronomy
Eccles, Ecclesiastes
Eph, Ephesians
Esther, Esther
Ex, Exodus
Ezek, Ezekiel
Ezra, Ezra
Gal, Galatians
Gen, Genesis
Hab, Habakkuk
Hag, Haggai
Heb, Hebrews
Hos, Hosea
Is, Isaiah
Jas, James
Jer, Jeremiah
Jn, John
1 Jn, 1 John
2 Jn, 2 John
3 Jn, 3 John
Job, Job
Joel, Joel
Jon, Jonah
Josh, Joshua
Jud, Judith
Jude, Jude
Judg, Judges
1 Kings, 1 Kings
2 Kings, 2 Kings
Lam, Lamentations
Lev, Leviticus
Lk, Luke
1 Mac, 1 Maccabees
2 Mac, 2 Maccabees
Mal, Malachi
Mic, Micah
Mk, Mark
Mt, Matthew
Nahum, Nahum
Neh, Nehemiah
Num, Numbers
Obad, Obadiah
1 Pet, 1 Peter
2 Pet, 2 Peter
Phil, Philippians
Philem, Philemon
Prov, Proverbs
Ps, Psalms
Rev, Revelation
Rom, Romans
Ruth, Ruth
1 Sam, 1 Samuel
2 Sam, 2 Samuel
Sg, Song of Songs
Sir, Sirach
1 Thess, 1 Thessalonians
2 Thess, 2 Thessalonians
1 Tim, 1 Timothy
2 Tim, 2 Timothy
Tit, Titus
Tob, Tobit
Wis, Wisdom
Zech, Zechariah
Zep, Zephaniah

Contents

SERMONS

Introduction 5

The Priesthood 7

The Great Dinner and the Discourteous Guests 39

Pentecost 73

Parable of the Good Samaritan 117

Prayer of Petition and the Love of Jesus Christ 133

Born a Deaf–Mute vs. Deaf and Dumb for Convenience 151

Death as the End or as the Beginning 171

The Good Shepherd 197

The Laborers Sent to the Vineyard 237

The Cross and the Mystery of Sorrow 255

The Mystery of Priesthood 269

Epilogue 297

Ingram Content Group UK Ltd.
Milton Keynes UK
UKHW051852080323
418216UK00007B/256